Sexual Textualities

Texas Pan American Series

Sexual Textualities

Essays on Queer/ing
Latin American Writing

by David William Foster

University of Texas Press
Austin

Copyright © 1997 by the University of Texas Press
All rights reserved
Printed in the United States of America
First edition, 1997

Requests for permission to reproduce material from this work
should be sent to Permissions, University of Texas Press,
P.O. Box 7819, Austin, TX 78713-7819.

♾ The paper used in this publication meets the minimum
requirements of American National Standard for Information
Sciences—Permanence of Paper for Printed Library Materials,
ANSI Z39.48-1984.

Library of Congress Cataloging-in-Publication Data

Foster, David William.
    Sexual textualities : essays on queer/ing Latin American writing /
by David William Foster. — 1st ed.
        p.   cm.
    Includes bibliographical references and index.
    ISBN 0-292-72501-9 (cl : alk. paper). — ISBN 0-292-72502-7
(pbk. : alk. paper)
    1. Latin American literature—20th century—History and criti-
cism.   2. Homosexuality in literature.   3. Sex role in literature.
4. Homosexuality and literature—Latin America.   5. Literature
and society—Latin America.   I. Title.
PQ7081.F635   1997
860.9'353—dc21   96-51597

091298-18

C ontents

Acknowledgments

I wish to acknowledge the contributions of my research assistants: Fabio Correa-Uribe, José María García Sánchez, Arthur Hughes, Francisco Manzo-Robledo, and Jeff Ritchie. In addition, Daniel Altamiranda read the manuscript and made valuable suggestions.

Preface

Several years ago, when I published *Gay and Lesbian Themes in Latin American Literature* (1991), queer issues were just beginning to gain a place in Hispanic studies. More recently, with the assistance of over sixty scholars in the United States, Latin America, and Europe, I edited *Latin American Writers on Gay and Lesbian Themes: A Bio-Critical Sourcebook* (1994), which provides coverage for approximately one hundred authors.[1] Since the publication of these two volumes, I have continued to write on gay and lesbian topics and, more important, to direct theses and dissertations on these topics in my home department, Spanish, as well as in English and the Interdisciplinary Graduate Program in Humanities. The current compilation includes some of this additional work. It incorporates much more of a theoretical base than *Gay and Lesbian Themes,* primarily because the bibliography that has sought to develop a queer theory in general and specific applications for Latin America only dates from the early part of this decade.

Because queer issues have recently begun to constitute an integral part of a research agenda for Hispanic studies, I begin with an overview of what a gay male heritage for Latin America might look like. Although feminist dimensions will be addressed elsewhere in this study, this chapter is male-oriented because gay male authors have received the bulk of critical attention, and have been translated into foreign languages and reviewed in the literary supplements.

I take up feminine figures in the following two chapters. Eva Perón, whom I discuss in Chapter 2, has always been an intriguing political and cultural icon. Scholars are divided over the degree to which she ought properly to be allied with feminist issues—whether her activist agenda represented an empowerment of women through the empowerment of her political persona, or whether she was nothing more than a stand-in for her husband with little personal identity, as she repeated the gestures of masculinism. However, I am less interested in interpreting Eva Perón as a historical figure than I am in her as a cultural icon and the degree to which her body, her persona, and her social concerns can be of interest to a queer culture.

The attempt to define a feminist pornography for Latin America is inspired less by the desire to fill a gap in literary historiography than by the desire to engage a controversial issue: i.e., whether to even speak of feminine pornography is to make use of a disturbing oxymoron. However, the opposition to pornography and the attempt to relate it to male violence against women is typically an American concern. American writers on sexuality such as Pat Califia and Camille Paglia, both of whom endorse pornography as a form of sexual liberation and argue for its first-amendment protection, are arguably much more in concert with Latin American feminists than are writers such as Andrea Dworkin and Catherine MacKinnon. In Chapter 3 I make this possibly questionable assertion, while considering the defense made by Califia and Paglia for the visible display of sexuality and the deep imbrication of sexuality and human rights. The sort of social engineering to achieve a sex-safe environment championed by the antipornographers stands in sharp contrast to the strong tradition in most Latin American societies of the defense of the freedom of the body. This freedom is necessarily curtailed by the restrictions the antipornographers have in mind, which for many Latin Americans sound very much like the moral agenda of recent neofascist military dictatorships. Of specific interest here, however, will be how the focus on the body entailed by pornography may also include queer dimensions.

Jaime Hermosillo's film *Doña Herlinda y su hijo,* which I discuss in Chapter 4, has become something of a cult classic among gay American audiences. More about a feminine figure than about homoerotic sexuality in Mexico, it too raises serious questions about whether the accommodating mother of one of the protagonists is, in her concern for appearances, in the end reduplicating the rules of the patriarchy, or whether her collaborative efforts to create a privileged space for her son constitute a viable queering of the social text.

Chicano literature, especially that which is oriented toward male experiences, has been slow to accept queer perspectives, despite the impressive bibliography that now exists on Chicana lesbian sexuality. I argue in Chapter 5 that Chicano culture, as it struggles to address both its Hispanic and its Anglo components, exemplifies the phenomena of liminality. Sexuality is no exception, and even less so homoeroticism. Among the authors of interest in this regard, John Rechy exemplifies especially the marginations involved in Chicano culture, including his own internal margination because of his self-identified sexual outlawry. Cherríe Moraga, the author of the stunningly provocative essay "Queer Aztlán: The Re-formation of Chicano Tribe" (1993), is notable for the ways in which she has attempted to create homologies around questions of sexual identity, cultural place, and language usage.

Exilio (1988), by the Cuban-American dramatist Matías Montes Huidobro—the topic of Chapter 6—raises other issues of homoerotic identity. Montes Huidobro, who has produced numerous literary works, most of them in the narrative and theater, has not been generally concerned with a gay-marked cultural production. Nevertheless, several of his plays address erotic issues in Cuban culture, and it is possible to read into these plays, perhaps even despite the author's conscious interests,[2] perspectives than can be labeled queer. In the case of *Exilio,* however, sexual identity is a marker for questions of political expediency and oppression in Castro's Cuba. This issue has been revisited with more positive results in Tomás Gutiérrez Alea's 1983 movie, *Fresa y chocolate,* which has done much to call attention to a changing sexual environment in Cuba. What is of interest, then, is how unanalyzed questions of sexuality can be used in an essentially heterosexist context as a metaphor for political interpretations.

Although Alejandra Pizarnik has been extensively identified with lesbian-marked writing in Argentina, my examination in Chapter 7 of the representation of the body in her poetry is not directly concerned with lesbian erotics.[3] Rather, I am interested in questioning the affiliations with surrealism that have been established for her poetry, affiliations which in my mind detract from the materiality of the body to the extent that they imply a separation from concrete sociohistorical contexts. An exploration of the materiality of the body in Pizarnik, furthermore, would seem to be absolutely crucial for a study of queer, and not just lesbian, erotics.

In Chapter 8, I take a different approach to an investigation of queer perspectives by examining the crisis of masculinity in Argentine fiction in the 1950s. During this period the outlines of compulsory heterosexuality in Argentina become even more clearly drawn in the context of the machismo represented by the figure of Juan Domingo Perón. In a sense this question is the contrary of the queer dimensions associated with the figure of Eva Perón and her gender-challenging personality, while at the same time it complements the hyperfemininity of her persona and her (largely unsuccessful) attempts to assimilate to the oligarchic matriarchy. Concomitantly, Evita served as a dream fulfillment for many Argentine women. By examining texts from differing and conflicting social vantage points—the high bourgeoisie occupied by Sylvina Bullrich, the militant left by David Viñas, the traditional oligarchy by Manuel Mujica Láinez—I wish to chart the distance between the general social ideology of compulsory heterosexuality (along with the privileges of the patriarchy) and the specific machismo of the Peronista regime on the one hand, and the interpretations of the breakdown of that ideology on the other. It is precisely the space that is created by this distance in which a queer reading of society is made possible—which is what characterizes, in a global fashion, the fiction of Mujica Láinez.

1   Agenda and Canon
Some Necessary Priorities

Alguma coisa está fora de ordem
Fora da nova ordem mundial

CAETANO VELOSO

Any attempt to engage in a discussion of a lesbian and gay heritage for Latin America must inevitably and immediately confront the problem of dominant cultures, such as those of major world centers (usually European) and recognized establishment groups (typically white, middle-class, and male).[1] It is necessary from the very outset to conceptualize an interlocking array of dominant cultures, which affect a cluster of societies that might at one time have been characterized as Third World or dependent and perhaps now could be examined profitably from the perspective of marginality. Both the medico-criminal concept of homosexuality (homosexuality as illness or as crime) and the agenda which affirms homosexuality as a legitimate sexual identity (today often called queer theory, as a privileged term to cover both gay and lesbian sensibilities in their commonalities and their differences) are dominant-society constructs that have only an imperfect and even a distorting applicability to Latin America. Such a misapplication is even greater if we take into account Latin America's enormously different regions, cultures, linguistic practices, classes, and ethnic and racial traditions. If

2

one speaks globally about Latin America, it is difficult to avoid being superficial, and if one speaks about specific Latin American societies, there is the risk of partializing phenomena, in the sense that the range of data may not be extensive enough to allow for persuasive conclusions.

To be sure, Brazil is virtually a continent to itself , and its own homoerotic traditions reveal considerable complexity. Adolfo Caminha's *Bom-Crioulo* (1895; The Good Nigger) is the first Latin American novel to deal with homosexuality as a theme, while Aluísio Azevedo's *O cortiço* (1890; The Tenement) contains the first scene of lesbian seduction and lesbian acts. While he did not eschew the tragic mode of homosexuality as a psychological problem, Caminha attracts attention today for dwelling on the sincerity of the black seaman's passion and on the persecution of his homoeroticism by agents of the patriarchal order, who enforced military discipline, self-serving compulsive heterosexuality, and white racial superiority. Caminha introduces into Latin American sociocultural thought a view of homosexuality, which lasts to the present day, as tied to larger issues of the patriarchal social order rather than to the emphasis one finds in American writing on questions of personal identity and internal psychological processes. That is, from *Bom-Crioulo* on (although with some exceptions), homoeroticism is repeatedly linked to collective history. It is no coincidence that the emergence of numerous writings about homosexuality in Latin America goes hand in hand with resistance to authoritarian military dictatorships that view anything other than monogamous heterosexual procreative matrimony as a threat to the social fabric. Concomitantly, one must stress that, by attributing a homosexual identity only to the insertee in sexual relations, these writings implicitly question the legitimacy of femininity, in its various "natural" and "imitated" versions. This is one reason why the carnival, with its strong (albeit contained) element of male-to-female cross-dressing (especially in Brazil), and transvestism in general may be more outrageous in Latin America than in Europe or the United States.

Azevedo's novel *O cortiço,* while it does initiate a tradition that recognizes lesbian sexuality in Brazil and Latin America, is written from a masculinist point of view. Depicting the seduction of a local girl by a French courtesan, Azevedo is quite forthright in describing the details of lesbian passion. The experience unleashes the young girl's blocked menstrual development, to the joy of her family. Here, then, lesbian passion is, if rather dubiously, legitimated as a threshold experience that leads to procreative normalcy. Thanks to the agency of the foreign libertine, French sexual practices, like French culture in general, prove beneficial to native flowerings—all within a context of the harshest facts of life as strictly economic transactions. Neither denouncing nor glorifying sexuality, Azevedo treats lesbian encounters as part of the maturational process of his modest Brazilian protagonists, who are on their way out of the tenement.

The divergence, then, that must be recorded for the constructs of homosexuality and gay sensibility, in terms of foreign dominance, is an initial recognition of both their impropriety and their improbability. The terms are improper to the extent that they describe a configuration of the social order that may correspond to British or American society, but not to Latin America. In Latin America homosocialism and the division between private and public life have always included opportunities for same-sex relations that do not necessarily provide for anything like the construction of a homosexual identity. One ought not ignore the entire question of the substratum of indigenous cultures in Latin America, which reveal numerous traces of both ritual homosexuality and pansexual eroticism. They are traces of a sexuality that both complements procreative heterosexuality and resists five hundred years of an imposed Judeo-Christian sexual morality. Moreover, some of the most diverse societies in Latin America offer examples, codified in their cultural production, of the macho who makes it with both men and women without ever yielding an iota of his masculine persona. The figure of the *maricón* (fag or queer, as understood in the most stereotypic terms) is reserved exclusively for the insertee. The issue that insistently recurs is the disjunction between the ideology of the macho insertor and the *maricón* insertee and the intimate details and confusing nonbinarism of their actual sexual practices.

Thus, Latin American culture may define homosexuality in two ways: either in terms of the Euro-American medico-criminal discourse where any sexual commerce between individuals of the same sex makes them both homosexual; or, more paradigmatically, in terms of a disjunction between the insertor, who never loses his alignment with establishment masculinity, and the insertee, to whom alone a deviant sexual persona is attributed. In Manuel Puig's *El beso de la mujer araña* (1976; *Kiss of the Spider Woman*, 1979), the queer is Molina. Even when Valentín has sex with Molina, thereby fulfilling the latter's illusion of subscribing to the feminine mystique, there is never any question about Valentín's masculinity. Babenco's film version for American and European audiences is disconcerting

4

because Valentín is never "gayified," even when he and Molina exchange commitments. Valentín recognizes the justice of nonhetero-
sexuality, while Molina assumes Valentín's revolutionary political
activism.

But it is an unavoidable fact of Latin American fiction that the insertee—aside from any characterization as morally, emotionally, and
psychologically disadvantaged—is routinely portrayed as the victim
of macho exploitation, whether in terms of male rage, power politics, personal and social revenge, or opportunistic randiness (a point
made by Reinaldo Arenas about the experience of gay men in Cuban
concentration camps during the early years of the Castro government). In *El lugar sin límites* (1966; *Hell Has No Limits,* 1972), by the
Chilean José Donoso, the figure of the transvestite maricón serves
only to reaffirm the masculinist code. The macho who turns on the
maricón is as much a victim of the social structure as the latter is, for
he loses the object of his erotic attachment. Only when the masculinity of the macho is challenged publicly is there any questioning
of the division of sexual roles. And when the macho's preferences
are challenged, the violent—and murderous—reaffirmation of the
male code must take place. But until that point, the separation of the
public and the private, in which everything is permitted although
nothing is discussed, allows for a fluid sexual satisfaction that does
not gibe with the Euro-American discourse on homosexuality.

Of course, there are examples in Latin American culture of the en-
dorsement of rigid demarcations between heterosexuality and homosexuality, with the latter looming large with any transgression of
the former and affecting equally both partners in the transaction.
Luis Zapata is the most prominent gay writer in Mexico at the moment. But his half-dozen novels, though they represent dimensions
of sexual liberation and the Latin American conflation of the personal and the political, have routinely been criticized for reproduc-
ing older European stereotypes and a typically American model of
homosexual tragedy. Zapata may not subscribe to any proposition
concerning the inherent wrongness of homosexuality. Nonetheless,
many of his Mexican characters, moving in what is often alleged to
be the gayest of Latin American societies, do not achieve anything re-
motely akin to erotic fulfillment. One can understand the terrible
fate of characters whose sexuality collides with tyranny, as is the case
with characters by Puig in Argentina or Reinaldo Arenas in Cuba.
But Zapata's characters exist within relatively open and noncoercive
social contracts in contemporary Mexico.

Alternatively, one could argue that Mexico's passive liberalism—

which reflects the U.S. pattern of a condescending acceptance of the assimilation, on the margins, of its uncomfortable minorities—provides Zapata with a model of even greater human aggression than military tyranny. The latter is so explicit that it makes clear what the battle lines are, while the former is ambiguous enough to make it impossible to define the question in the concrete terms of human-rights violations. This greater tragedy, therefore, emerges in Zapata's Mexican novels and in texts from similar "liberal" societies like Isaac Chocrón's Venezuela, Luis Rafael Sánchez's Puerto Rico, or João Trevisan's Brazil. Here it would be appropriate to emphasize how military tyranny only provides homophobia with its greatest value as spectacle. Under authoritarian governments, homophobia, which must always be present and is only to varying degrees submerged, enters into the dictatorial/dictated reconstruction of the public dimensions of personal identity and behavior, as proffered very loudly and repeatedly in the press, from the pulpit, by official decree, and in exemplary acts of aggression against alleged deviants.

As thorny an issue as homosexual identity is, gay sensibility presents an even greater problem. Some resistance to simply making "gay" a nonbiased synonym for the negatively charged term "homosexual" continues in Latin America, especially since, as a foreign-sounding word in Spanish and Portuguese, "gay" is viewed as an index of a foreign ideology. The notion of gayness has two fundamental problems. The first is that it tends to become associated with a middle class that is privileged in terms of its economic status, its professionalism, and its opportunities to consume foreign culture (either in the original or in local translations) and to travel abroad in order to assimilate an international style. This is evident in Jaime Humberto Hermosillo's 1985 film, *Doña Herlinda y su hijo* (Doña Herlinda and Her Son [the only Latin American film, discounting Babenco's English-language *Kiss of the Spider Woman,* to be included in the revised edition of Vito Russo's *The Celluloid Closet*]). The film may be a brilliant utopian vision of the restructuring of the patriarchal family, whereby bisexuality allows a young doctor to have both a wife (herself a professional) and a child by her and to have his male lover, all of them living happily ever after together with his mother in a house that she has built for them.

The displacement of a rigid heterosexist patriarchal order by a more open matriarchal order is undoubtedly meaningful for Mexican and Latin American viewers. This significance derives from matriarchy's strength in the private sphere, where it has customarily been accommodating toward gayness even when it is also complic-

6

itous with the patriarchy in wanting sons to produce grandsons—which is what Doña Herlinda clearly also wants. But Doña Herlinda is a well-to-do widow, and her son belongs to one of the most prestigious and well-paying professions in his society. Thus there is little danger that the insulated cocoon they inhabit, surrounded by the international trappings of their class and protected by the walls, hedges, and grills of their estate, will ever be disturbed by the police, who harass less-advantaged gays in the public spaces that are all they can afford to inhabit. Part of the meaning of Hermosillo's film for Mexicans is that it is set in Guadalajara, which is not only one of Mexico's most traditionally Catholic cities (the opening shot is of the 450-year-old Cathedral) but also one where homoeroticism is very much on display—and frequently repressed with vigor, at least in its many public manifestations.

Major gay novels such as Darcy Penteado's *Nivaldo e Jerônimo* (1981; Nivaldo and Jeronimo) in Brazil, Zapata's *En jirones* (1985; In Tatters) or José Rafael Calva's *Utopía gay* (1983; Gay Utopia) in Mexico, Oscar Hermes Villordo's *La otra mejilla* (1986; The Other Cheek) in Argentina, or Isaac Chocrón's *Toda una dama* (1988; A Real Lady) in Venezuela all depict members of the middle class, especially professionals, who are more able to construct their lives in accordance with international models than are working-class gay men and women. Indeed, they view both their conflict with their society and their opportunities for an alternate sensibility as consequences of their access to extranational perspectives. This implies not that there is something amiss with these texts, but that they cannot avoid the controversies of national versus international culture in Latin American artistic and critical circles.

The second problem associated with a gay identity as it has been promulgated within Euro-American culture is the danger of systematically excluding homoerotic practices among social groups unacknowledged by the Euro-American model. In the United States, the pursuit of marginalized identities has resulted in the recovery of a submerged homoeroticism in some Native American societies (whether tagged as berdache clans, ritual practices, or quotidian behavior) as well as the inquiry into similar phenomena among other marginalized groups. For example, Cherríe Moraga, in both her play *Giving Up the Ghost* (1986) and her personal ethnic memoir *Loving in the War Years* (1983), discriminates between an Anglo destructive lesbianism (which she sees as reduplicating macho stereotypes) and a productive Chicana lesbianism (in which the Hispanic emphasis on the dignity and sensitivity of interpersonal relations counters the violence of the Anglo world). Moraga affirms a strong and vibrant lesbian continuum in Hispanic culture that affords her a way of coming to terms with her own personhood. Terri de la Peña's much more schematic novel, *Margins* (1992), details a similar pattern. And one of the sustaining themes of anthologies of Chicana lesbianism such as *Compañeras: Latina Lesbians (An Anthology)* (Ramos, 1987), *Chicana Lesbians: The Girls Our Mothers Warned Us About* (Trujillo, 1991), and the Chicana material in *This Bridge Called My Back: Writings by Radical Women of Color* (1981), of which Cherríe Moraga is the first editor, is the coordination of Chicana/Latina culture and a profoundly spiritual lesbian identity that is disconsonant with images of white, middle-class, heterosexist leisure society.

The existence, and the sustained survival, of a homoerotics among large segments of the socially disadvantaged, or at least among those who only sporadically accede to positions of public privilege, may have escaped recognition because it cannot be captured within the parameters of an internationalist gay sensibility. Carlos Monsiváis's probing and entertaining cultural critiques have, while underscoring the deep homoeroticism of the poets of the internationalist Contemporáneos group in Mexico (active from the late 1920s to the mid-1940s), delved into a wide array of popular-culture practices in that country that can be said to be marked by alternate sexuality, including homoerotics. Manuel Puig was also interested in sexual modalities among subordinate groups, among individuals who did not recognize themselves as homosexuals not because they practiced a denial of their "true nature," but because what their society was calling homosexuality or a gay sensibility failed to match the business of their own lives. This was one of the reasons why Puig on several occasions energetically repudiated the validity of the concept of homosexuality. His first—and, for many, his best—novel, *La traición de Rita Hayworth* (1968; *Betrayed by Rita Hayworth,* 1971) establishes his interest in erotic feelings and practices that match poorly both the medico-criminal concept of homosexuality and the politics of a gay identity. Puig pursued this interest throughout his writing. His last novel, *Cae la noche tropical* (1988; *Tropical Night Falling,* 1991), although superficially dealing with marginalized older women, may be read as a homoerotic text where gender roles have ceased to be carefully distributed.

Many working-class men populate the pages of Puig's novels. Their machismo is tinged with emotions and experiences that fail to confirm the conventional stereotypes of the heterosexual Latin lover. This is also true of novels by Mexico's José Joaquín Blanco, narrative essays by Brazil's Glauco Mattoso (one of which also has a comic-book version), and the social anthropological narratives of Néstor Perlongher, an Argentine who worked in Brazil. There has been no adequate analysis of homoeroticism among the marginal social figures in the Cuban author Severo Sarduy's fiction—especially in texts like *Cobra* (1972), *Maitreya* (1978), and *Colibrí* (1984)—and one suspects this is because these figures cannot be dealt with conveniently by the models of an internationalist gay sensibility. Moreover, discussions of Sarduy's poetry always seem to stop short of his remarkably explicit homoerotic writing in *El Cristo de la rue Jacob* (1987; The Christ of the Rue Jacob) and *Un testigo fugaz y disfrazado* (1985; A Fleeting and Masked Witness). Similarly, critical studies of José Lezama Lima's dense novel *Paradiso* (1966) have been unable to offer convincing conclusions regarding the question of homoeroticism in the novel (a question whose interest is compounded by the publication of the text in Cuba at a time when those accused of homosexuality still suffered draconian persecution). Virgilio Piñera's expressionist-surrealist narratives have also been resistant to transparent gay readings, despite the fact that Piñera was himself a victim of Cuba's revolutionary morality.

In addition to Puig and Sarduy, what might be called a gay sensibility or a gay aesthetics can be detected in such prominent writers as Brazil's Aguinaldo Silva, João Trevisan, and Silviano Santiago; Colombia's Fernando Vallejo and Gustavo Alvarez Gardeazábal; Mexico's Luis González del Alba; Puerto Rico's Luis Rafael Sánchez; and Argentina's Juan José Hernández—without anything like a homosexual thematics necessarily being present (although it is, of course, in selected texts). Yet there is still no systematic treatment of this aspect of their work, perhaps in part because of the absence of adequate models that take into account the general configurations of Latin American society and the specific circumstances of individual national cultures. Examples of specific national circumstances may be found in the dual status of Puerto Rico, caught between U.S. and Hispanic social practices; the structural violence that characterizes life in Colombia for Alvarez Gardeazábal (and also for his compatriot, Gabriel García Márquez, who has attained fame and fortune without ever hinting at homoeroticism in his narrative world); and the repression of the combined threats of the social outcast, the young, the mestizo, and the always threatening urban specter in Blanco's Mexico City.

It would also be appropriate to reemphasize here the importance of correlating, in the majority of these writers, the personal with the political, since questions of sexual politics are inevitably related to larger issues of social construction. This is emphatically evident in Alvarez Gardeazábal's novel *El divino* (1986; The Divine One), in which a favorably portrayed gay man is also a drug trafficker. Any minimally satisfactory critical exegesis of this novel must work through the challenging correlations established by the author, beginning with the questions of whether his homoeroticism is compromised by what is usually understood as a criminal activity or whether both homoeroticism and drug trafficking are to be interpreted, conjunctively and disjunctively, as indicative of the author's revised interpretation of what is "good" and "bad" in Colombian society, evaluated independently of internationally dictated value systems regarding sex and commercial ventures.

The foregoing discussion has referred primarily to male sexuality. Turning to lesbian culture, it is important to stress that it is substantively different from gay male culture both in Latin America and the United States. Moreover, Latin American lesbian culture must be seen as different from lesbian culture in the United States, with the possible exception of unifying phenomena to be tracked among marginalized women of color. One necessarily returns to the question of international cultural models as opposed to models specific to each society.

Sylvia Molloy is the author of one of the only two Latin American lesbian novels to be translated into English, *En breve cárcel* (1981; published in English as *Certificate of Absence*). Molloy, an Argentine educated in Paris who has been a professor at several ivy-league schools in the United States—and who currently holds an Albert Schweitzer chair at New York University—has written a novel in which lesbianism and First World feminism intersect. While Argentina forms the background of her protagonist's experiences, these experiences are set in France and the United States. Molloy's recording of them has to do with the private struggle of the writer to find an authentic self-expression. Clearly, these factors are all privileged, white, middle-class dimensions that make the novel immediately accessible to foreign readers.

In contrast is the performance theater of Mexico City's Jesusa Rodríguez. In Rodriguez's work the limited-access space of a private bar (Teatro La Capilla/Bar El Hábito, which experiences repeated police harassment), the lack of published texts, and the enactment of female proletarian subjectivities—as well as the distaste her work has provoked among more establishment feminists—point to a lesbian framing that escapes customary international definitions, even when it may be coextensive with the Chicana/Latina lesbian identity described above.

Lesbian writing remains very much of a minority voice in Latin America, even though the publication of women's work, including previously lost and forgotten texts, has increased dramatically in the past two decades. Several factors are probably involved here, at the very least a reluctance, in the face of opposition to feminist writing in general, to use literature as a means of advocating for lesbian issues. But more important may be the serious matter of critical optics: too few critics have been able to see a sustained lesbian tradition among women writers. Octavio Paz's book on the seventeenth-century Mexican nun, Sor Juana Inés de la Cruz (1982), is profoundly ambiguous and ultimately contradictory in its handling of the poems Sor Juana addressed to one of her patronesses, the Marquesa de La Laguna (Condesa de Paredes). At times he recognizes homoerotic sentiments, while at other moments he seems to dismiss such details as part of the conventional amatory rhetoric of the period. This ambiguous response parallels the division in Shakespearean criticism over what to do with the love sonnets addressed to a young man. Yet, it is now generally agreed (and research in the area of lesbian nuns is cited as support) that Sor Juana's poetry must be taken as the point of departure for a lesbian literary tradition in Mexico and Latin America, both in terms of the tenor of much of her writing, which is now enthusiastically endorsed as central to a Hispanic feminist descendence, and in terms of her personal biography, despite all of the shadowy factual areas that render it so perplexing. Most interest in her biography has focused on attempting to determine if she abandoned court life in favor of the convent because her condition as an illegitimate child blocked her amorous aspirations—which is a heterosexist line of inquiry that ignores the possibility that she may simply have preferred the exclusive company of other women.

But if Sor Juana is a lesbian foremother for Mexican writers, it will require much intensive literary historiography and some powerful analytical models to fill in the gaps between her death in 1695 and the publication of the first lesbian novel in Mexico, Rosamaría Roffiel's *Amora* (1989).[2] Roffiel had already written some excellent homoerotic poetry before the publication of *Amora,* thus joining the ranks of writers (which also include Sabina Berman) who affirm poetry as a privileged space of lesbian expression that picks up on Sor Juana's example. But *Amora,* as a narrative, allows for a full play of social concerns: it introduces intersecting lines between a generalized feminism that resists the overwhelming machismo of Mexican patriarchal society, and a specifically lesbian sensibility that characterizes the intimacies between women who are brought together because of their shared sense of marginalization, repression, and oppression. One could argue that Roffiel reenacts in Spanish, and in a narrative framework, a dominant society like that of Adrienne Rich's lesbian continuum,[3] with which the author is clearly familiar. The sort of utopian, ahistorical view of lesbianism championed by Rich, and which Roffiel's work echoes, may be the result of the urban internationalism of Mexico City. Or it may be part of a postmodern stance that necessarily transcends local ideological beliefs, whether those of Mexican machismo or those of Mexican *marianismo* (woman's compulsory adherence to a norm of demure sacrifice, as modeled by the Virgin Mary).

Sara Levi Calderón's *Dos mujeres* (1990; published in English as *The Two Mujeres*[4]) presents quite different issues, beginning with that of Jewish minority status in Mexico City and the author's use of a pseudonym in order, one suspects, to protect her family's honor. *Dos mujeres* is a novel of feminine rage in the face of a constellation of abusive forces, which engage in every physical and psychological strategy possible to coerce the protagonist into submission and subservience. Not surprisingly, and in response to an imperative to break with the (essentially gay male) prototype of homosexual tragedy, Levi Calderón's novel is the chronicle of triumphant liberation. But the cost is a tremendous one, as layers of conventionally successful feminine identity are stripped away: the protagonist's identity as a good Jewish daughter, her identity as a loyal wife, as an omnipresent and balsamic mother, and, most generally, as a dedicated guardian of the patriarchal order who fulfills her duty to uphold a social pact of exemplary respectability in order not to occasion *shande far di goyim* (shame in front of non-Jews).

Levi Calderón's novel evokes, of course, multiple levels of shame, in a rewriting of the social text whereby the provocation of a sense of shame and outrage is an index of the lesbian critique of an implacable heterosexist order. The novel involves a reinterpretation of the matriarchal model, both in terms of Jewish culture—the Sarah of the Tanakh on whom the author slyly bases her pseudonym—and in terms of the Guadalupan myth—the figure of the mother as the servant of the Virgin of Guadalupe, Mexico's patron saint. The immigrant daughter's rejection of Guadalupan motherhood is as scandalous as her separation from traditional Jewish family life. This conjunction of elements has ensured *Dos mujeres* an important place in

contemporary Mexican fiction—much, I should add, to the conster-
nation of heterosexist feminists whose affinities lie within a Christian Mexican tradition that Levi Calderón appears to spurn. All of
which may be why Mexico's most important contemporary woman
writer, Elena Poniatowska, herself an immigrant daughter, has studiously eschewed any lesbian resonances in her own influential
oeuvre.[5]

To the best of my knowledge, the only scholarly study on lesbianism in a Latin American society is Luiz Mott's *O lesbianismo no Brasil*
(1987). The personal document *Amor de mujeres: el lesbianismo en la
Argentina, hoy* by Ilse Fuskova and Claudina Marek (1994; Woman's
Love: Lesbianism in Argentina, Today) is, as far as I know, the first
book-length work relating to Argentina and the first work in which
women themselves recount their own experiences. It should be
noted that the authors are identified as "Ilse Fuskova en diálogo con
Silvia Schmid. Claudina Marek." This is important because much of
the text consists of a long dialogue between Fuskova and Schmid,
while approximately the last fourth is Marek's independent text.

Fuskova and Marek are partners, and the selection of photographs
includes material relating to the officialization of their union in the
Iglesia de la Comunidad Metropolitana in June 1992. As a couple
they have participated in numerous lesbian events and programs in
Argentina, the United States, and various countries in Europe. Their
book is unquestionably the best statement of Out and Proud that has
come from Argentina, where there have been considerable struggles
and frustrating setbacks in launching a lesbian and gay movement
since the return to constitutional democracy in the mid-1980s.

The material included in their book demonstrates that Fuskova
and Marek are committed to the international movement of homoerotic liberation and have little interest in analyzing the patterns of
resistance to such a movement, whether this resistance is homophobia in Argentina (which itself has multiple origins) or an understanding of homoeroticism that does not fit comfortably into the
context of the international movement (i.e., an interpretation of
homoeroticism in Latin America that resists its correlation with identity politics). Clearly, the authors and the movement represented by
them draw inspiration from the internationalist climate in contemporary Argentina, which for now may be the only way to effectively
promote a gay and lesbian agenda.

The separate documents by Fuskova and Marek depict a lesbian
coming-of-age in Argentine society. In addition to discussing their
immigrant backgrounds, they also focus on their respective mar-

riages and motherhoods; an important detail is that they both enjoy good relations with their children and former husbands. The dialogue between Fuskova and Schmid is very solidly structured, and it is apparent that they agreed beforehand about the essential points to be covered. In addition to exploring the crucial points of lesbian identity and its construction as a refutation to the patriarchy, and more importantly, they explore lesbianism in the context of Latin America and Argentina. They make no attempt to minimize the ways in which lesbianism is a forthright challenge to the patriarchy, and they use no euphemisms. Nor do they pander to the squeamishness and the defensive smugness of so much of the Argentine media. Their exposition of lesbianism draws heavily from Adrienne Rich's "lesbian continuum," thereby confirming the influence her proposals have had in Latin America.[6]

When reading Latin American literature, one must seek out homoerotic commitments in areas not immediately apparent to a foreigner or to a Latin American inscribed within a patriarchal order (an order that is as much internationalizing as nationalistic, and that systematically denies the possibility of public discourse about alternate sexualities). In this spirit one could propose that, much as in the case of gay male cultural production, one should look for materials that escape privileged generic or conceptual categories. In Mexico, this means attending to the song lyrics of Chavela Vargas, which are really quite stunning in their unabashed lesbian positioning. They include a same-sex marking in the narrator/narratee relationship that is unique in female-voiced compositions in Hispanic society, where for either male or female singers a potentially homoerotic relationship (e.g., the ballads of Federico García Lorca, the love songs of the Mexican gay popular singer Juan Gabriel) requires either conventional sex roles or, at best, common-gender ambiguities.

In Argentina, the children's songs of María Elena Walsh and her fiction for children are not clearly marked by a lesbian consciousness. Yet it is significant that a woman who is publicly identified as a lesbian has devoted virtually all of her creative efforts to the production of literature for children. One of Walsh's songs is the leitmotif for Luis Puenzo's Academy Award–winning film *The Official Story* (1985), a movie about women's consciousness and feminist solidarity in the face of a masculinist military dictatorship, concentrated in the figure of a little girl who is the tragic figure of a sociohistoric anarchy provoked not by rebellious women but by tyrannical men.

Finally, one needs to examine even commercially motivated popular art, such as the novels of the Brazilian writer Cassandra Rios.

14

These novels are unabashedly written to be read on the beach during the lazy days of summer. Nonetheless, their audacious sexual transgressions—including nonchalant lesbian encounters—are as much indexes of shifting erotic sensibilities as they are signs of the commercial advantages associated with the exotic, outrageous comings and goings of her socioeconomically privileged characters. Rios sells most of her novels to bored philistines, who enjoy the mild jolts of deviant sexuality provided by these potboilers. But one should note that middle-class popular-culture texts in Brazil are transgressive in a way that is impossible in the United States. Thus they represent an opportunity for articulating a lesbian identity and incorporating it— inasmuch as it too refuses to perpetuate the commonplaces of homophobic tragedy—into a dominant-society text.

Avenues of future research on lesbian and gay motifs in Latin America follow clearly from what has been discussed up to this point. First, it is important to recognize that a way of talking about homosexuality as illness and as crime has been incorporated into Latin American social consciousness as a consequence of international influences. Any attempt to conceptualize Latin American gay sensibility as unified should also be understood to derive from international influences. Yet the essential fluidity of the concept of gay sensibility allows it to include both the remnants of pre-Hispanic homoeroticism in Latin American society that transcend contemporary political movements, and the framing of cultural and literary practices as homoerotic in ways that escape the dominant society's impositional categories. Lesbian issues and identity in Latin America likewise mirror aspects of the dominant internationalizing society, while at the same time reflecting unique Latin American experiences. The imperative to make the personal political—either on the level of primary texts or on the level of critical readings—uniquely colors Latin American homoerotics and, across gender and ideological lines, is its most abiding and cohesive feature.

What might a canon look like for Latin American literature? Such a canon would resemble a basic reading list either for a specific course on Latin American gay writing or for a course on contemporary Latin American fiction that would seek to include an adequate representation of authors of a gay-marked fiction.[7] Latin American nations are extraordinarily diverse in terms of geography, climate, demography, economy, political development, and social symbolism. Since, as Manuel Puig (following Alfred C. Kinsey and Gore Vidal) has asserted, they by and large lack the sense of gay identity found in the advanced industrial countries of Western Europe and North America, it generally makes more sense to speak of homosexual acts, but not of a homosexual or gay identity. What Puig seems to be seeking is the dismantling of fixed gender identities and hierarchies. In fact, a broad approach based on the concept of sexual dissidence might open up an array of practical and theoretical considerations that fruitfully address the problematic character of the homosexual concept for particular categories of writing in Latin America. One cannot, as I have already stressed, productively examine "homosexual writing" in Latin America through the lens of U.S. critical and political priorities. It is true that, at least in urban centers in Latin America, North American concepts that encourage identity politics have enjoyed a renewed influence. However, although there are some identity movements in Latin America (e.g., the Comité Argentino de Derechos Homosexuales or the Grupo Gay de Bahia), there is nothing like a project or an agenda of dissident sexual analysis for any segment of Latin American culture. Hence the problem of applying to the literature of other countries the critical parameters of one's own persists.

How to situate Chicano and other Latino literature in this canon is another question. Works by Hispanic-identified authors in English are now, but not without some blurring of cultural boundaries between the American and the Hispanic, customarily used as disjunctive terms, generally considered American writing (e.g., work by John Rechy). Yet, to the extent that Chicano literature constitutes frontier writing, tied as it is to the specific space of the southwestern border between the United States and Latin America, one must take into account how it manifests both issues of general U.S. queer culture and issues of a particularly Latin American consciousness of sexuality.

Argentina

The Argentine Manuel Puig (1932–1990) is necessarily the point of reference for a discussion of gay writing in Latin America, not so much because of the abundant references to homosexuality in his novels, but because of the concern with questions of sexual dissidence manifested throughout his oeuvre. *El beso de la mujer araña* (*Woman*) is Puig's most famous novel, in part because it was subsequently made into an Oscar-winning movie by fellow Argentine Héctor Babenco. Yet the novel is exceptional in its own right for its demonstration of how sexual and political liberation must be viewed as integral parts of the same process. Though the novel has many dimensions, the two that stand out are the relationship between popular culture and political ideology, and the intersection of one man's pursuit of sexuality with another man's striving for political liberation. The seduction of the latter by the campy cultural icons of the former and the former's acceptance of the political project of the other leads to their sexual union and to a deep emotional involvement.

In addition to underscoring the imbrication of the personal and the political in a homophobic, authoritarian society, Puig's novel models an interpretation of the social text in which liberation must involve more than a change in the structure of the political process. In this interpretation, diverse cultural materials that are contestatorial, resistant of the heterosexist hegemony, and defiant of social hierarchies are useful because they provide representations of alternate ways of living. Puig demonstrates how camp, both as a parody of cultural norms and as a bricolage of multiple cultural forms and genres, is an important site for the critical evaluation of sexual ideologies. Although a similar view of camp has prevailed within the U.S. homosexual culture—because of the interplay of the hegemonic and the subaltern, and the international versus the national and regional—the novel has nonetheless had a fascinating freshness for English-language readers. Its fame in the United States and in Europe has, in turn, fueled its reputation in Latin America.

Puig's writing as a whole, virtually all of which is available in English translation, is informed by perceptions of sexual dissidence and the queering of the patriarchy, from the sentimental education of a gay child in his first novel, *La traición de Rita Hayworth,* to the touchingly melancholic pairing of two elderly women in *Cae la noche tropical.* Puig published most of his work in exile.

Other Argentine writers who are also of major significance include Oscar Hermes Villordo (1928–1994), Manuel Mujica Láinez (1910–1984), José María Borghello (b. 194?), Carlos Arcidiácono (b. 1929), and Ernesto Schóó (b. 1925).

Mexico

Mexico's Luis Zapata (b. 1951), who is as famous as Puig among Latin American readers, has not enjoyed the same fortune among English-language readers. His novel *Las aventuras, desventuras y sueños de Adonis García, el vampiro de la colonia Roma* (1979; *Adonis García: A Picaresque Novel,* 1981), although available in English, has failed to reach a general reading public; nor is it supported by an internationally acclaimed film version. Zapata's novel seems not to address issues as compelling as those broached by Puig—or not to address them in as compelling a manner. A middle-class youth who, because of a conflict with his father, leaves home and turns to hustling in one of downtown Mexico City's "zones of sophisticated nightlife," Adonis García articulates a critique of bourgeois orderliness and its accompanying norm of sexual discipline. The novel is typically unclear, however, about the degree to which Adonis García has a modern "gay" identity (although the Mexico City setting of the novel exemplifies a modernizing project). Nor is it evident if the protagonist's incursion into the world of gay hustlers is anything more than an act of defiance against the patriarchy, through sexual disorderliness. Yet what emerges in the narrative is a useful depiction of a sexual underworld in which economic opportunism intersects with significant deviations from compulsory heterosexism. (Gay hustlers do not necessarily identify themselves as gay, and "gay" is usually taken to refer to the sexuality of the clients they hustle. However, in Zapata's novel, Adonis is clearly marked as gay.)

Zapata has a greater interest than Puig in specifically gay characters—or at least in those who can be identified as gay in terms of the prevailing Latin American definition of "effeminate passives." His recent novels like *La hermana secreta de Angélica María* (1989b; Angélica María's Secret Sister) and *¿Por qué mejor no nos vamos?* (1992; Why Don't We Just Leave?) provide very complex, often highly entertaining depictions of the subjectivities radically at variance with the Mexican sociosexual norm. Zapata has also been quite successful in teasing out of both the popular culture that is integral to capitalism and its supporting ideology of compulsory heterosexism dimensions of sexual dissidence and erotic disorderliness, which effectively question attempts to determine sexual normalcy. This dimension of Zapata's writing is especially evident in the short story collection *Este amor que hasta ayer nos quemaba* (1989a; This Love That until Yesterday Burned Us).

Zapata's fellow Mexican writers on gay themes include José Rafael Calva (b. 1953), Carlos Monsiváis (b. 1938), José Joaquín Blanco (b. 1951), and Miguel Barbachano Ponce (b. 1930).

Puerto Rico

Perhaps the best example in Latin American writing of the primacy of a queer optic rather than a specific representation of homosexuals or self-identified gays is Puerto Rico's Luis Rafael Sánchez (b. 1936). I have written elsewhere that

> Where Sánchez's writing is of particular relevance for queer theory beyond congealed images, identities and plot schemata is in the area of the display of sexual turbulence, shifting sex-

ual models and an eroticism that is transgressive in the ways it transcends and overcomes the attempts to contain it in a conservative, repressive society and in the ways it is fundamentally at odds with circumscribed sexual identities and behaviors. (1994c, 401)

La guaracha del Macho Camacho (1976; *Macho Camacho's Beat,* 1980), which has yet to be published in Puerto Rico,[8] is built around a popular song. The virtually meaningless lyrics of this song, which are repeated insistently, signal the flux of urban life that belies fixed moral codes and putatively unassailable social roles. Sánchez mocks the view of the tropics as a sexual paradise, while at the same time exposing the moral hypocrisy of the social elite and the official social culture it defends. It is in the gaps between official culture and lived experience, between cultural myths and the dirty business of life, where patterns of sexual disorderliness and realignments of the patriarchy are to be perceived.

This reading of the underside of the social tapestry is also present in *La importancia de llamarse Daniel Santos* (1988; The Importance of Being Named Daniel Santos), a fictionalized autobiography of the famous bolero songster. Sánchez cleverly demonstrates the bolero's erotic potential and its attendant cultural projections, the paneroticism it promotes, and a kind of romantic sentimentalization that contravenes the sobriety of (male) heterosexual discipline. When Sánchez begins to describe the eroticization of the bolero, as sung by a man for another man, the reader understands that here is another example of the queersome potential of popular culture.

Cuba

Antes que anochezca: autobiografía (1992; *Before Night Falls: A Memoir,* 1993) by the Cuban Reinaldo Arenas (1943–1990) is virtually iconic in its representation of the issues that lie on the border between modernism and postmodernism in Latin American narrative. First, there is the intersection of Arenas's homosexuality with his condition as probably the only Cuban exile in the United States— certainly the only exile who landed with the *marielitos*—to have received sizable recognition among members of the U.S. cultural establishment. Arenas came to the United States at a time when it was becoming more and more difficult to endorse the Castro regime without acknowledging that a wide range of social problems were the consequence of it (not the consequence of what it hadn't yet gotten around to, or the fault of the U.S. blockade). Much has been written about the *marielito* phenomenon; suffice it here to note that Arenas became an eloquent spokesperson for the *marielitos*. Any facile interpretation of his memoir is thus complicated by the fact that his comments about the Cuban-American community in Miami are as scathing as the book as a whole is about life in revolutionary Cuba, and as scathing as the grand gesture of his suicide, an act of political protest against Fidel Castro.

Arenas arrived in the United States at the height of the gay liberation movement, where he fell victim to the HIV infection that would soon change the course of gay politics. The general sense of *Antes que anochezca* is, despite the enormously oppressive backdrop of political persecution the author puts forth, a triumphant and joyous celebration of unfettered homoeroticism. Arenas describes in loving detail the discovery of his sexuality and the wide range of adventures and misadventures undertaken in his Faustian quest for erotic experiences. He makes it clear that, despite an official homophobic discourse, in pre-Castro Cuba there were alternatives to compulsory heterosexuality (which disappeared with the Revolution). Thus, without engaging in a specifically political analysis, and without engaging in fictional allegory, Arenas encodes within the details of his own (sexual) life an interpretation of the homophobia that characterized the socialist experiment in the Cuba of his experience (I stress this qualifying clause, since a publicly displayed homoeroticism has once again emerged, at least in Havana, and it appears that any official policies of enforcing compulsory heterosexuality have been abandoned).

There is an element of sexual utopianism in Arenas's memoir. Yet it is seriously mediated by the AIDS infection that, while not part of the core narrative, is part of its essential framing, both within the text and as part of the conditions of its publication. This fact reminds us that Arenas, in his writing, was keenly aware of the different barriers to unrestrained homoeroticism in American society; this perception prevents his memoir from falling into the binarist trap common to so much anti-Castro writing. The personal is truly political for Arenas, and that the personal is focused on the boundary transgressions of homoeroticism makes his memoir (which also suspends the modernist distinction between fiction and nonfiction) particularly exemplary. Arenas left a legacy of exceptional novels on gay themes, but it is his personal memoir that is destined to serve as a master narrative of homoeroticism in Latin America.

Arenas's writing will, when the history of gay culture in Cuba is finally written, figure prominently as one culmination of a tradition that reaches back to the decadent poet Julián del Casal (1863–1893); the fiction writers Alfonso Hernández-Catá (1885–1940), Lino Novás Calvo (b. 1905), and Virgilio Piñera (1914–1979)[9]; and José Lezama Lima (1912–1976), the most important writer of his generation, whose poetry and prose has yet to be adequately read for its many homoerotic dimensions.

Brazil

In the case of Brazil, it is difficult to select one representative text. This is not because the legendary eroticism of Brazil leads to a particular abundance of riches: while there is much to be said about sexual tolerance in Brazil and the complex patterns of its erotic culture, there is an equally strong countervailing force of sexual orderliness that is part of the country's own interpretation of the project of modernity. Rather, the simple facts are that Brazil is an enormous country with a level of literary production to match, and that most subaltern groups participate in this vast production. Moreover, Brazil is one of the few Latin American countries that produces its own "supermarket" fiction. (In most Latin American countries, pulp fiction is likely to consist chiefly of translations of U.S. titles.) Much of this fiction offers sensationalist representations of sex, including homosexuality. Such images in Cassandra Rios and Adelaida Carrara are hardly commendable, but they do serve in a limited fashion to naturalize, within the context of a public discussion, dissident sexuality.

There are many conventional novelists to whom one may refer. Caio Fernando Abreu (b. 1948), Silviano Santiago (b. 1936), and Aguinaldo Silva (b. 1944) are perhaps the most representative of a gay discourse, while Gasparino Damata (1918–198?) and Darcy Penteado (1926–1987) exemplify a more explicit homosexual thematics, including the representation of the effeminate man in the case of the former and the conjunction of sexual liberation and political liberation in the case of the latter. Moreover, as I have stated above, *Bom-Crioulo,* by Adolfo Caminha, may be considered the founding text of Latin American gay writing. Nevertheless, for the purposes of discussion here, I would like to focus on a text by Glauco Mattoso (b. 1951; Glauco Mattoso is the pseudonym of Pedro José Ferreira da Silva), *Manual do pedólatra amador: aventuras & leituras de um tarado por pés* (1990b; Footlover's Manual: The Adventures and Readings of a Foot Fetishist). This text also has a comic-book version with drawings by Marcatti—*As aventuras de Glaucomix o pedólatra* (1990a; The Adventures of Glaucomix the Footlover)—the existence of which reaffirms the relationship between gay writing and popular culture in Latin America.

While *Manual* is more a semiautobiographical narrative than a novel, its textual nature serves to underscore another prominent feature of gay writing: the unconventional manipulation of literary modalities. Fixed forms of cultural discourse are a reflex of the repressive hierarchies of patriarchal society. Mattoso mixes scholarly information concerning the eroticization of the foot with freewheeling speculations about sexuality(ies), making his text one of the few attempts to provide a queer analysis of the technology of the body in Latin America. Mattoso's emphasis on foot fetishism is an example of not only a sexual dissidence that suspends gender imperatives but also the metonymic displacement of privileged sites of erotic stimulation among gay males to a bodily appendage that, according to the writer, has so far not been implicated in the transmission of AIDS. Moreover, it is as much a refutation of (pseudo)scientific and popular information regarding sex in his society as it is an outrageous proposal for a renewed energetic sexuality in the face of the trivialization of sexual pleasure in the extensive commercial culture of Brazil.

The outrageousness of Mattoso's proposals hinges on the valuing of the fetish; on a defense of dirty sex (represented here by unwashed and unkempt feet and, by extension, unwashed shoes and socks); on a correlation of footloving with the transgressive and therefore highly charged acts of fellatio and anal sex; on the revaluation of sex as an essential dimension of the economy of the body, beyond reproduction and circumstantial but transient recreational enjoyment; and on the establishment of the relations between sex and social power. Evoking Oriental acupuncture and manipulative massage, Mattoso displaces the narrative of Western sexual economics in a gesture that exposes its untested yet still dominant assumptions. That *Manual* is never categorically homoerotic (although Rex's illustrations in the original edition certainly imply the primacy of a gay primacy, and Mattoso's other writings leave no doubt as to the essential parameters of his sexual interests) underscores one significant dimension of sexual dissidence: if not the questioning of sex as gender-marked, at least the indication that sex need not always be defined, need not always be fetishist, in terms of binary sexual categories.

Evita Perón, Juan José Sebreli, and Gender

Una mujer decente es la que se lleva al mundo de los machos por delante.

AS ATTRIBUTED TO EVA DUARTE DE PERÓN BY ABEL POSSE,
IN *LA PASIÓN SEGÚN EVA*

"**S**i Evita viviera, sería tortillera."[1] With this play on the 1970s rallying cry of the guerrilla movement of the Argentine left—"Si Evita viviera, sería montonera"[2]—the late 1980s fledgling gay movement, which was only made possible by postdictatorship redemocratization and Argentina's abiding, unflagging determination to be *absolument moderne,* attempted to claim Eva Duarte de Perón as a potent symbol. For fifty years, Evita has served as a symbol of social liberation, under a host of different political banners. For example, the left used her during the 1960s and 1970s as a way to assert its identity both against and within Peronismo. Perón energetically moved to squelch the leftist component of Peronismo once he returned to power. Yet, taking a cue from Evita's successful efforts in 1947 to gain the vote for Argentine women, feminist movements both within and outside Latin America have accorded her prototypic status (see *Eva Perón* 1974; Hodges 1976).

It should be noted that there is no evidence that Evita ever showed any interest or participated in homosexual circles, aside from the inevitable contact with gays and lesbians in the entertainment world of 1930s Argentina, which enjoyed a relatively relaxed moral climate.[3] Indeed, it seems probable that she was basically asexual in her private life, ripe gossip to the contrary. But as a gay symbol, Evita joins the ranks of other famous women of power who have been notorious "fag hags": Imelda Marcos, Madame Chiang, and a host of divas (Maria Callas being perhaps the most famous) and Hollywood grand dames (including Mae West, Tallulah Bankhead, Barbara Stanwyck, and Joan Crawford). (Today such women are less likely to be dames than "personalities": e.g., Elizabeth Taylor, Barbra Streisand, Madonna, and Roseanne Barr).

In his 1995 novel *Santa Evita,* undoubtedly the best fictional treatment of Eva Perón to date, Tomás Eloy Martínez has several pages on Evita and gays, including the following passage: "Quienes mejor han entendido la yunta histórica de amor y muerte son los homosexuales. Todos se imaginan fornicando locamente con Evita. La chupan, la resucitan, la entierran, se la entierran, la idolatran. Son Ella, Ella hasta la extenuación" (199).[4] This passage is typical of the almost delirious texture of Martínez's account, where fact and fiction, sober analysis and grotesque fugues turn around the obsessive fetish that Eva Perón's body becomes for all concerned, but most especially the military government that overthrew her husband. Anxious to prevent the perfectly embalmed body from becoming an object of veneration by the supporters of the ousted president but refusing to destroy it (according to Martínez, out of conservative Catholic sentiment), the regime is faced with the dilemma of what exactly to do with the body.

Although there are other sources of information about this necrophiliac tale (including a fine essay by V. S. Naipaul [1981]), no one has told it with Martínez's degree of black humor. As part of his narration, Martínez creates a whole network of pseudoaccurate and specious bibliographic sources. It is therefore unlikely that his information about gay interest in Evita Perón (and even here it unclear how a desire to have sex with her body can itself be described as "gay"), while it may correspond to a valid cultural interpretation, has any documentary validity. For example, although Martinez's references to Copi's play are accurate (see below), my guess is that his references to Néstor Perlongher are invented. (On the other hand, the title of Perlongher's poem "El cadáver de la nación" [1989; The Cadaver of the Nation] is subsequently attributed to an unidentified ex-president's assessment of the long shadow cast by her body over recent Argentine history.)

Another recent book to underscore both the strength and the complex nature of the symbol of Eva Perón is Alicia Dujovne Ortiz's *Eva Perón: la biografía* (1995; Eva Perón: The Biography). Dujovne Ortiz, who originally published her book in French, is the daughter of leftist Argentine Jewish intellectuals and the niece of the important social essayist Raúl Scalabrini Ortiz. *Eva Perón* is in many ways a straightforward biography, complete with published and unpublished documentary sources. However, it is unique in other regards. In the first place, Dujovne Ortiz comes to the conclusion that, had Evita lived, she would have ended up affiliating herself with the left, which explains why someone of the author's background may have been interested in writing about her in the first place. Yet Dujovne Ortiz also makes it clear that, fifty years after the inaugural moves of Peronismo and over forty years since the death of Evita, one can no longer invest in either the myths of Eva Duarte as a whore or Evita Perón as a saint. Taking her cue from the American anthropologist Julie Taylor's widely influential work (1979) on Eva Perón as a socially symbolic figure, Dujovne Ortiz is interested in providing as balanced and detailed an account of the complexities of Perón's character as is possible. Although she does seem at times to fall under the sway of the soap-opera motifs that have always provided the master narratives of Evita's life, Dujovne Ortiz is primarily concerned with the "Rashomon effect": the belief that historical truth is elusive if not nonexistent, and that the narrator's real task is to create a mosaic of possible meanings that constitute ever-shifting reality effects. The result is a work of highly original observations and at times brilliant insights, particularly when the author demonstrates her thorough mastery of feminist ideological principles that other writers have been unable to utilize. This is most apparent in two major subthemes: the analysis of the construction of Evita's persona through dress; and the analysis of a woman's body in a perpetually delicate state of health, which prefigured her terminal cancer. In the context of masculinist principles of control, as exemplified by Perón as the Macho Triumphant, Dujovne Ortiz's analysis is particularly eloquent and effective.

Evita's basic allure has undoubtedly been that of the strong woman able to accrue power. This results in a portrait of a woman who defies macho-dominated society, often by assuming the macho's own trappings of power. Nevertheless, the woman does not become the macho, but rather displaces him through the deconstructive gestures of a skillfully crafted presence. Such a presence calls into question the "naturalness" of the masculinist pose, while at the same time underscoring how power and presence are complex construc-tions that entail equally complex performances (I am evoking here the form of analysis of gender identity pursued by Judith Butler [1990]). The rags-to-riches tale of someone like Evita is homologous with a program of personal construction—the body and sexual iden-tity as works in progress—that is central to so much of what is at-tributed to gay sensibility. And the parvenu as display text is coter-minous with drag, the latter understood not just as ostentatious cross-dressing but as any form of dress, and related phenomena, rep-resenting structures of dissident articulation: bodily adornments, body language, affective speech, narrative discourse, and spatial placement, all as "perversions" of the putatively and ideologically enforced "natural."

Moreover, the excesses of the self-constructed woman become part of a powerful semiosis. These excesses do not necessarily imply abuses of power, although they can involve, as in the case of La Señora, legendary stories told in disgust by her detractors but with awe by her supporters. Rather, these excesses have to do with pat-terns of overdetermination in the process of signifying femininity and feminine power, or the power of the feminine. Just as Evita found it necessary to overstate her newfound position and wealth, so may the sexual outsider find it necessary or advantageous to overstate difference, dissidence, and deviance (which is in great part the signi-fying power of the screaming queen). Finally, the circumstantial apo-ria and tropes in the behavior of the powerful woman—in the case of Evita, her famous rages, her strategic lapses into barroom and brothel language, her refusal to adhere to time-honored protocol—legitimate defiance in the face of the norm and the normal, provid-ing yet other opportunities for an enhanced elaboration of symbolic presence.

I do not mean to imply that there are easy and evident continu-ities between Evita and the libertarian and gay rights movements, or between Evita the power queen and gay sensibility. Rather, what I mean to underscore is how the surpluses of meaning generated by a public persona like Evita lend themselves to multiple appropriations, of which Evita as *tortillera* is only one. This appropriation may ap-pall traditional Peronistas, who had no ideological component cham-pioning a restructuring of sexuality beyond the vote for women and a concomitant greater role for women in the Peronista political pro-cess (which, to be sure, necessarily brought with it redefinitions of sexual roles, although apparently never as part of any conscious po-litical process: indeed, Evita's public declarations consistently maintained that suffrage for women meant the opportunity to enhance male-centered politics such as those manifested in General Perón's programs). I know of no research on how marginalized groups other than ethnic groups (notably the Jews) interacted with Peronismo. Nonetheless, it is safe to assume that the masculinism of the military establishment, which was always Perón's basic point of reference, and the generally homophobic climate of Argentina, offered little room for sexual dissidence—as, in the end, they really made little room for feminism understood in any way other than as power for the President's wife in her role as an adjunct of his programs. Any other serious feminist dimensions follow from historical assessments of the implications of Eva Duarte de Perón's political participation, rather than from programmatic proposals formulated by her or her circle.

The alliance between the historical and the iconographic Evita and the gay movement—and it remains to be sorted out if Evita is a more powerful image for certain gay males, for whom the powerful woman is meaningful, or for lesbians, who may appreciate her defiance of masculinist privilege—is equally a matter of interpretive projections. It is not so much a question of what Evita might have meant had she lived on into the 1980s or even had she been a power figure in that decade, than it is a question of what her position in the hypermasculinist, homophobic context of the 1940s and 1950s might be taken to mean.

Finally, Evita's operatic/soap-opera death, her cancer, her forced renunciation of the vice-presidential candidacy in Perón's second bid for the Presidency, the pathetic valor of her appearance at his reinauguration, and the grand theatrics of her state funeral and subsequent veneration by a regime desperate to shore itself up against its inevitable decline (leading to the widespread belief that Perón could not function without Evita) are all the stuff of gay tragedy, whether as the kitsch of the theater of the ridiculous (one can only surmise why major performance artists like Enrique Pinti and Antonio Gasalla have yet to mine this rich lode) or as actually bespeaking the inevitable death of hyperfeminine beauty and all that it metonymizes for sexual dissidence.

It is perhaps not surprising that, although the bibliography of historical and political assessments of Eva Duarte de Perón abounds with contrasting interpretive opinions (especially if one takes into account material published outside of Argentina and scholarship free of the sectarian debate grounded in the immediate humus of the national political process, which has included both the demonization and mythification of Peronismo), there has not been much in the way of rich cultural production on Evita. A legacy of partisan poetry endures, as well as Nacha Guevara's rock opera *Eva,* a rather grimly messy attempt to counteract the offhanded fictions of Lloyd Webber and Rice's *Evita.* Yet the fact that *Evita* has never been performed in Argentina (although "Don't Cry for Me, Argentina" [sung in Spanish as "No llores por mí, Argentina"] was a popular song hit) speaks eloquently to the virtual taboo in Argentine culture regarding narrative, theatrical, or filmic interpretations (other than partisan documentaries) of Evita. Abel Posse's *La pasión según Evita* (1994; The Passion according to Evita), an account of Evita's last year of life as culled from documentary sources, is indicative of the abiding problem of writing fiction in the context of intransigent sectarian politics. Posse—not surprisingly although rather disappointingly—provides an essentially dithyrambic portrait of Evita, which fails to reach the core of her subjectivity or to place her in any nonsuperficial way with respect to sociohistorical coordinates. The book is interesting, but no significant new insights are provided beyond those of Posse's cited documentary sources.

Posse's book is made possible, one assumes, by the new face of Peronismo in Argentina.[5] Menem has been widely recognized, and widely denounced, for having substantially modified the nature of Peronismo, most specifically by eliminating the imperative social conflict (often interpreted as social resentment), trade-union domination, and welfare bureaucracy (see for example, Galasso 1990). For many, this means that there is nothing Peronista (or Justicialista) left in Peronismo—except perhaps for its principal exponents' lower-middle-class and immigrant social origins—and that contemporary Peronismo is only an appropriation of Liberalism (see Posse's tirade against the "new" Peronismo, 276–277). Menem would insist that his neoliberalist administration is popular because his policies ultimately benefit the broad electorate that supported his party. And one might also characterize Menem as following in the best Peronista tradition because of his artful ability to govern so often by virtual fiat. What all of this has meant is a radical revision of the icons of Peronismo. It is probably unnecessary to determine if this radical revision has been required for the formulation of Menem's unique definition of Peronismo, or whether that uniqueness has rendered many of the icons meaningless or incoherent.

One such icon is that of Evita (see Geltman 1969; Taylor 1979; Goldar 1971, 63–71). Evita remains one of the most effective Peronista images, and examples abound of the government's support for her continuing importance among Argentines. Nevertheless, when one recalls the potent uses of her symbolism in the context of the relegitimation of Peronismo in the early 1970s and the return of Perón in 1973, current images of Evita are pale indeed. When Perón's third wife became President in 1974, it was customary both to comment on how far short she fell of Evita's model and to observe that she was in a sense usurping a position that should have been Evita's: María Estela (a.k.a. Isabelita) Martínez became President upon Perón's death because she was able to be his vice-presidential candidate in 1973, while Evita had been kept by the military from a similar position on the Peronista ticket in 1950. The attenuation of the Evitine iconography provides a major context for Posse's novel, both in the sense of giving it resonance—its basically hagiographic portrait of Evita, a renewal of the legend for a new generation, and the pathos of the painful agony of her declining health—and in allowing it to have narrative significance outside the official version of Peronismo. Evita's agony is shown to parallel significantly the decline of the Peronista experiment, and Perón's appearances in the novel hardly rise above his portrayal as a military hack and a boorish buffoon, which only serves to reconfirm the belief that Peronista mythopoesis gives credit either to Perón or to Evita, but never to both in a balanced fashion.

Perhaps the most fascinating cultural interpretation of Evita is Copi's 1969 play *Eva Perón*. Although he wrote most of his works (principally novels and plays) in French, Copi (1941–1987; his real name was Raúl Damonte) was Argentine. Only a scant amount of his dramatic production has been translated into Spanish (see Wetsel 1994). There was a 1994 Spanish-language production of *Eva Perón* in San Juan, Puerto Rico, directed by Rafael Acevedo; the play was re-produced in the 1992–1993 season in Paris under the direction of Laurent Pelly.[6] In the play's original productions, Copi is reputed to have played the part of Eva Perón, and his drag interpretation was abetted by his public homosexuality. Like Posse's novel,[7] Copi's play focuses on Evita's final days.[8] But unlike Posse's novel, Copi's play stresses her rage: rage against the power structure that denies her and that blocks her desires, rage over her disease (which is also given sociopolitical meanings), and rage over her realization that she will be monumentalized, turned into a public icon to serve the interests of others.

The first word of Evita's opening speech is "Shit" (9; this word becomes a veritable motif). The play closes with Perón's words of beatification: "Eva Perón, ladies and gentlemen, is more alive now than

EVITA PERÓN, JUAN JOSÉ SEBRELI, AND GENDER

ever before" (35). Perón's words are doubly ironic, because they allude to not only how mythification makes one larger than life, but also how, in the play, the character of Eva Perón has absconded with the numbers of her secret bank accounts, leaving her nurse to take her place on the death bed. It is Evita as survivor whom Copi wishes to enshrine (clearly, Evita the martyr is the one who interests Posse), and it is this Evita, in all of her creatural presence and her bodily materiality, who is the drag queen's unholy icon, and who has nothing to do with the worn political pieties of Perón himself. "Don't talk such fucking rubbish" (30), she tells him at one point, and she tells her brother (who in the play is named Ibiza): "You left me all alone to sink into the depths of my cancer. You're a pair [Ibiza and Perón] of skunks. . . . You watched me die like an animal at the slaughter house" (32).[9]

Copi's play is wickedly anti-Peronista. Copi was from a diplomatic family who left Argentina because of Perón; one of his first books, ¿A dónde va Perón? De Berlín a Wall Street (1955), was a denunciation of Peronismo. While he was uninterested in buying into the Santa Evita myth that Peronismo has repeatedly staged so well, Copi was attempting to represent Eva Perón's oppositional character and her ability to prevail against the three patriarchal figures in the play: Perón, her brother, and her mother. In this sense, Copi's characterization of Eva Duarte is in line with my characterization of the ways in which she would interest a gay audience.

In contrast to Copi's play, Juan José Sebreli's Eva Perón: ¿aventurera o militante? (1971; Eva Perón: Adventuress or Militant?) is a much more sober (and regrettably nonhilarious) effort to establish distance between Evita and Peronismo. This book, which has been issued in numerous editions and widely cited, is the first to be written from a markedly leftist perspective. It seeks to find in Evita's public persona a defense of Marxist ideals that would be radically at variance with the Peronista establishment—which, as has been firmly established, repudiated Marxism and leftist ideologies in general and persecuted their adherents in Argentina as apátridas (persons without a country; i.e., anti-Argentines). In this sense, Sebreli's book anticipates the leftist appropriation of Evita by the Montoneros and other radical movements of the late sixties and early seventies, with, as previously stated, their apogee coming in their collaboration with institutional Peronismo in Perón's return to power in 1973.[10]

Sebreli (b. 1930), Argentina's major extra-academic sociologist, has produced an extensive body of research, mostly in the form of interpretive essays and characterized by the absence of the sort of original statistical evidence that typically accompanies the academic exercise of sociology. His writings have centered on three main themes: the Argentine oligarchy (Sebreli 1986); the Marxist interpretation of cultural phenomena, including popular culture (Sebreli 1960, 1964, 1971, 1981)[11]; and the exploration of homoeroticism. The latter has been more of an implied subtext in Sebreli's writing. It emerges explicitly, albeit guardedly, in his examination of the homosociality of soccer (Sebreli 1981, 93–98). This theme should be examined in full detail in Sebreli's much promised but as yet unpublished book on homosexuality in Argentina.

Eva Perón: ¿aventurera o militante? was written under the aegis of the intellectual left of the postwar years. The intellectual left exercised a considerable impact in Argentina during a time when opposition to Perón and general economic prosperity combined to renew fulsomely the commitment of Argentine writers and artists to European, especially French, culture. Victoria Ocampo's literary and intellectual review, *Sur* (first published in the 1930s; South), devoted considerable space to Spanish translations of the best of postwar writing in Europe and the United States. The publication of these translations was intended to counteract the official culture of Peronismo, which had come to prevail in many public and private sectors (particularly in university-sponsored and commercial publishing). *Sur* also had its own publishing imprint, which brought out an extensive list of non-Peronista writers and book-length translations from English and French: a typical publication was the 1956 translation by Jorge Luis Borges of Virginia Woolf's *A Room of One's Own.*

Sebreli served for a time as an assiduous contributor to *Sur,* and in 1953 he published in its pages a classic existential interpretation of Roberto Arlt (1900–1942), one of a number of important Argentine authors who were rediscovered by the left in the 1960s. (Sebreli also collaborated with *Contorno,* the major leftist intellectual review in Argentina during the period 1953–1959, and in a 1956 issue dedicated to Peronismo he made statements in defense of certain aspects of the movement [see Katra 1988, 76–79]). To be sure, *Sur* was hardly a left-wing journal. Ocampo's cultural ties were with the old oligarchy, which was one of the major objects of scorn of the Peronista regime, and Sebreli was subsequently to break with Ocampo and to criticize her and the journal openly (King 1986, 156–157). But in the way in which difficult times make for strange bedfellows, *Sur* involved the participation of Argentine writers whose affinities lay more with the postwar left, and the magazine saw fit to oppose Peronismo with texts by Sartre and company in the name of a serious cultural tradition.

Eva Perón: ¿aventurera o militante? contains specific acknowledgments of the French left. It is dedicated to Simone de Beauvoir, one of the foremothers of contemporary feminism (thereby suggesting from the outset Evita's affiliation with feminism), and it opens with a long epigraph from Sartre's *Crítica de la razón dialéctica* (Critique of Dialectical Reason), a passage that speaks of the dynamic and dialectical relationship between the individual and the social group: "Hay que ir más lejos y considerar en cada caso el papel del individuo en el acontecimiento histórico" (9).[12] This epigraph makes it clear that Sebreli wishes to examine Evita from an existential perspective; that he wishes to place her in a social context in which she and that context are involved in a single process of mutual and reciprocal determination of meaning; and that, by virtue of the implications of choosing to analyze her life in the first place, Evita may be viewed as complying favorably with Sartre's understanding of historical agency.

Thirty years later Sebreli will revise his interpretation of Evita, moving more into line with the interpretation of her as embodying fascist characteristics (see below for further discussion of this point). However, in the 1950s, in the period of transition between Evita's death, the collapse of Perón's second Evita-less government, and the military takeover of 1955, Sebreli is able to frame Evita as a revolutionary figure. He significantly re-echos this position in the fourth, expanded edition of *Eva Perón: ¿aventurera o militante?*, published in 1971, precisely the period in which the urban guerrilla movement emerges. That movement will claim Evita as one of its icons using the aforementioned slogan, "Si Evita viviera, sería montonera." (A few years later, in 1978, Andrew Lloyd Webber and Tim Rice depict this left-wing identification of Evita by pairing her in a dialectical relationship with Che Guevara (1928–1967), thus lending their rock opera *Evita* significant additional meaning. Noting, however, that Che Guevara had no known contact with Evita, both the radical left and traditional Peronistas have focused on this conjunction as a grand metonym of the serious historical inaccuracies that plague the work—a master example of the impossibility of adequate interpretations by foreigners of Argentine social history.)

Sebreli quickly establishes the parameters of his interpretation of Evita's militancy, and it becomes obvious that his subtitle is purely rhetorical:

> Su breve vida, su espectacular conversión, su acción desenfrenada, las circunstancias dramáticas de su muerte han devenido una leyenda, haciendo de ella una heroína romántica. (11)[13]

This quote is marked by two intersecting discursive strategies: the utilization of unanalyzed assumptions (expressed in either adjectives or adjectival phrases such as "espectacular" and "heroína romántica"); and an *accumulatio* that establishes a network of qualities for Evita which, less than synthesizing the militancy of her life, provide it with the dimensions of operatic pathos. One will recall that the pathetic functions to a large degree through the deployment of unanalyzed assumptions about human behavior, such as one finds typically in the soap opera. Indeed, I would argue that the quality of Sebreli's interpretation of Evita which evokes gay sensibility is that of Evita as an operatic persona, as a Camille or a Manon struck down while almost a child, after a heroic and romantic struggle during a febrile emotional period. In order to pursue this theatrical casting of Evita, Sebreli must necessarily compromise with the sober historical agency that Sartre has in mind. After all, Eva Perón as an individual whose life is marked by a *"conversión"* can hardly be equated with one of Sartre's paradigmatic dark angels—for example, Jean Genet, who for a long time was for Sartre the embodiment of the existential hero, precisely because of his strenuous acts of separation from social institutions (in contrast to Evita, whose existence was solely defined through interactions with social institutions).

Sebreli makes it clear that Evita is a heroine in the way in which she struggled to prevail against the forces in which she was caught up. In this sense, the meaning of her life is more operatically pathetic than that of the tragic hero of existentialism, whose struggle is to disengage from established institutions. By all accounts, Evita struggled *against* conventional social norms, *against* the institutions of class structure, and *against* the processes of social margination. Yet there is, with the exception of the alienation imposed by the intense pain of her final agony, a paucity of evidence for the willed, sustained disengagement that one associates with the classic existential paradigm.

This mismatch between canonical existentialism and Sebreli's operatic interpretation of Evita does not make all that much difference—not because it is unimportant whether or not Argentine thinkers capture exactly the conceptual framework of their French models, but rather because their interface creates fields of interpretation that are more interesting (at least today) than any strict intellectual accuracy. This issue could be fruitfully explored with regard to the general relationship between Argentine and foreign models. And it should be raised with respect to other major cultural analyses of the day, such as Adolfo Prieto's monograph on Borges, *Borges y la nueva generación* (1954; Borges and the New Generation), a text that also reflected the influence of French existentialism (it was the first monograph to be published on Borges, and one of the opening salvos in the parricidal criticism of Borges that prevailed at least until his death in 1986).

It would seem reasonable to be less interested in the rigor of Sebreli's existentialist line of thought than in his use of it to legitimate an interpretation of Evita that is, from the opening characterization of her life, marked more by the narrative schemata of grand opera than by those of the "stranger": Evita may have been an outcast, but she was not an outlaw, especially when one accepts the proposition that the black legend of her fabled rise to fame through diligent prostitution and shrewd courtesanship is mostly nothing but the nasty fabrication of her enemies on numerous fronts (presumably even within macho Peronismo). Of course, in order to demonstrate the authenticity (this is a key word, certainly) of Evita's personal commitment to militancy—a militancy that derived from her personal story, and not from any role imposed on her by a Peronismo that was, in any event, insensitive to the specific dimensions of social activism embodied by her—Sebreli must emphasize those interpretational strategies that separate her from the Peronista apparatus and that ground her activism in other spheres.

In the former case, this means repudiating her affiliation with the Peronista machine: "Tampoco es admisible . . . una variante de interpretación antiperonista que muestra a Eva Perón como un mero producto mecánico de la máquina de Estado, el aparato político y la propaganda masiva" (17).[14] As regards the latter, Sebreli easily bases his interpretation on the rich lore of Evita's background of social, cultural, and economic deprivation. Such a background was hardly unique for the time, but was nevertheless one from which she was able to draw inspiration, so to speak, in her exercise of individual power. Posse, who cites Sebreli in his bibliography, pursues the same line of narrative exposition; this is confirmed by Perón's virtual absence from the novel, or his appearance only in passing, in buffoonish poses.

It should be noted that, while I have continued to use "Evita" to evoke not so much the historical figure as the cultural icon, Sebreli rarely uses the familiar diminutive, which was exploited so effectively by Peronista propaganda in the 1950s and again in the 1970s and by certain left-wing ideologues of the late 1960s and 1970s. Rather—and this is also true of Posse, whose novel is titled *La pasión según Eva*—Sebreli prefers the more neutral and presumably more respectful "Eva Perón," both in the title of his book and in the body of his text. It is interesting to speculate why Sebreli would not have preferred "Eva Duarte" or "Eva Duarte de Perón." While the former was not her legal name, it would have underscored better her pre-Peronista roots; the latter, a sequence that articulates sequentially her origins and her separable relationship with Perón, would have evoked her legal status as Perón's wife.[15] I suspect that Sebreli prefers "Eva Perón" to refer to her problematical relationship to Peronismo, and eschews "Eva Duarte de Perón" as cumbersomely resounding the society pages of the oligarchy. Rather, as suggested by the icon of her exclusively personal name, Eva Perón, Evita is "creación y creadora a la vez, producto y a la vez productora, reflejo y reflejante, punto de llegada y punto de partida, [quien] padece la historia y a la vez la elige" (20).[16] This formulation echoes both the existential concepts of a forged self-identity and the subsequent gay adherence to constructionist principles. Such adherence means, among other things, that one's identity—which is not just sexual, since it is important to disavow the identification of individuals in terms of some kind of magnified sexual disposition—is a project of constant elaboration.

The recurring grounding of Evita in the overarching narratives of opera is particularly evident when Sebreli begins to sum up her character in the concluding chapter "Lo vivo y lo muerto" (What Is Alive and What Is Dead), where once again the myth of Evita must be rejected in order to achieve a proper historicization of Eva Perón, a *historical* romantic heroine:

> El mito de Evita [sic] como expresión simbólica de los anhelos de justicia e igualdad de las mujeres y los trabajadores argentinos, sólo a medias realizados en la realidad, y a la vez como expresión del temor por la pérdida de sus privilegios por parte de las clases burguesas, fue como tal un mito de carácter dinámico, creador y progresivo, estaba dirigido hacia el futuro y no hacia el pasado, como los mitos regresivos. . . .
>
> La característica del mito regresivo es el eterno retorno al pasado y la negación del tiempo histórico, del progreso. La muerte de Eva Perón fue una contingencia histórica, pero tal vez coincidió con una necesidad que su ciclo estaba cumplido: no nos podemos imaginar a una Evita envejeciendo en la inacción del destierro. La muerte de Evita viene a coincidir con el fin del poder del ala plebeya del peronismo. . . .
>
> Es por ello que entre las masas populares, se repetía insistentemente en el 55: "Si Evita viviera esto no hubiera pasado". Se intuía vagamente que la caída del peronismo se debía antes que nada al freno puesto por el propio Perón a la clase obrera,

a la que Evita representaba dentro del gobierno, más que al
propio Perón. (109–110)[17]

At this point, one could well ask to what extent Sebreli has been
successful in establishing a distance between Perón/Peronismo and
Evita, and to what extent he has displaced Evita in favor of Eva
Perón. Sebreli does consistently argue for the proper historicization
of Evita and the demonstration that her character formation and
her conduct in power responded to concrete sociohistorical circumstances. He also argues that she was neither an adjunct to Perón's ideology—its more "human" face—nor the consequence of some tel-
luric process, which seems to lie at the root of her quasi canonization
that exceeds the boundaries of Peronismo itself. But I would also
submit that, while Sebreli is consistent in his evocation of the existentialist concept of the dialectic relationship between individuals and their sociohistorical circumstance, such that the predicates
"made" and "making" work in both directions at once, the grandeur
conferred by his essay upon Evita strains the parameters of history
by reaching toward the ahistorically operatic, the Evita who is somehow "larger than history."

This perception is necessary in order to account for the surplus of
meanings that as early as the mid-1950s had begun to accrue to her.
And these are, in turn, excesses that are juxtaposed to the masculinism of Perón and Peronismo, such that they inexorably point out its
inadequacies, its flaws, and finally its failures. These are Sebreli's concluding comments, and it is significant to note that, in this 1971 edition, he has added a specific reference to Che Guevara, who was mur-
dered in captivity by the Bolivian police in 1967:

> Contra las necrofilias de ciertos peronistas que reclaman la
> momia de Evita para convertirla en un objeto mágico de ado-
> ración mística, prefiero que la tumba de Evita siga abierta y
> que su fantasma siga perturbando las conciencias. Los héroes
> que de una u otra manera mueren por la libertad de los pue-
> blos de América latina no tienen sepultura; los cadáveres de
> Evita y del Che no tienen descanso ni han comenzado a mode-
> larse sus estatuas. Profanar el tabú, descaralizar el mito, tanto
> en su versión angélica como diabólica, develando el verdadero
> significado histórico de Evita, haciendo aflorar a la conciencia
> el secreto de su poder que una severa censura interna y externa
> nos impone ocultar, es una de las maneras—la que corresponde
> al escritor más que al político—de contribuir al esclarecimiento
> de la concienca de la clase trabajadora y de las mujeres argen-
> tinas, o por lo menos de sus posibles dirigentes, de los cuadros,

> de quienes depende que la transformación social del país, el cambio histórico, deje de ser un mito nostálgico en el que se proyectan las esperanzas y los sueños más ardientes de una gran parte del pueblo. (113)[18]

I have quoted so extensively from the conclusion to the 1971 edition, with its added reference to Che, because it demonstrates that over fifteen years after the original publication of *Eva Perón,* Sebreli is still committed to propagating the excesses of meaning attributed to her figure, whereby a very emotional understanding of historical meaning is juxtaposed to the futility of both "angelical" and "diabolical" myths surrounding her. However, by 1983, Sebreli, with the publication of *Los deseos imaginarios del peronismo* (The Imaginary Desires of Peronismo), definitively liquidates any belief in a positive political meaning for Eva Perón, ascribing his earlier enthusiasms to "la rebelión juvenil típicamente pequeñoburguesa contra las convenciones y tabúes de la familia y la sociedad, el deseo bohemio de *épater le bourgeois*" (12).[19] Furthermore, he confesses that he was moved especially by his literary commitments:

> No pudiendo tampoco sustraerme a las influencias literarias, identifiqué a Evita con el bastardo sartreano, ese personaje a quien la condena de la sociedad transforma en censor implacable de la misma. . . . [La] exaltación lírica de la juventud, la borrachera heroica de un joven, si por añadidura es intelectual de izquierda, no se detiene ante los triviales hechos cotidianos. (13)[20]

Thus, Sebreli falls into line with current historical assessments of Peronismo that resist any attachment of socialist meaning to either Peronismo or to the biography of Evita, and Eva Perón is barely mentioned in the remaining two hundred pages of the book. Indeed, as Francesca Miller has argued, it is difficult to attach even much of a feminist meaning to Evita: "Eva Perón had little or no interest in or understanding of women's rights, and she expressed disdain for feminists as 'women who did not know how to be women'" (123).

What Sebreli provides in *Los deseos imaginarios* is a minute analysis of the irrefutable fascist underpinnings of Peronismo and the conclusion that Evita was simply an integral, if flamboyant, component of its propaganda apparatus (see Ciria 1983, 305–307). Sebreli is still unable or unwilling to step back and analyze the cultural meanings of Evita apart from Peronismo, to return to his interpretation of her as an operatic heroine and to discuss why the excesses of her public persona may have had cultural meanings impinging on issues of masculinity other than those that (rather uncomfortably) conform to his idea of the Sartrean bastard. Nor, as he proceeds to reinterpret her as a weft in the fabric of Peronista fascism, is he interested in the still vibrant connotations she evokes in Argentina. It is simply not enough to dismiss her as part and parcel of a set of "imaginary desires." In the best of the Argentine Lacanian tradition, imaginary desires have potent, nonsuperfluous meanings, which, as a Peronista like Menem realizes, include yet cannot be reduced to the meanings of exhausted political systems.

"Si Evita viviera, sería tortillera." Both Foster (1985) and Katra (1980) have examined the relationship between Evita and Argentine popular culture, but no one has yet connected her with issues like gay sensibility, sexual dissidence, or masculine subjectivity. The essays on her participation in popular culture begin to build a bridge toward the notion of "queering culture," in Alexander Doty's sense in *Making Things Perfectly Queer*, as to how mass culture necessarily escapes the sharp boundaries of the stable signifiers of compulsory heterosexuality. Yet it can come as no surprise that Sebreli, committed to homosexual issues, either as the young bohemian rebel who wrote *Eva Perón: ¿aventurera o militante?* or as the jaded social analyst of *Los deseos imaginarios*, declines the opportunity to place the figure of Eva Perón in larger cultural contexts, which might involve dissident sexual identities.

In addition to characterizing the extremely difficult history of homosexual liberation in Argentina, Zelmar Acevedo (1985), in fifteen pages of chronicle, mentions no names of individuals involved with movements, publications, or cultural acts. The stakes are too high. Of course, Sebreli might find it outrageous to establish links between Evita and gay sensibility, for there can be no question of the homophobia of the Peronista movement, with its military roots, as part of a deadening historical record of homophobia in Argentina. But the excesses of meaning surrounding Evita Perón do exist, and Sebreli's interpretation of them in the framework of the Sartrean bastard is only one approach. Though Sebreli may no longer be interested in Evita as a militant, he was in the mid-1950s, and his book exercised a considerable amount of influence at that time and subsequently. Sebreli's book stood alone, because although many other books about Evita were published in Argentina after her death, they were all hagiographic, and none attempted to establish larger historical, social, and cultural connections (indeed, the very goal of hagiography is to define the uniqueness of the individual). But when *Eva*

Perón is read today from the point of view of new cultural parameters in Argentina and an emerging interest in sexual dissidence, the coincidences between the gay slogan, the meanings of Evita as a popular-culture icon, and the excesses of meaning that derive from her characterization by Sebreli as, alternately, a Sartrean bastard or a romantic-operatic heroine point toward the possibility of a productive queer reading.

The Case for Feminine Pornography in Latin America

Estás confusa porque te relato tudo isto?

HILDA HILST, *CARTAS DE UM SEDUTOR*

Porque cada um de nós . . . tem que achar o seu próprio porco. (Atenção, não confundir com corpo.) Porco, gente, porco, o corpo às avessas.[1]

HILDA HILST, *CONTOS D'ESCARNIO*

Few topics in contemporary cultural production are more controversial, and more likely to create entrenched divisions among individuals, than pornography.[2] While pornography may be a central fact of human artistic expression, as archeological and historical studies have amply demonstrated (see Hunt 1993 for a discussion of the general relationship of pornography to modern culture), there has been no adequate resolution of the issue of how to interpret its role in cultural production. Some believe that pornography should be not only condemned but also legally banned. This group includes such implausible bedfellows as religious fundamentalists (whose views are voiced in the so-called Meese Report of the Attorney General's Commission on Pornography [1986]) and politically correct, interventionist feminists (paradigmatically, Andrea Dworkin and Catherine MacKinnon, separately and as coauthors). The former see pornography as the work of the Antichrist, while for the latter, as the famous formulation goes, "rape is the practice; pornography the theory."

Others, most notably Kendrick, see pornography as part of a continuum of human artistic expression, where it functions as a form of cultural resistance, a Bakhtinian polyphony, a defiant countercultural manifestation. Marcuse was able to see in the erotic and its cultural expressions a liberating corrective to the destructive demands of civilization, while Soble develops an explicitly Marxist defense of pornography as a liberating discourse. In all of these formulations, the relationship between the erotic and pornography remains either underdistinguished or undertheorized (one significant exception is the papers in Gubar and Hoff 1989). It has been said (though by whom I do not recall) that erotica is pornography for the well-to-do, invoking perhaps the image of Anaïs Nin, writing elegant, pay-by-the-word texts for a wealthy client, or the exquisite silk-screen creations of classical Chinese and Japanese culture.

The possibility of a pornographic discourse (and allow me to propose for the purposes of this discussion that we understand pornography to be an explicitly sexual narrative production privileging the genital or that which is considered synecdochally genital) continues to be energetically debated, particularly within feminism. Thus, while those like Dworkin and MacKinnon see it as a repugnant reduplication of patriarchal power, contrary opinions are offered in the collection *Pornography and Feminism* (Rodgerson and Wilson 1991) and by others such as Pat Califia, Nancy Friday, and Lisa Henderson, who see in a specifically feminist pornography both a site for the examination of the dynamics of patriarchal violence and the possibility for constructing an erotics that re-images relations of sexual power.

Specifically pornographic production by Latin American women writers continues to be scant. Instead, work by these writers reveals a greater emphasis on an erotic imagination that reterritorializes the body in order to escape the genital privileging of patriarchal sexuality:

> No partimos de la premisa de que la sexualidad constituye una categoría metodológica exclusiva, o que es la base única para examinar la identidad personal. Sin embargo, dado que la opresión y la represión sexual se encuentran entre las múltiples manifestaciones de la desigualdad entre los sexos, ¿cómo logramos que la cultura dominante sea más representativa de los intereses de la mujer? Para transformar las definiciones y categorías culturales opresivas debemos recurrir a la experiencia femenina, y tratar de comprender sus códigos, sus discursos y sus sistemas de signos; es decir, emprender el

tipo de estudio que el análisis de la imaginación sexual en la creación literaria femenina haría posible. (Fernández Olmos and Paravisini-Gebert 1991, xviii).[3]

Nevertheless, novelists like Cristina Peri Rossi, Alicia Steimberg, Diana Raznovich, and María Luisa Mendoza (see Foster 1984) have authored texts that constitute experiments in feminine pornography. Indeed, Brazil's Cassandra Rios (see Foster 1991a, 120–124) and Adelaida Carrara have even authored mass-consumer, soft-porn texts, complete with appropriately lurid covers. That this production originates in Brazil, a large-market society, has to do with the greater incorporation in that country of a project of modernity, which incorporates explicit space for cultural products that can be loosely termed "pornographic." Other clear examples of modernized Latin American societies are Mexico and Argentina, and Claudia Schaefer-Rodríguez (1989) has examined how the emergence in the former of an incipient lesbian narrative is related to neoliberal market forces. Argentina presents a different dynamic: while modernity has long been a byword of Argentine society, much of its cultural production that is of interest to this discussion either remains clandestine (as has been true of so much production even during the military dictatorship's neoliberal periods); or is excoriated on multiple fronts, some of which are really smoke screens for censorship (as, for example, when Enrique Medina's fiction is dismissed as bad writing, since it can no longer be legally banned); or is simply published abroad, as in the case of the texts by Alicia Steimberg (1990) and Diana Raznovich (1992) (both of which are examined below).

Perhaps the only prominent, self-acknowledged female pornographer is Brazil's Hilda Hilst (b. 1930).[4] Hilst's writing can best be described as fuguelike. Now, although academic/formal writing in all languages generally reveals some goal of achieving discursive cohesion, there is probably no reliable metric of discursive cohesion. Such a principle is based, however, on the degree to which it is immediately apparent that components of a text interlock with each other, a feature of writing reflected in the etymological meaning of the word "text." If one of the characteristics of colloquiality is a relaxation of the academic/formal principles of textual cohesion—which is usually quickly apparent in the attempts to transcribe colloquiality or to make it the basis of a narrative exposition beyond the level of quoted direct speech (as in, for example, *Tres tristes tigres* by Cuba's Guillermo Cabrera Infante [1967; Three Sad Tigers])—then colloquiality is especially notable in a language like Portuguese, which shares with French a rigidly codified standard for learned speech and writing.

Since the last decade Hilst, known as one of the most brilliant craftspersons of contemporary Brazilian prose, has, by her own admission, decided to devote her fiction to pornography. Without substantively altering the principles of textual production based on complex fuguelike patterns of semantic and narrative configuration, such that her texts often remain stunningly impenetrable after the most assiduous of (re)readings, Hilst has produced a number of works in which the multiple facets of sexual experience are sketched via an expository style that careens vertiginously from one image to another. It is impossible to explain away this writing as perceptive erotic analysis, in the way in which it has been claimed that the pornographic redeems itself as the erotic by virtue of the latter's emphasis on inscribing the former in a structure of sufficient psychosociological introspection.

If the pornographic involves the representation of sexual activity that appears motivated either solely by "animal lust" or—in a presumable perversion of the lust which might be seen as a beneficent feature of the noble savage—by what we have come to consider the distinctive features of rape (violence in which the sex organs, paradigmatically the penis, are the weapons of assault), then it is questionable whether one can comfortably distinguish Hilst's writings on sex as erotic. Indeed, a text like *Cartas de um sedutor* (1991; Letters of a Seducer), written by a woman presumably familiar with the general debate in Western society over sexual violence and the extended consideration given the topic in Brazil since the return to democracy in 1985 (when that country became one of the first in the world to establish police stations specifically serving the needs of female assault victims), derives much of its impact from the way in which it appears to conform to the hoariest notions of pornography. This conformity is manifest in the narrative accounts of sexual exploits by men perpetrated on the bodies of women (there is some reference to homosexual acts in the text, not the woman-woman activity characteristic of male pornography but rather male-male sex, which, presumably because of the psychological dynamics of rape pornography, is virtually never found in traditional scripts).

Two specific features of Hilst's text relate it to conventional forms of male pornography. The first concerns the primacy of the voice of a male narrator. As the letter of a seducer, *Cartas* originates with a male speaker who sounds very much like the narrator of Henry Miller's paradigmatic reveries of phallic hegemony. This does not mean, to be sure, that the text is an unrelievedly jouissant record of the satyr triumphant. Precisely because the narrator recounts his failures and limitations, his self-doubts and his occasional remorse, does his story become all the more satisfying when he is able to overcome the obstacles to male supremacy and realize, through acts on the female body (or the male body, in homosexual versions of the same script), the full measure of his potency.

The narrative voice of the satyr triumphant expands to occupy every structural dimension of the text, such that there is no room for any other voice to be heard, nothing that contradicts the imposing speaker: pornographic discourse is the paradigm of the monologic text as conceptualized by Bakhtin. While there may be some stray instances of dialogue, these serve to sustain the master's voice. In no way do they represent an opening toward a dialogism that might be another way in which a theorizing over the difference between pornography and the erotic could take place. Essentially the text of Karl directed toward his sister, Cordélia, along with other narrative segments that appear to be either extrapolations of his letters or parallel narratives by him, *Cartas* underscores the lopsided preeminence of the discourse of male sexuality by providing the reader only with Karl's letters and never with Cordélia's response to them (which could take the form of written replies to Karl, interior monologues, diary entries, or some other mode of reaction). Therefore, Karl speaks for himself and for Cordélia, by either explicitly or implicitly replying for her, if no more than by pursuing an epistolary production on the assumption that yet another letter is called for and, indeed, welcome.

Within this framework, Hilst's narrator strives for a maximum degree of sexual transgression, so much so his letters could be characterized as delirious masturbatory fantasies, wishful thinking having little correspondence to actual life. Thus Karl reminds Cordélia of their sexual couplings, and then compounds the incest taboo by bringing their mother and father into the erotic ars combinatoria and by adding a homosexual liaison for their father with a fifth party. Karl's recounting of these exploits, which is reinforced by the privileged second-person form characteristic of intimate letters, makes use of the Portuguese *tu* form in two special senses. The first is the presence of direct address in pornographic narratives, whereby the male voice ascribes to and prescribes for the woman her role in the sexual drama. As might be expected, the indicative mode of exposition is frequently exchanged for the imperative and subjunctive/jussive modes that enjoin—directly and indirectly, respectively—the woman's actions.

The second use of *tu* in Hilst's text has to do with this pronoun's special status. Without going into the details of the extremely complex pattern of the second person in Brazilian Portuguese, a pattern more complex than the corresponding system in Latin American Spanish, suffice it to say that the *tu* in *Cartas* establishes much more than a trace of intimate familiarity between the narrator and interlocutor. The *tu* form in Brazilian Portuguese has basically fallen into disuse, except in some regional dialects: the familiar form *você* is universally used, except in very restrictively defined formal contexts, in which *o senhor/a senhora* is the equivalent of the Spanish *usted* (both *você* and *a senhora/o senhor* use third-person verb forms; in Biblical and liturgical texts, the pronoun of divine address is *vos,* the second-person plural form, unlike Spanish, which uses the singular *tú*). Except in traditional lyric poetry, the Portuguese *tu* in its Peninsular uses is virtually unknown in Brazil. Thus, when Karl addresses his sister in the *tu* form, it creates a lyrical connotation that, depending on how one wishes to view it, either accentuates the sexual exchanges or rudely clashes with them.

What complicates this assessment, however, is that Karl's use of *tu* is fundamentally divided. On occasion he resorts to the "poetic conjugation": the use of the pronoun with its matching historical forms: *tu és,* etc. But on other occasions, *tu* simply alternates with *você* and is used with the third-person verb forms of the latter: *tu é.* This usage is distinctly colloquial, if not essentially untutored, and thus Karl's address moves between the conventionally lyrical and what one might call a hard-edged colloquial intimacy (hard-edged because it enjoys none of the attenuating factors of a presumably conscious effort at verbal refinement). This hard-edged colloquiality is carried out metonymically by the fact that it would be hard to find another text of Brazilian literature that so resolutely engages in inventorying every possible lexical item for the vagina, the penis, the nipple, and the anus, with an impressive array of other erogenous zones, including the nostril and the ear, surveyed as well.

The union of traditional pornographic discourse features and a colloquiality pursued in terms of expository style, verbal forms, and sexual slang provides the specific texture of *Cartas de um sedutor.* One associates with parody a fairly transparent reinscription of the base text, such that the work's parodic value is unmistakable; an initial reading of Hilst's text leaves scant room for viewing it as anything other than parodic. Certainly, the sustained exploitation of the female body makes it difficult, if not impossible, to view *Cartas* as a defense of female sexuality. Even in the case of the woman Karl features, grossly nicknamed "Cuzinho" (little asshole; it may also imply a trope of *cuzinha,* kitchen, the subjugated woman's special realm), who is obsessed with her desire to practice anilingus, she is less an agent of her own erotic fulfillment than one of Karl's pornographic fantasies, developed in all of the fuguelike extrapolations that characterize his narrative production.

In a sense, the fuguelike nature of Hilst's text (another characteristic might be surrealist delirium, which is reminiscent of William S. Burroughs's writing) excludes the possibility of any counternarrative, or any dialogic interaction, as the pornographic is a textual coordinate of a sexual violence that excludes any resistance, any alternative, any antiphonic response. If Hilst is producing something other than pornography understood in this way, it is a sexual discourse that, because of its univocal imperiousness, bars any alternative to it, whether in the form of human experience other than the erotic, a program of human passion other than the one it provides, or an articulation of a point of view regarding sexual history other than the one supplied by Karl and his equally hegemonic masculine surrogates. Karl writes to his sister on one occasion to prompt, provoke, force her memory:

> Palomita, lembras-te que mergulhavas o meu pau na tua xícara de chocolate e em seguida me lambias o ganso? Ahh! tua formosa língua! Evoco todos os ruídos, todos os tons da paisagem daquelas tardes . . . cigarras, os anus pretos (aves cuculiformes da família dos cuculídeos . . . meus Deus!) e os cheiros . . . o jasmim-manga, os limoeiros . . . e teus movimentos suaves, alongados, meus movimentos frenéticos . . . Ahhh! Marcel, se te lembras, sentiu todo un universo com as dele madeleines . . . (65)[5]

Hilst's expository form provides only glimmers of satisfaction for the reader accustomed to the dogged if always shocking transparency of conventional pornography. Certainly there might be room to correct the present assessment of what this text is about, by insisting that fugue and erotic ars combinatoria function to enunciate a liberated sexuality where semantics and narrative action are demonstrated to be releasable from closed paradigms of the safe and the conventional. But, in either case, Hilst's text represents the intersection of the superficially pornographic with a form of narrative exposition that is unique among the texts being considered here.

> Sabia que não era para a gente se perguntar muito, que a vida é viável enquanto se fica na superfície, nos matizes, nas aquarelas. (Hilst, *Contos d'escárnio,* 83)[6]

Hilst's *Contos d'escárnio* (1990; Stories of Derision), explicitly published as part of the author's commitment to producing pornographic literature (this avowal appears in the text of the back jacket
flap), centers on two oxymorons. The first is rather obvious: that of
how a configuration such as the "feminine pornographic" is possible, unless it signals the female author's affiliation with a masculinist criterion of the sexual abuse and exploitation of woman (either
as her conscious alliance with hegemonic patriarchal structures, or as
her unwitting collaboration with the instruments of her own degra-
dation, the most obvious of which would be, precisely, her being
made into an unwitting accomplice), which would constitute a use
of the adjective "feminine" as identifying only the sexual identity of
the author and not her feminist ideology. Yet this oxymoron can be
understood in terms of the extent to which we have come to associate the pornographic not with the libidinous display of erotic activity—which in such an affirmation is implied to be unfettered by exploitative power and, quite the contrary, to be an evasion of it, as seen
in the forces that would suppress the pornographic—but instead
with a return to the root meaning of the term: writing about prostitutes. Such a return entails the concomitant assertion that prostitutes
are paradigms of the violent exploitation of the female body, and
the pornographic is the absolute icon of violence against women:
Dworkin's image of intercourse as unremittingly the display text of
the masculinist expropriation of the feminine other. If the erotic
is to transcend pornography for the well-to-do, it can only do so by
freeing itself from the semantic anchoring in prostitution to which
an understanding of the pornographic has returned, which might
be why a term like "feminine erotic" does not strike one as oxymo-
ronic, but only tropic to the extent that it leaves open whether it
has freed itself from the imperatives of the master masculine erotic.

Equally contradictory in appearance is the second term associated with Hilst's text: a "humorous pornographic." Violence, when
understood as lacking any mediating discursive strategies, cannot be
regarded as funny whereas violence in, say, a Bugs Bunny comic book
is putatively mediated by its framing as simple fun that involves
nonhumans, where no matter how much mayhem the characters experience, they always reappear intact in the next frame or strip; alternative readings may peel away these mediating conventions, but
they first appear as a not-to-be-challenged given that makes violence
humorous. This especially so if the text inscribes the reader into the
position of the victim, which would seem to be a routine strategy of
most writing and unquestionably of any attempt to lead the reader
to repudiate the social scenario being portrayed.

But it is exactly in its dimensions as a humorous text that *Contos* is able to resolve the contradiction of the idea of a feminine pornography. Hilst does this by seeking to drain the sexual encounter of its dramatic tensions: sex is, after all is said (the text) and done (the act), no big deal. One might immediately object that sex is certainly a big deal for those obliged through physical and ideological coercion to engage in it. But Hilst's rejoinder could well be that either she is talking about sex when it is uncoerced—when it is sex and not violence in which sexual organs and their extensions are the bludgeons—or that what is often read as sexual coercion, especially seduction, corruption, and entrapment, merits possible revisionary consideration. This is precisely the circumstance of feminine S/M, whether the idea is outrageously disingenuous—S/M viewed as reenacting masculinist violence—or it is reinterpreted as consenting sexual theatrics, one of whose virtues may be a catharsis of oppression (see Califia's introduction to her erotic fiction in *Macho Sluts* [1988], as well as her *Sensuous Magic* [1993]; see also Henderson [1992]; Brown [1994]; Dunn [1990]; and Sontag [1982]).

Hilst's text claims neither that sexual coercion does not exist nor that there is a pornography properly speaking that is its abetting record, but rather that there is a domain of sexuality that can be scrutinized within the parameters of the operant terms of her title, *escárnio* and *grotesco*. The former term is of venerable ancestry in Luso-Hispanic letters, referring to that mode of textual production that is designed to outrage. In modern terms, this means a discourse of transgression, defiance, resistance, or polyphony. It is the return of the repressed, the speech of the subaltern, and multivocalness in the face of the monologic. This is why in its origins in medieval literature, *escarnio/escárnio* (cf. the English word "scarn," or "dung"; the former probably has the same Germanic roots attributed to the Spanish word) was one of the popular modes opposed to the monologic discourse of the Church; indeed, some its practitioners, like Spain's fourteenth-century Juan Ruiz, author of *El libro de buen amor* (The Book of Good Love), were clerics who rewrote *a lo profano* (in a profane manner) the master texts. Hilst's other key qualifier, *grotesco* (grotesque), is understood to be a modern attribute, in which less an opposition than a shifted reading is involved: the grotesque discovers deeper, hidden levels of meaning that frighten rather than affront, repulse rather than outrage.

These dual attributes work in Hilst's narrative to underscore a strategy of trivialization—the basis of her demonstration of the non-transcendence of erotic encounters. Crasso and Clódia (note the classical resonances of their names) engage in geometrically multiplied erotic encounters that are compounded by his efforts as a writer (the text is one example of the production of erotic experience) and her efforts as a painter; Clódia specializes, in the tradition of Georgia O'Keeffe, in vaginal abstractions. Their sexual exercises, a freewheeling set of bodily conjunctions, are indiscriminate as regards subject and object, agent and patient, pursuer and pursued. The multiplicity of their erotic field is reduplicated by the mosaic of Hilst's (or Crasso's) text, which also encourages the reader to view sexual acts as the accumulation of superficial detail, in which the depth meaning of the Freudian tradition and the cultural tradition it has inspired are absent. Thus, sex is demystified as personal sin, as psychological complex, as social tragedy, as existential liberation, and as the compulsive nucleus of the Western tradition of cultural production. Although *Contos* is about sex, it is also about how writing need not depict sex as a metonym of the whole of human experience.

Toward the demythification of sex, Hilst engages in a series of metatextualities that, because they are mocked and trivialized, induce scorn for a certain cultural frame of mind: that which attributes to the genres represented by the metatextualities vast and profound interpretations of personal and collective life as sexual dramas. In one sequence the devil appears, ostensibly to torment the narrator of another author's writings (fragments supposedly of interest for their Oedipal constructions that Crasso has included) for his sexual transgressions, and to give him a glimpse of the hell fires of damnation that will punish him for his sins:

> Senti náuseas de repente e uma dor profunda no peito. Ainda pude perguntar-lhe: há uma outra vida?
> Sim. Milhoães de crianças como eu. Você será uma delas.
> É tedioso e até inaceitável mas é assim. (93)[7]

Elsewhere, theatrical fragments mock the turgid sexual dramatics of Shakespeare (53–66), the Freudian theme of father-son competition (67–69), and the exquisite scatologies of Sade (70–74), in his guise as a forefather of erotic liberation (and not, as Angela Carter would see him, as a critic of power won through sexual domination).

Hilst's text is hardly one of sexual ludics, in that the erotic has an ulterior meaning, either as the enactment of political oppression or as an opportunity for the ultimate jouissance. Male sexuality, as the central scene of the Oedipal family romance and the site of subjugation (of women as a global social construction), is trivialized by Hilst's text. This is not because the exercise of sex as power does not take place, but because it can be shown as not always endowed with the transcendent signifier that the Judeo-Christian, the Freudian, and the feminist traditions in turn have unequivocally attributed to it. It is for this reason that Hilst has no feminine/feminist agenda to offer in the place of the meanings that have been drained from sex (in contrast, say, to Griselda Gambaro's experimentation with pornography in *Lo impenetrable* [1984; *The Impenetrable Madam X*, 1991]; cf. Foster 1995b, 157–172). At the end of the novel, the narrator informs Clódia that he has been first in Paris and then in New York, where he has found a publisher for his manuscript—leading one to wonder if the text is not mocking the two poles of feminist understandings of sexuality, those that have restored the etymological meaning of pornography. Much fucking takes place in Hilst's pornographic writing, but it is all surface narrative, devoid of the resonances "fuck" has acquired as a vulgarism that is dirty not because it is vulgar, but because of the violence that its very utterance is said to enact (see MacKinnon 1993).

Hilst's texts point, then, in two directions. On the one hand they undermine the profound meanings attached to the sexual by most of the Judeo-Christian tradition (not to mention others); in this sense they resound with the postmodernist repudiation of depth psychology and master narratives. On the other hand they mock dominant feminist interpretations of sex, at least sex involving female participants, as necessarily exploitative and violent. It may be going too far to say that Hilst has turned to narrative pornography as a particular positioning from the margins of her subalternity as a Brazilian writer, in what may seem from the Third World to be the overheated debates of First World feminism: it has often been noted that First World feminism seems to be irrelevant to the Third World, where socioeconomic violence, assuredly a masculinist patriarchal system, leaves most of society unempowered, men and women alike. Yet Hilst's complex narratives are far removed from touristy representations of Brazil as a happy-go-lucky sexual haven (Parker 1990). Rather, her humorous pornography stakes a claim to the validity of the proliferation of surface meanings, whether on the page, the canvas, or the body: "Resolvi escrever este livro porque ao longo da minha vida tenho lido tanto lixo que resolvi escrever o meu" (10).[8] It is symptomatic of Hilst's enigmatic writing that we are left unable to decide whether the antecedent of "o meu" is "livro" or "lixo," two words which, after all, in the dominant practice of Luso-Hispanic assonance, are a paired rhyme.

Hilst's most recent collection of texts, *Rútilo nada: a obscena senhora D. Qadós* (1993; Glittering Nothingness: The Obscene Ms. D.

Qadós), contains two narratives originally published in *Com meus ohlos de cão e outras novelas* (1986; With My Eyes of a Dog and Other Stories). These narratives demonstrate the impressive flexibility of her utilization of a highly writerly version of Portuguese literary dialects, employed to probe the obscenity of human experience as it relates to the attempt, especially for the feminine consciousness, to escape the patriarchal repressiveness of fleshly pleasure. To the extent that such pleasure cannot be signified by the patriarchal code, language—the immediate and highly normalized embodiment of that code—must be explored in a fuguelike way, in order to discern the semantic configurations that make possible a signing of the transgressive erotic in general and the feminine erotic in particular. A feminine erotic—or, perhaps more specifically, a feminine pornographic—because it falls outside the legitimacy of social discourse as fixed in language, constitutes an especially intransigent position in the defense of the materiality of the feminine body, whether viewed from an essentialist or a constructivist point of view.

Of specific interest in Hilst's latest publication is the lead story, which is published here for the first time. "Rútilo nada," which I take to mean "no brilliance whatever," is a tale of the revenge of homosexual transgression. Lucius is the (apparently unattached?) son of an important banker who falls in love with Lucas, his daughter's fiancé. Lucius's father protests furiously—because of the scandal of the two being seen together in public, and because of the outrageousness of his son's having expropriated his own daughter's lover—and then arranges for a *serviço* (job): two hired thugs will visit Lucas in order to convince Lucius of the error of his ways. The central part of the narrative describes this *serviço*. Lucas is trapped by the two men, one of whom sodomizes him while the other obliges him to perform fellatio; then one of them whips him with the buckle-end of a belt while the other ejaculates. Lucas, left broken and bleeding in his blood- and semen-smeared apartment, is visited by the banker, who gives him a pistol with which to commit suicide, kisses him on the lips, and departs; Lucas, realizing that his life is over, that not to commit suicide will result in his being slowly beat to death, complies with the inevitable. Lucas's martyrdom turns on parodic posturings by his tormentors of the clichés of gay love: anal penetration, nonvaginal ejaculation, and the sadomasochistic reterritorialization of pleasure. This scenario's accommodation of the narratives of violent pornography against women, as enactments of a punishment directed against an individual for her transgression (if only by omission) of the patriarchal order, constitutes one of the most suggestive dimensions of Hilst's text.

The banker, at the wake for Lucas, informs his son that he should follow his lover's lead, and that obviously Lucas was the *machão* (stud) since he was man enough to commit suicide. The narrative concludes with seven of Lucas's poems on the theme of walls: walls as barriers, as prisons, as the backdrop of repression (one's repression is projected against the walls, one is thrown against or off of walls), as entombment.

Homosexual desire/passion/love is an inevitable component of socioeconomic power in Hilst's narrative, both as a transgression of the patriarchal code (one does not disrupt the line of transmitted power by falling in love with one's daughter's fiancé) and as a violation of the code prohibiting the public display of nonconformity, which challenges orderly transmission of patriarchal power from father to son, and from son to son-in-law as surrogate father of the overdetermined female body in its role as the token of civilized decency. While homosexual desire may exist as a clandestine text in Brazilian society, its public display is a violation of the social pact; the degree of punishment of such a violation is in direct proportion to the extent of power that is at play. Having made a display text out of his transgressive love for Lucas, Lucius must endure the excruciating agony of seeing his lover's body made into a display text (through the whip marks still visible on the body, as it lies in the open casket during the wake) of the consequences of transgression.

Were one to jejunely subscribe to the proposition that Brazilian culture offers multiple sexual options, Hilst's text provides a necessary corrective: sex may not always be a component of power, but where it does intersect with power, sex must yield to the priority of power. This is why the banker, who has no need to prove his power, can afford himself the luxury of kissing the battered lips of his son's and granddaughter's beautiful lover, but why his son, in a subservient position within the power apparatus, must feign a kiss for his dead lover through the crystal of the coffin. No other Latin American writer, not even Manuel Puig, who was a master of the representation of sexual abjection, has written such a terrifying story of sexual revenge, and one in which transgression—here only circumstantially inscribed in terms of gay love—clashes so strikingly with Latin American historical necessity.

One venerable scenographic topos in literature is that of life aboard ship. The shipboard romance in particular has undoubtedly been a frequently recurring narrative formula for a wide spectrum of fiction. Indeed, passenger ships today exist primarily as "Love Boats," and in the best tradition of expanding markets, they offer cruise packages tailored to a variety of sexual tastes. The Caribbean cruise, with its stations-of-the-cross approach to the tropical islands, whose diversity derives from their crisscross of cultural influences, is an inevitable setting for the most delirious of shipboard romances.

La última noche que pasé contigo (1991; The Last Night I Spent with You) by the Cuban writer Mayra Montero (b. 1952), part of Tusquets's La Sonrisa Vertical prizewinning pornography series, is the story of mid-life sexual discovery and erotic recovery. Having just married off their only daughter, Fernando and Celia embark on a cruise through the islands in an effort to redefine and reinvigorate their relationship. During the cruise they meet Julieta, who is something of a sexual shifter: the conflicting stories she tells about herself and her reasons for being alone on the cruise are correlates of the crucial differences in her personal and erotic relations with Celia and Fernando as individuals and as a couple. The reader discovers at the end of the novel that someone also named Julieta was the woman to whom Fernando's grandmother lost her lesbian lover—although it is probably not the same Julieta alluded to previously (what to make of the author's confusing playfulness here is not clear). Fernando as a child carried letters between his grandmother and her lover, Angela, and texts of those letters are interspersed in the novel, despite the fact that they are signed with a masculine pseudonym. Furthermore, it turns out that Julieta's husband is one of Celia's former lovers.

This brief characterization of the sexual pairings presented in the novel seems like too much coincidence. Nonetheless, because Julieta is viewed as a shifter, as a convenient element for bringing to the fore relationships between others, there is less need to raise the question of whether Montero's novel is a put-on or a challenge to the reader to admire the labyrinthine combinations, in the fashion of a daisy chain, of everyone appearing to have sexual relations with everyone else, not exactly in perfect structural balance, but as an index of the counterimage to the patriarchal matrimony Fernando initially strives to impose.

Carlos Esterrich (1994) has written accurately of the lesbian grounding of Montero's novel, both the lesbian relationship which Fernando witnessed as a child and which provided him with a potent image of a hidden female sexuality, and the lesbianism in his own wife's involvement with Julieta. The point that I would like to underscore here is the way in which that lesbianism is a determining factor in Fernando's interactions with his own wife and with Julieta. Although some miscellaneous eroticism takes place in the novel, both on board ship and in the form of flashbacks (mostly of Celia's affairs with other men), the grand sexual scenes of the novel involve the juxtaposed seductions of the two female protagonists by island men. Both men are black, and both provide transport services: Celia's seducer ferries passengers between the mainland and an island in his boat, and Julieta's is a taxi driver. The narrator describes both seductions in considerable detail, with both men appearing to be paradigms of the racist stereotype of the generously endowed buck. In both cases, the sexual act is described in details that evoke a rape fantasy—that is, the erotic encounter is based on the men violently taking the women, whose intense shock and pain are transformed into intense, unforgettable pleasure. Montero uses the narrative arsenal of numerous fictional works that represent violent, anonymous sex as a woman's glorious sexual awakening, and in which the supposed pleasure for both the woman and the reader (who witnesses the woman's orgasm through the medium of literature) is enhanced by the crucial transgressive primitivism of the agent (a role that is routinely assigned to black men).

But there is a crucial difference between Celia's and Julieta's experiences. Celia goes off on her own, and even if she is only quasi-conscious of her actions (and it is important to note that the event is narrated by her, in the first person, thereby forestalling the possibility of another narrator or character misinterpreting her responses and feelings), she offers herself for sexual seduction. Afterward, in what is almost a parody of closing tags in popular fiction, she states: "tuve la corozonada de que aquélla era la tarde más importante de mi vida" (154),[9] and she returns from the encounter "[sangrando] como una virgencita" (154).[10] There is little doubt that Celia has codified her sexual experience with the *botero* in such a way that it will become an integral, positive part of her psychological identity:

> Me despedí besándole la boca, el implacable filete de esos labios, una lengua que no se me negaba más, unos dientes que se me quedaron clavados en la carne, para que me acordara de su sabor en esa noche, para que me acordara mañana por la noche, y para que me acordara ahora y en la hora de mi muerte, y por el resto de las noches que iba a vivir sin él. (154)[11]

"Ahora y en la hora de mi muerte": this accommodation of the topos of the Marian protectorate definitively empties the description of Celia's sexual adventure of any implication of rape and converts it into the erotic core of the novel.

As opposed to the lesbian subtext, especially evident in Fernando's experience with female sexuality, genital heterosexism is rather triumphantly vindicated. Such a vindication necessarily involves the liquidation of the lesbian subtext, and this is effected through Julieta's seduction. Like Celia's, it also takes place in Guadalupe (the description of this setting contains appropriate allusions to Josephine and Victor Hugues, perhaps as primes of female sexuality and revolution, respectively, although it is unclear whether they refer to anything other than the circumstances of tourism). But in this case, it is impossible to doubt that a rape has taken place. Riding in a cab with Julieta, Fernando engages in heavy foreplay with her. The cab driver, realizing what is happening, pulls over and turns around to watch. Fernando silently offers Julieta's body to him, and the man descends from behind the wheel and takes Fernando's place in the back seat. As he once watched, although surreptitiously, the lovemaking of his grandmother and the woman who would leave her for Julieta, Fernando contemplates the sexual encounter between the cab driver and Julieta. In this case, Fernando narrates. At the end of the chapter, Fernando continues the rape by forcing a reluctant Julieta to confess that she enjoyed the encounter stage-managed by him.

Significantly, the imposed confession of pleasure is dominated by the imperative to confess as well to the pain she has endured. These are the closing words of the chapter: "¿le había dolido o no?, dijo que sí, más alto, perra, y ella gritó que sí, que sí, que sí . . ." (172).[12] Fernando here may be avenging himself through Julieta's multiple rape for what he intuits to have been Celia's pleasure with another man, or her understanding with Julieta, lesbian-defined or not, that has excluded him. But also, in retrospect (like the unsent letter that closes Manuel Puig's *La traición de Rita Hayworth* [1967; *Betrayed by Rita Hayworth*]), seen in terms of the unsent letter in which the lesbian lover of Fernando's grandmother informs her that she is abandoning her for Julieta, Fernando's act of violence is motivated by the ghosts of the sexual apprenticeship provided him by his grandmother and the controlling motifs of the boleros that permeate all of the narrative schemata of the novel, beginning with its title. It is not clear to what extent Fernando recognizes Julieta. Nor is it evident that he ever understands the role she played in his early life, even after Celia, in the last scene between them, provides him with some new information about her. But Celia destroys, in his face, a letter Julieta had left for Fernando before deciding to leave the cruise and remain permanently in Guadalupe (with the cab driver?—which would be the culmination of the rape fantasy, in contrast to the rupture of the rape fantasy that occurs in Celia's codification of her seduction). Thus if Fernando is somehow settling accounts with Julieta for her role in his grandmother's unhappiness, he is unaware of it.

This adds a dimension of feminist irony, because the patriarchal agent is, by virtue of his structural role, unable to grasp what is happening: "he just doesn't get it."

Yet of course there is a problem here, revealed by the irony, and which cannot be disavowed in the face of Celia's erotic fulfillment and its feminist meanings. I am referring to the triumph of Celia's genital heterosexism over the lesbian experience. Leave aside the pathetic dimension of the final unhappiness of Fernando's grandmother (because only a reactionary sexual code would prevent her lover from acting on her desire for another woman, or would deny Julieta the right to seduce the grandmother's lover). Bolero-drenched clichés of betrayal and abandonment have little place in a narrative of sexual liberation. Indeed, they can only serve to mark the source of oppression—and it goes without saying that, ideologically, bolero lyrics echo masculinism (even if it is true that a closeted, denied gay sensibility expresses itself to some degree in the sentimentality of the male singing voice: see Luis Rafael Sánchez's *La importancia de llamarse Daniel Santos* [1988; The Importance of Being Named Daniel Santos]).

What is crucial here is that, at the same time and in virtually the same exotic, tropical setting, the heterosexual Celia (who calls Fernando's grandmother *la maricona*, the feminine form of *maricón* [fag]) has a momentous sexual adventure, while the lesbian Julieta is raped by two men, one of whom is possibly acting out of revenge. One could argue that Montero depicts Julieta's rape as evidence of the power of the patriarchy, which becomes even more violent when confronted with lesbianism (cf. the references to Fernando's grandfather and the priest who hears his grandmother's deathbed confession), and with Celia's sexual satisfaction, as proof of women's ability to manage their own erotic life. Nonetheless, there remains an irresolvable conflict between heterosexualism and lesbianism (which is never shown in any light more positive than the frustrated romanticism of the grandmother's affair), a conflict that is in turn overshadowed by the masculinist bolero.

There has never been any doubt as to the direction of Diana Raznovich's work: in all three major genres, the Argentine writer (b. 1945) has addressed in highly imaginative ways topics relating to gender and sexual identity, and has undertaken the enormous project of constructing an erotic discourse with sociopolitical meaning. *Mater erótica* (1992; Erotic Mother) consists of two narratives, the first approximately twice as long as the second. In both narratives, the fall of the Berlin Wall is the backdrop to an erotic experience. In the first one, the erotic encounter involves the wife of a member of the East German high command and a friend of her teenage son; in the second, it involves a double agent of both Germanys who, under a death threat, lives out a sexual idyll with a sixteen-year-old woman. In both cases, the stories are told in the first person by the older person; elements of bisexuality and gender-role exchange are involved; and there is reference to the climate of sexual repression that functions in all of Western society, with establishment socialism depicted as being equally draconian as capitalist democracy.

However, in the case of the older woman there is more of a narrative of transgression, while in the second case there is more of a narrative of sexual exploitation. What Raznovich seems to be staging here is a juxtaposition of radical differences in perspective. In the second narrative, it is a masculinist perspective—the cynical double agent who lives out the hours before his assassination by availing himself effortlessly of the body of an essentially powerless woman, all in the context of free, libertine Paris, the capital of "love" in all of its heterosexist mythology. In the first and longer narrative, a feminist discourse is forged (in the context of the masculinist repression of female sexuality in an establishment socialism that is homologous to traditional Western and Christian systems of values), in which the fleshquakes of an awakened sexuality foreshadow the structural earthquakes the woman will later produce in the society around her.

Raznovich uses many conventions of masculinist pornography, beginning with the urban Iberian dialect which provides her with a voice that is jarringly different from her other "Argentine" writings yet much like the stilted language of her generic models. Moreover, setting both stories in non-Spanish-speaking societies reinforces the otherness of her texts, although the first one is more marked than the second in this regard. From a feminist point of view, pornography (which is what Raznovich seems to be reiterating in the second, masculinist-based story) is a profound dystopia that overlaps significantly with the actual society of the male abuser, the female victim, and voyeuristic readers, whose gender identities variously position them with respect to that dystopia and may even remodel it as a fantastic utopia capable of leading one out of the real world's sexual conflicts (both for those who abuse and those who have internalized the abuse as an ideal to be sought out). Raznovich begins the first and feminist narrative by configuring a dystopia. The non-Communist-block reader is asked to grasp that this dystopia reduplicates capitalist society, and then to accept that a utopian space can be created within it. Such a space is based on a series of transgressions that install woman as sexual agent, with an agency that replaces feminine lack with a force capable of invalidating masculinist male phallic power. The first-person narrative underscores the greater presence of the woman who no longer speaks the stasis of the *stabat Mater* (see Kristeva 1986), but instead articulates the agency of the *Mater erótica*, who will reconfigure society in a liberating, nonphallic fashion.

Despite the element of bisexuality in both narratives, Raznovich's texts are resolutely heterosexist and genitalist—which means that she focuses on female/male sexual politics rather than on alternate sexualities. Nevertheless, within this role frame (which also reduplicates conventional pornography), there is enough erotic delirium to demonstrate that even traditional male/female roles offer some promise of sexual liberation.

Masturbation has always gotten something of a bum rap. Biblical injunctions prohibited the needless waste of man's seed. They were part of a male-biased law that was surely the reflex of a society obsessed with the need to maintain a level of population growth that would sustain its tribal or ethnic identity (if not enhance its power through numbers). In modern times, when population size became less of an issue, health and hygiene technologies viewed masturbation as a moral threat because of the alleged weakening of the mind brought about by the intensely self-centering act of onanism. The major threat still appeared to exist for males, although there was also a growing awareness that women had sexual urges which were not just a perversion leading them to licentiousness and prostitution. Finally (although there may now be a growing recognition of the validity, if for no other reason than its persistent practice, of masturbation as a natural sexual release), one major dimension of the contemporary sexual revolution has been to decry masturbation as a deviation from sexual unions made possible by the final overthrow of constraining taboos: masturbation is viewed as a selfish act to the extent that it rejects communion with others, the barriers to which the sexual revolution is supposed to demolish. Masturbation is a negation of the free sexual marketplace. Nevertheless, in a post-AIDS society, masturbation may be the only real form of safe sex (not abstinence, unless nonrelease can be promoted as a form of frustrated, and therefore even more pleasurable, eroticism). The need to substitute new erotic practices for those at high risk of HIV contamination has opened up the possibility of encouraging masturbation, whether solitary or mutual, reflexive or reciprocal.

Steimberg's *Amatista* (1990; Amethyst) enters the discourse on masturbation from the perspective of a feminine narrator. It is perhaps the first Hispanic novel to have masturbation as its central theme, although in a few other texts masturbation appears as one narrative incident (e.g., the disquisition on male masturbatory techniques in Enrique Medina's *Strip-tease* [1976]). *Amatista* depicts a series of encounters between an unidentified woman, whose recounting of them constitutes the text of the novel, and a *doctor,* whom she initiates into an enhanced enjoyment of the sexual act. The text is specifically, insistently heterosexist because it is centered on the conceit of a woman of unspecified qualifications serving as an erotic guide for a professionally titled man. The woman overtly assumes a series of sexual privileges that are conventionally denied her sex: she possesses a superior knowledge of erotic dynamics, despite the man's status as a *doctor* (a title that, in Spanish, is not synonymous with medicine but conserves the etymological meaning of one who is professionally or academically learned); she serves as the agent, the initiator, the controller of the sexual act; she possesses specialized knowledge about techniques and accessories that enhance and sustain pleasure; and she is the one who has the right to talk about sex, both as an element of the sex act—talk as a technique of sexual stimulation—and as a consequence of sex—the formal recollection of sex in the form of a report, a memoir, or a novel.

Yet this vocalization of a woman as sexual agent is not without its ideological problems. While it may be important for a woman to recount her sexual agency, in *Amatista* the female narrator remains devoted to male heterosexual satisfaction. The issue of female eroticism experienced in concert with anyone other than a socially powerful man never arises, and there is no exploration of what it might be like for a woman to speak her sexual desire separate from a masculine figure of power. Thus, the initial audacity of Steimberg's text is significantly attenuated by its masculinist and heterosexist anchoring. This anchoring is, however, attenuated in turn by the reader's constant sense that the whole story is a feminist put-on.

Narrativized sex in Steimberg's novel has three dimensions. All three are attributed to the narrator-participant, and all are transgressive insofar as conventional Western, and especially Hispanic, images of female sexuality are concerned. In the first place, the first-person narrator grants herself the privilege of narrating her erotic education of the *doctor,* a student as ideally responsive as any teacher could hope for, and who, in his compliance with her performance instructions, is as ideally obedient a character as any pornographer could desire. That the student is a man and the teacher a woman inverts a pornographic norm, albeit not an exclusive one, and that the woman's sexual knowledge is inversely proportional to the *doctor's* ignorance about sexual pleasure contravenes the principle of masculine superiority in the realms of knowledge and experience.

In order to fulfill her role as teacher, the narrator explains to her pupil practices that will increase erotic pleasure. Part of the controlling conceit of *Amatista* that begins with the identification of the *doctor* as pupil concerns the use of a stylized primer designed for teaching the alphabet, a reference to which opens the novel: "Era un alfabeto de letras traslúcidas y cambiantes, con arabescos, proyectado en una pantalla. Lo seguí letra a letra [. . .]" (9).[13] The narrator recounts to the reader how she explains to her student what he is to do in order to profit from her knowledge, what techniques she will teach to him, and of what strategies she will avail herself in order to maximize his pleasure. This role of woman as the speaking agent of sex, which is complemented by the virtual mutism of the man (for whom she often speaks, either by telling him what to say or by directly attributing words to him), transgresses the conventions of pornography. Though in a novel like John Cleland's *Fanny Hill* (1749) the woman is the narrator, she is only circumstantially the sexual agent, since she is clearly enacting and recounting the sexual fantasies of the male discourse, which include the woman's compliant receptivity. In *Amatista*, it is the man who complies with a sexual script that is articulated by a woman, which she patiently yet efficiently expounds.

Finally, the novel is transgressive in a third narrative dimension by virtue of the often droll sexual anecdotes the teacher tells her student, veritable Boccaccian exempla of sexual performance. The narrative pivot of all of these anecdotes is Amatista, who is either autobiographical or a fantasy doubling of the narrator/pedagogue. As she explains to her student: "Escuche, doctor, que hasta un hombre de mundo como usted necesita a veces que le cuenten historias" (9).[14] These *historias* are all tales of idealized sexual accomplishments—idealized in that climax is always triumphantly achieved without antagonistic forces ever intervening to thwart it. In short, in the glorious beauty, superb proportions, and unfettered lugubricity of the performers evoked by the narrator, these anecdotes are the quintessence of the classical pornography genre of erotic exploits. That a woman recounts them to a man in the context of an erotic education underscores the feminist conceit of Steimberg's novel.

But another dimension of this conceit relates to the question of masturbation. The narrator's exempla are reminiscent of classical pornography (which she ironizes through metacommentary asides on the language she cannot avoid using, begging his pardon for words that are too technical, too graphic, or too colloquial), but her own encounters with the *doctor* deviate significantly from the narrative schema framing her anecdotes. Although compulsory heterosexuality is maintained throughout as part of the woman-teaches-man conceit, two significant departures point toward the author's feminist consciousness. One involves the degenitalization of the sexual act. The Amatista anecdotes, as befits their stock narrative formulas, center on genital interaction, yet the female pedagogue is concerned with the total eroticization of the body. And while there is not as complete a survey of corporal geography as the demanding reader might want, the teacher's attentions to her student's body studiously concentrate on nonpenile stimulation:

> Voy a usar una crema suavizante con aceite de pepitas de durazno y muy delicado perfume. Sólo sentirá un frío juguetón con el primer contacto y enseguida el masaje generará calor. Comenzaré por los huecos detrás de los dedos del pie izquierdo. No habrá centímetro de su piel por donde no pasen mis dedos. (23)[15]

A concomitant aspect of total eroticization is the enhancement of sexual release through delay and displacement. In order to overcome the brutish macho practice of the quick exploitation of the feminine body and the subsequent casting aside of the woman—the practice of the wham-bang, the three-minute fuck—the woman wishes to teach the man the virtues of prolonged sexual involvement. Not just a courting ritual that is the prelude to sex, with or without sustained foreplay, it is an arousal whose culmination is almost indefinitely postponed, such that it is a brief stage in the entire erotic narrative, but for all that a much more intensely climactic one.

Yet another aspect of the man's sexual (re)education hinges on the merits of displacement, whereby sexual utilization of the other's body is not a necessary imperative in the erotic narrative. This is where the recodification of masturbation comes in: masturbation not as an ingredient of foreplay or as a form of *faut de mieux* release (as transient homosexuality in all-male environments is often touted to be), but as a sexually climactic experience for the individual, even when an appropriate sexual partner is present. The narrator encourages her pupil to engage in masturbation, and she explains its virtues to him, instructs him on how to do it, and even commands him at certain points to jack off. Although masturbation does not emerge from *Amatista* as the master sexual act, the fact that the narrator uses it as an essential ingredient in her pedagogy is in sharp contrast to the conventional intergenital sex on which the Amatista anecdotes are based.

Another dimension of masturbation in Steimberg's novel, however, justifies the way in which I have fronted this sexual practice in my presentation of *Amatista*. I refer to the conventional wisdom on pornography as a form of voyeurism that is fundamentally an inducement to masturbation: the image of teenage boys engaged in the solitary vice behind locked bathroom doors, hunched over raunchy girlie magazines they smuggle past their parents' vigilance. But surely all cultural production prospers through some form of voyeurism, in that it provides the reader/spectator with something like a sanitary, privileged access to the life, thoughts, and conduct of others. This is especially evident in the reader's access to the innermost feelings and fantasies of characters in stream-of-consciousness formats: the scandal over the closing Molly Bloom episode in Joyce's *Ulysses* may have had as much to do with embarrassment over the intrusion of privacy promoted by the novel as it did with the content of Molly's ruminations. In any case, pornography at best foregrounds the voyeuristic dynamic of display texts in culture. Any promotion of masturbation may be a reflex of the solitary nature of both reading and onanism, especially since reading, like culture in general, presumably stimulates all sorts of psychosomatic responses, sexual arousal being only one of them.

The point about Steimberg's novel is that the interdependence of reading and masturbation are foregrounded through the use of the pedagogue's inner texts in the arousal of the *doctor*. She channels this arousal into masturbatory practices as a complement to enhanced sexual fulfillment, genital deterritorialization (even when a return to the penis is the end result of the lesson), and the deferral of climax in order to augment its intensity. If, however, there is anything specifically feminist in this program centering on a woman's espousal of sexual practices that exceed the strict limits of brief, territorialized, and unreflexive macho sex, it lies not so much with the highlighting of masturbation. It is located instead in the disruption of a masculine dominance that has traditionally denounced onanism as unmanly—for disrupting reproductive sex, for excluding the other (i.e., the woman's body), and for reflexively indulging in erotic fantasies, all of which are at issue in the teacher's program of instruction for the *doctor*.

The texts examined in this study do not belong to the category of violent pornography that is the main concern for the Dworkin/

MacKinnon tradition and the theorizing that underpins *For Adult Users Only,* whose subtitle is *The Dilemma of Violent Pornography* (Gubar and Hoff 1989). Clearly, what is debatable is the definition of violence, and whether there is any significant distinction between violent pornography and pornographic (i.e., genitally based) erotics on the one hand and between real rape and theatrical sex (Califia's "sensuous magic") on the other (although a collection like *Feminist Views on Pornography* [Russell 1993] would argue that pornography is indeed distinct from erotica).

Steimberg's text approximates, as closely as any Spanish text, theatrical erotics as a form of cultural resistance to compulsory heterosexuality and to normative "straight" definitions of sexual enactments. These issues inform Raznovich's and Montero's narratives but do not attain the same degree of characterization as in *Amatista.*

It is Hilst's texts, in their writerliness, that offer the most complex depictions of erotic revisionism in Latin America. This has to do in large measure with a tradition of erotic culture in Brazil that sustains Hilst's perspectives. Brazilian erotic culture cannot, any more than other societies, escape its own legacy of heterosexism, racism, and sexism by contemporary feminist standards. But it does provide the reader with semantic horizons against which to understand Hilst's figurations of sexuality—indeed, even to accept them as legitimate public-access cultural products (something which, I venture to say, would be more difficult in Spanish-speaking societies, including Argentina).

It is evident that one must be careful not to apply hegemonic English- and French-language cultural priorities to an assessment of this writing, a danger that is present for feminism in general and for lesbian/gay thematics. Yet it would also be unacceptable to frame this writing in such a way that it loses specificity as a definable corpus of cultural production, which would be the case if it were subsumed under a more general category of the feminine erotic. That Montero, Steimberg, and Raznovich all published their novels outside their native countries (in Montero's case, this is true whether her native country is taken to be Cuba or Puerto Rico) and that there is a clear difference in the readers implied by the complex language of Hilst's texts and the cliché-ridden transparencies of Rios's and Carrara's hyped bestsellers, means that this writing has some problematical dimensions. (Rios is wont to say that she is the most banned writer in Brazil, a statement that is directly contradicted by her sales statistics.) Whether or not it will constitute a significant block of

Latin American feminist cultural production, or whether or not it will be overridden by the dominant emphasis on an erotics that supersedes genital sexuality, as in the case of the texts in *El placer de la palabra* (Fernández Olmos and Paravisini-Gebert 1991; The Pleasure of the Word) or Denser's two collections for Brazil (1982, 1985), will depend on the particular directions taken by feminist writing.

Queering the Patriarchy in Hermosillo's *Doña Herlinda y su hijo*

Haz patria: ten hijos.

OFFICIAL MEXICAN GOVERNMENT SLOGAN
DURING THE 1930S AND 1940S

It is frequently assumed, not only within dominant representation, but within certain kinds of psychoanalytic discourse, that there are only two possible subject positions— that occupied on the one hand by heterosexual men and homosexual women, and that occupied on the other by heterosexual women and homosexual men. Not only does this formulation afford a preposterously monolithic reading of male homosexuality, but it depends upon a radically insufficient theory of subjectivity.

KAJA SILVERMAN, *MALE SUBJECTIVITY AT THE MARGINS*

One long final sequence occurs in Jaime Humberto Hermosillo's 1985 film, *Doña Herlinda y su hijo* (Doña Herlinda and Her Son), undoubtedly the most notable film made in Mexico in the last decade. The sequence ends with the baptism of Rodolfo's infant child. Surrounded by his loving wife, adoring mother, closest friends, Rodolfo presents his son to the world to the strains of a saccharine song in praise of motherhood. As she has done throughout the film, Rodolfo's mother, Doña Herlinda, presides with a look of serene triumph, confident that she has successfully fulfilled her maternal role of overseeing the reproduction of society. This serenely triumphant look contains significant resonances. The look is an important tool of social control, and mothers often caution their children by claiming they have eyes in the back of their heads. The look of scrutiny is a radar sweep that seeks to detect social deviancy, and its sequel, the look of disapproval, seeks to rectify deviancy detected. Doña Herlinda has indeed looked into her son's life and detected his sexual deviancy, but after her mediating efforts and maternal machinations, her look communicates to her son and to the world around them not disapproval but a beatitude deriving from viewing the social code upheld—at least those aspects of the social code that are available for public scrutiny.

One could argue that Doña Herlinda's demeanor is ironic, in that it masks that which can no longer be available for public scrutiny. I would like to believe that irony yields to bliss, the radiant smile of accomplishment, which in this case means the happiness of her family members. Doña Herlinda may have inherited the patriarchal mantle from her deceased husband, but Hermosillo means for us to understand that Doña Herlinda's social otherness as a woman is the source of her effective queering of the patriarchy she is called upon to uphold.

As one might expect, Doña Herlinda's poise has a suitable masculine counterpart. Yet, as the viewer of this droll comedy knows by now, that counterpart is not Doña Herlinda's husband (a formulation that would, in any case, invert the male primacy in the masculinist world perpetuated by Rodolfo the son). Rather, her counterpart, the individual who stands alongside Rodolfo's wife (but who in one portrait holds the baby), moving back and forth and keeping the festivities going, is Ramón, Rodolfo's male lover.

Prior to the film's concluding minutes, as Rodolfo's wife begins to experience final contractions of labor, the viewer is called upon to contemplate/cheer/abhor the explicit scene of Ramón and Rodolfo leisurely making love, in the private space Doña Herlinda has created for them in a specially renovated wing of her house. Although Ramón is generally portrayed in the feminized role of the insertee, in this scene—and marking Hermosillo's earnest attempt to defy canonical conjugations of male homosexual bodies—it is Rodolfo, on the verge of assuming the patriarchal role of reproductive father, who is leisurely serviced by Ramón. In this context it is also important to note (in line with Hermosillo's general question about fixed sexual roles, including the role of the "total homosexual uninterested in women"), that, in the only scene showing an expression of intimacy between Rodolfo and Olga, he lies back on the couch while she proceeds to seduce him.

This series of implausible acts, all carried out without any social or interpersonal tension, marks the problematical utopian space postulated by Hermosillo in the film. Transcending the tired clichés of tragic homosexual love (understood as same-sex eroticism dominated by a heterosexist medico-legal codification) that are found in early novels such as José Ceballos Maldonado's *Después de todo* (1968;

After All) and Miguel Barbachano Ponce's *El diario de José Toledo* (1964; The Diary of José Toledo) (Barbachano Ponce is the producer of *Doña Herlinda*), or even the rather thinly configured gay identity of Luis Zapata's groundbreaking *Adonis García, el vampiro de la colonia Roma* (1979; *Adonis García, a Picaresque Novel*), Hermosillo's film defies classification in terms of hegemonic homoerotic primes. Indeed, it transcends those formulations that, like José Rafael Calva's *Utopía gay* (1983; Gay Utopia)—however interesting this text may be as a radical reinscription of reproductive marriage in Mexican society— can only have meaning if it is clear who the "man" and "woman" (the one who ends up pregnant) are (see Foster 1991a, 136–139). Hermosillo significantly modifies the Mexican representation of homoeroticism by confusing the issues of male/female identity, although it would be safe to say that Rodolfo is generally assigned the male role. For example, in one important scene Ramón receives an "anniversary" gift from Rodolfo that includes a container of Nivea, presumably to be used as a lubricant in order to enhance his role as the insertee. Yet while Ramón plays the jealous lover on those occasions when, in order to maintain appearances, Rodolfo escorts women in public, he also plays the male counterpart to Doña Herlinda in her orchestration of patriarchal bliss in the baptismal denouement.

But the crucial axis of the film, however, is Doña Herlinda herself. The crucial question is, To what extent is she a token arbiter in the reduplication of patriarchal structures, and to what extent does she engage in their subversion? This subversion turns on the refusal to abide by the "epistemology of the closet" (Sedgwick 1990), which involves the definition of homosexuality as a dark, dirty secret that sustains compulsory heterosexuality out of the constant threat of being revealed as the damning identifying mark of an individual.

Clearly, Doña Herlinda is fully capable of engineering the social space such that the closet is no longer a precarious site of public scrutiny. She invites Ramón to live in the same house with her son, while at the same time she maneuvers Rodolfo into an engagement with Olga. She also remodels her house so that Ramón can live in separate quarters, as she does also, while Rodolfo and Olga, the apparently happily married professional couple, occupy with their son the main part of the house. And she balances with equanimity the relationship between Ramón and Olga, fully supporting the latter's desire to have her own career, which will involve a fellowship in Germany: while Ramón will be a companion to Rodolfo, she will be a loyal wife but not a dependent, subservient helpmate.

That lower-class, provincial Ramón will occupy this slot in the social structure in Olga's stead is one of the unexplored ideological issues of the film. When Ramón's parents come to visit their son in Guadalajara and find him living in Doña Herlinda's house, they are confused and even a bit suspicious. But the ever-attentive Doña Herlinda ends up winning them over, in a victory that is both a measure of her maternal efficiency and also a reflection of the uncertainties surrounding Ramón's social role. Thus Hermosillo glosses over class differences—those based on economic criteria (Doña Herlinda is a wealthy widow, while Ramón's parents are working-class provincials), profession (Rodolfo is a successful pediatrician while Ramón is studying the French horn), and culture (Rodolfo is a big-city sophisticate, while Ramón is a relatively humble provincial).

The major emphasis in his film, however, concerns the question of public versus private space, and the conflicts that cluster around the divergence between social obligations and private needs. Once again, Doña Herlinda is the pivotal figure. On the most explicit level, she is the one who undertakes to move her son and Ramón out of the sphere of public scrutiny into the privacy of the home. This assumes four stages. In the opening scene of the film, we see her son Rodolfo in front of the early sixteenth-century Guadalajara cathedral, a monument to traditional Catholicism and a symbol of the rigid moral code of Mexico's second-largest city. For the viewer who is more of a Mexican film buff than I, this scene must have parodic intertextual connections with classic Mexican films and with the master narrative conjunction of mariachi music (which is typical in Guadalajara and which permeates *Doña Herlinda*), machismo (in the style of Pedro Armendáriz), and nationalist sentiment (iconized by the Guadalajara cathedral). Rodolfo's stance evokes Armendáriz's paradigmatic figure of the Mexican macho. Armendáriz is reputed to have countered Luis Buñuel's suggestion that he wear a short-sleeved shirt in a scene with the curt "eso es de maricones" (that's for queers); in this scene, Rodolfo is wearing short sleeves.

However, in an irony not lost on the cognoscenti, Rodolfo is also standing in one of the several interconnected squares in downtown Guadalajara that serve as the major cruising area of the city, and nearby side streets contain several of the city's quasi-gay bars, including the Bar Corona, which appears in the film. (Yet it should be noted that gay pairs in Guadalajara blend in rather indistinguishably with the traditional all-male clientele of most Mexican nontourist bars, and that some of the city's bars more known for their legendary bohemian past blend this past with a specifically gay ambiance). In the opening scene, Rodolfo is on his way to meet Ramón in his room at a boardinghouse catering to out-of-town students. In a series of comic contretemps, it becomes evident that the boardinghouse cannot be a reliable trysting place since its public space, which is reminiscent of the public space of the plaza, is unconducive to intimacy in general, and much less to gay intimacy. Everyone knows Rodolfo at the boardinghouse and is appropriately deferential to him given his social rank, but it is clear that he and Ramón cannot pursue their relationship there.

The second stage involves Ramón's move into the house of Rodolfo and his mother. As I have indicated, this move is engineered by Doña Herlinda. In an often-cited scene in the film (see Berg 1992, 131), after the three have had dinner and the two men have retired to Rodolfo's bedroom to engage in intimacies now protected by the walls of the mother's home, Doña Herlinda settles down in her room to thumb through magazines, looking at pictures of bridal gowns. A third stage follows the marriage of Rodolfo and Olga. While the newlyweds inhabit their own apartment, Doña Herlinda and Ramón remain at home as though they were the proud parents of the couple. In one sequence they all assemble at the newlyweds' apartment to view the slides of their honeymoon in the United States and Hawaii. Afterward, Doña Herlinda explains to them how she is remodeling her house so that all of them—along with any children—can live together comfortably. The fourth stage involves the closing sequence described above, which juxtaposes the fullness of Ramón's and Rodolfo's protected erotic intimacies (in the film's most explicit sexual scene) with the fullness of Rodolfo's and Olga's domestic tranquility, all presided over by the beaming Doña Herlinda, who as usual has little to say, her face gently fixed in a beatific but knowing smile.

Doña Herlinda is a pivotal figure in another sense as well. Olga is a key female figure in the film, signaling a modern sophisticate who is able to combine both her career and motherhood—which she is able to do specifically because her husband has a male lover willing to assume parenting responsibilities. It would be inappropriate to lament Olga's being shoved to the margins as a wife: to do so would involve interpreting the film in terms of social coordinates other than those with which Hermosillo frames his narrative. Olga is fully aware of the arrangements Doña Herlinda has made. She has become good friends with Ramón and realizes that in the context of Doña Herlinda's world she will be able both to fulfill herself as a wife and as a professional; moreover, she will be able to accept the fellowship in Germany that has been offered to her, confident that she is abandoning neither her husband nor her child.

Doña Herlinda, therefore, does not overshadow or marginate

Olga; and Olga's role could be understood as marginal only in terms of a heterosexist, socially reactionary standard. Rather, Doña Herlinda binds together the public and the private. As a wealthy widow, she is able to move comfortably in the public world, where she is called upon to exemplify maternal discretion. This she does on several occasions, the most notable one being at the beginning of the film when she mediates the initially tense situation between Rodolfo and his two "dates," Olga and Ramón, who have yet to forge an alliance between themselves. But, most important, she exemplifies and ensures compliance with the social code of compulsory heterosexual monogamous reproductive marriage, at least as regards its crucial requirement of reproductive marriage. Mexican society, perhaps more than U.S. society, admits the possibility of the conjunction of reproductive marriage and the transgression of the criterion of monogamous heterosexuality (whether through the traditional practice of men's extramarital affairs or through the varying degrees of homosociality and homoeroticism that can be associated with Mexican male bonding). I do not wish to insinuate that male bonding in Mexico is the same as gay sexuality, but rather that a continuum stretches from basic *compadrismo*[1] to the various manifestations of physical intimacy (what I have in mind here is something like a masculine version of Adrienne Rich's lesbian continuum). By contrast, in the United States the concept of buddyism is either viewed as a youthful phenomenon that one outgrows with marriage, or it is seen as a characteristic of ethnics and other subaltern groups. This is especially so since the "reheterosexualization" of American society in the 1950s, which was in large measure a reaction to the strong male bonding romanticized in cultural productions like war films (see Silverman 1992, especially Chapter 2, "Historical Trauma and Male Subjectivity"). Nor do I mean to imply that Mexico is more "morally flexible" than the United States, at least as regards wandering husbands. But there appears to be a level of male-perspective cultural production that models such opportunities without the aura of condemnation that customarily surrounds such narratives in the United States.

Concomitantly, Doña Herlinda exemplifies the private space of Mexican life. As a woman, her realm of power is her home, and therefore to a large degree whatever she does to enhance life within its walls is socially legitimate. Sexual intimacy is a private matter, which is why Mexican law and Latin American law in general have been historically less concerned with the nature of acts than with their distribution between public and private realms (this is detailed by Lumsden 1991 [51ff.] and confirmed by other commentators on the place of male homoeroticism in the Latin American social dynamic [see Acevedo 1985; Trevisan 1986; Murray 1987; homoeroticism in Mexico is examined in Núñez Noriega 1994 and Taylor 1986]). Transgression involves not the acts themselves but making private acts public, which is why the public display of heterosexual eroticism is as vigorously defended as homosexual display (both as acts of defiance against norms of public decency). This does not translate into any greater respect in Mexico for gay rights. But it means that the American concept of the long arm of the law reaching into the bedroom of consenting adults is an alien judicial principle in most Hispanic societies. Therefore, when Doña Herlinda creates within the confines of her own home a love nest for Ramón and Rodolfo, although she is flaunting a Catholic moral convention she is also affirming the sanctity of the home and the privileging of her private domain. While the film might be decried as immoral by viewers who subscribe to institutional Catholicism, Doña Herlinda cannot be faulted for having "rescued" her son from the risks involved in the semipublic display of his sexuality in the boardinghouse, with its ill-fitting doors, and protecting this display behind the vine-covered walls of her home.

The question has been raised as to whether or not *Doña Herlinda y su hijo* is an adequate example of gay liberation, or whether or not it ends up reinscribing patriarchal values (Lozano 1989, 30). I believe this question is an inappropriate formulation of the issues, because it implies the possibility of somehow transcending patriarchal values, whatever these may be. (That is, is reproductive sexuality in contemporary society necessarily patriarchal, or is modern medical technology enabling conception and pregnancy to circumvent patriarchalism and even heterosexuality?) Hermosillo's film might be viewed as utopian in that it supersedes the either/or disjunction—*either* heterosexual marriage for Rodolfo *or* the "gay lifestyle"—by modeling a conjunctive arrangement in which no one is victimized (except for the possible unresolved social subalternity of Ramón). Yet to the extent that the arrangement *is* possible in the real world, rather than being a social fantasy or a science-fiction proposal, *Doña Herlinda y su hijo* is hardly utopian. Embodying micropolitics at its best, Hermosillo's film constitutes a gesture of resistance that does not wait for the totally revolutionary restructuring of society in order to bring about the fulfillment of personal needs.

It is less a question of reinscribing the patriarchy than of living at cross-purposes to it, less a question of resigning oneself to accepting the impositions of society (Rodolfo does not seem displeased at becoming a father) than of taking advantage of the gaps or the contra-dictions in the system in order to construct dimensions of an alter-nate world (see the proposals of Jonathan Dollimore [1991]). In this case, the criterion of privacy, especially for the professional class, can displace fulfillment of the social code of compulsory heterosexual-ity. What audiences have likely identified with in Hermosillo's film (an identification that has been repeated in subsequent films such as María Novaro's *Danzón* [1992; Big Dance]), is the image of personal subversion in an alienating though not exactly hostile environment. For example, at least in the universe of the film, there is no organized persecution of Rodolfo and Ramón, no sense of threat or danger, only the discomfort of the semipublic location of their meetings. Devel-oping of the practice of seeking fissures in the social edifice allows for the subversive pursuit of personal needs, without this pursuit be-coming a utopian confrontation with the deeply sunk pillars of that social edifice.

Rather than a reinscription of the patriarchy (albeit a singularly defective one) or a utopian imaging of an impossibly polysexual world of alternative family arrangements, Hermosillo's film is, I would argue, an example of what Alexander Doty (1993) has de-scribed as the queer potential of popular-cultural production. Doty develops the proposal that the queer is anything that challenges or subverts the straight, the compulsory heterosexual, through either an ironizing of its limited view of human potential or through the overt defiance of its conventions. The so-called gay sensibility and its lesbian counterpart are necessarily queer (although lesbians and gays may in some contexts endorse the straight), but queerness is something larger than gayness and lesbianism:

> I ultimately use [queerness] to question the cultural demarca-tions between the queer and the straight (made by both queers and straights) by pointing out the queerness of and in straight couples, as well as that of individuals and groups who have been told they inhabit the boundaries between the binaries of gender and sexuality: transsexuals, bisexuals, transvestites, and other binary outlaws. Therefore, when I use the terms "queer" or "queerness" as adjectives or nouns, I do so to suggest a range of nonstraight expression in, or in response to, mass culture. This range includes specifically gay, lesbian, and bisexual expressions; but it also includes all other potential (and potentially unclassifiable) nonstraight positions.
>
> This being the case, I like those uses of "queer" that make it more than just an umbrella term in the ways that "homo-

sexual" and "gay" have been used to mean lesbian *or* gay *or* bisexual, because queerness can also be about the intersecting or combining of more than one specific form of nonstraight sexuality. (Doty 1993, xv–xvi)

Doty goes on to analyze major popular-culture manifestations, finding that such productions are particularly privileged spaces for the elaboration of queer perspectives. Doty does not say whether this is the result of the need for mass culture to be constantly seeking new, usually superficially elaborated, combinations as part of product consumerism, or whether mass culture is only the most public face of a cultural production that is inherently queer because the straight mind has little need for practices that are premised on questioning the given. Such an understanding of the queer may end up by draining it of most of its transgressive value (indeed, many of the examples analyzed by Doty—such as *I Love Lucy* or *The Jack Benny Show*—have never been viewed as particularly transgressive). It may also serve to undermine the primacy of alternate sexualities viewed as alternate sexual practices and not just cute gender-bending. Nevertheless, Doty's formulations are valuable for defending the notion of queer as a global concept and not just a pejorative synonym of gay, and for proposing that the queer be sought beyond the limited confines of the texts of those in the know.

John King describes *Doña Herlinda* as one of Hermosillo's gay *divertissements* (1990, 141). Although this description may not be intended as dismissive, it nevertheless gives the impression that the film only has meaning for a specifically gay audience. By contrast, I am proposing that Hermosillo's film be viewed as a significant reinterpretation of clan arrangements that are not utopian in any fantastic way but are instead legitimated by the full participation of the actors involved. Furthermore, I am suggesting that *Doña Herlinda* be viewed under the purview of Doty's concept of queer culture, as a proposal for subverting the Mexican patriarchy through, significantly, the agency of Doña Herlinda herself, the one figure in the film most charged with defending the heterosexist system. Doña Herlinda "naturalizes" the perversion of the system as, perversely, a way of ensuring its reproduction (evident in the arrival of the newborn, whose baptism at the end of the film is a ritual of his entrance into that system). A good measure of the success of Hermosillo's film lies in the astuteness of his treatment of the borderlines between inscription and perversion (a "sweet subversion," according to Russo [1987, 313]), between legitimacy and transgression.

5 Homoerotic Writing and Chicano Authors

> In June, 1989, I was asked to speak at the Texas Lesbian Conference in Houston, Texas, where "diversity" was stressed. Many different groups belonging to Chicana, Latina, German, Italian and other white ethnic Texan groups attended. There was an assumption that all these groups were in the same boat—after all, all the women were lesbians. But ethnic colored people in this country are *not* on an equal footing with other ethnic American groups. We're never just "one of the guys."
>
> GLORIA ANZALDÚA, *MAKING FACE, MAKING SOUL*

> [T]he sexual significance of writing is not simply a matter of sexual content or of an author's overt sexual commitment (or orientation), but also of the work's engagement with a culture's literary ordering of the world . . . Homosexuality is a style, not a subject matter.
>
> ROBERT K. MARTIN, "ROLAND BARTHES"

I

Any attempt to legitimate a discussion of homoeroticism in Chicano/Chicana writing requires attending to two crucial issues. My interest here lies not in exploring a potential bibliography on the subject but in thinking through some theoretical issues, and some issues of practical criticism, entailed by a discussion of the subject. For there is no reason to believe that we have at hand either a well-defined corpus, a well-defined conceptual apparatus, or even a legitimate basis for approaching the topic as an already given of cultural studies in general and of Chicano/Chicana studies in particular.[1] An initial concern, therefore, turns on the question of the legitimation of such an inquiry. And as I have stated, two crucial matters must be dealt with at the outset.

The first concerns the larger theoretical issues of where one wishes to locate the site of Chicano/Chicana culture and its attendant cultural production. It may not be essential for every inquiry to determine whether the location of this site is to be construed as, alternately, a subaltern space within the hegemonic Anglo society of the United States or as a deterritorialized projection of Latin American culture—or even as a third dimension that, strategically to one degree or another, marks itself off from either of the two aforementioned and disjunctive options. But I would postulate that, as regards sexual ideology, especially as it affects the homoerotic, Chicano/Chicana society is positioned between two contradictory and mutually exclusive paradigms. It seems to me that this is less a question of an intersection between a traditional, premodern paradigm and a modern paradigm, such as we could propose is the case for sexual ideology in general, especially as it affects images of matrimony and the family. Rather, it has to do with whether or not the homosexual as a cultural ideologeme even exists, or under what circumstances it might exist.

Traditional Hispanic/Mediterranean society has had little ideological investment in the concept of the homosexual, instead preferring concepts like *maricón* (queer, faggot, fairy) and *sodomita* (sodomite). In modern Western medico-legal discourse the latter ideologemes have been subsumed under the term "homosexual," although they are not coextensive with it. Yet in Spanish it is questionable whether "homosexual" has any linguistic validity outside of an urban parlance circumscribed by "modern" social thought. While there can be no doubt that *maricón* and *sodomita* refer to human types, traditional Hispanic culture, as it perdures in Spain and Latin America today, views these terms as defining ways of acting and being rather than fixed personality types—existences rather than essences. The *maricón,* in particular, is characterized by his behavior and not necessarily by either his sexual preferences or his sexual acts: he is a man who displays himself publicly as a "woman," a marker, as contemporary terminology would have it, of gender performance. By contrast, the *sodomita* is more narrowly characterized, circumscribed by the practice of anal sex; tradition underscores the use of the term for the insertee rather than the insertor (without questioning how this in turn may not be a stable or suitable binarism), while also recording that it is a matter of circumstantial activity and not a fixed, exclusive preference.

One might pursue the complex images associated with these two ideologemes in the historical record, and consider the exceptions, revisions, and amplifications of the parameters I have noted; one might want to examine how these terms are applied to analogous female cases and, also, how the separate history of women and woman's sexuality creates significant differences. Here I will only refer to this ideological underpinning, in order to emphasize that a vast Western, Judeo-Christian, and Hispanic/Mediterranean tradition does not record the existence of the "homosexual person," but instead condemns certain acts and certain forms of gender performance.

With the emergence of the medico-legal concept of the homosexual at the end of the nineteenth century, first in German and then in the scientific discourses of other languages in societies embarked on a project of modernity, a personality or psychological type is created, whose nature, character, worldview, and total life experience are marked by same-sex preference. This preference is universally viewed as a compulsion, a depraved weakness, and a fatal alienation. As we are all aware, this ideology prevailed from the latter decades of the last century until the 1960s and 1970s, when new ways of viewing sexuality emerged as part of the incipient paradigm shift in the social status of the marginal and the subaltern; subsequent shifts have led from the "rights of the oppressed" to the "valuing of the Other" as a condition that affects us all. Indeed, at the present moment, under the sign of Queer Theory, the entire superstructure apparatus of the distinction between the heterosexual (a category that emerged at a significantly later time) and the homosexual has begun to crumble (but this shift is not immediately pertinent to our discussion here). Nevertheless, the construction of the homosexual is part of a modern scientific discourse, originating in hegemonic urban centers yet spreading out from them via colloquial registers that provide terms like "queer" and its synonyms, as part of the irradiating, all-consuming effects of the discourse of modernity.

Chicano/Chicana culture is as much a recipient of this discourse of modernity as any other sector of American society, and any other cultural group that still reveals vestiges of a traditional way of life—and, in this regard, Chicano/Chicana society is no different from other subaltern groups such as Afro-American society, Native American society, and all immigrant societies, or, for that matter, all rural societies, in which conflicting, contradictory ideological beliefs are sustained in uneasy concert. On some occasions, the discussion of nonsanctioned sexuality may evoke the traditional ideology, while on other occasions it may evoke medico-legal categories. And at times these evocations may be complementary (the town fairy alongside the gym teacher accused of improper advances toward her students), and at times they may be contradictory (as in the belief that an effeminate man is necessarily committed to same-sex preferences). The medico-legal discourse of homosexuality sought to assimilate the older categories of sexual transgressions, creating a master narrative of putatively seamless homologies (a particular way of appearing equaled a particular way of acting equaled a particular way of being equaled a particular way of existing in the world), but the competing scientific need for discriminating subcategories always led to a semiotic overflow from the master narrative.

Moreover, the difference between the stasis of scientific classification and the praxis of technology led to the problem of claiming the existence of a homosexual type and to the belief that medicine and psychiatry could cure a sickness called "homosexuality." The whole superstructural apparatus was doomed to collapse under the weight of its own frenzied homologizing (which reached a peak of hysteria in the reheterosexualization of the 1950s in the United States, where the menace of the Red Scare became yet another theme in the master narrative) and its ultimately irresolvable internal contradictions. But this collapse did not take place without first generating a great deal of social and personal suffering, and also yielding some rather awful examples of cultural production. (My favorite has always been Robert W. Anderson's 1953 play, *Tea and Sympathy,* in which the wife of a hairy, thick-wristed macho coach cures one of her husband's students of his sexual insecurities and suspected effeminacy by generously lending the boy her body so that he may discover that he is, after all, a red-blooded American heterosexual).

How this concerns Chicano/Chicana literature is that the discourse of modernity, as part of the configuration of a specific Chicano/Chicana cultural production, has led to some rather grim and repudiable passages, which are found especially in narrative fiction by men. The early fiction of John Rechy is particularly problematic. (Rechy is also interesting for the reluctance of pioneer scholars of Chicano/Chicana literature to accord him bibliographic and critical status. His work does not become part of the Chicano canon until 1979, when *Minority Voices* published in its fall issue the section "A Focus on John Rechy," with essays by Bruce-Novoa, Charles M. Tatum, and Carlos Zamora). For writers like Miguel Méndez-M. or José Antonio Villarreal (at least in key passage in their novels), the homosexual is either a category of the predatory Anglo, or an example of Chicano youth who are corrupted by Anglo ways—seduced by some agent of Anglo authority or contaminated by cohabitation with the barrio-destroying Anglo society—who are thus infused with a shame that must be zealously concealed so as not to appear to fall short of the highly esteemed Mexican male ideal. But Rechy, who from his earliest writings made no secret of his own homosexual identity, nevertheless provided an equally deleterious view of homoerotic preferences by failing to break away from the tragic mode that marked virtually every depiction of homosexual existence. Those who wrote to expose the depravities of homosexuality and those who wrote to depict their own relentless victimization by an ignorant society both depicted the homosexual as inevitably doomed to unremitting suffering: that the queer must either die or go crazy was the narrative order of the day. Such was the norm until, at least, a novel like Gore Vidal's *Myra Breckinridge* (1968). (And in this regard there is true gender equality, since lesbian-identified writing shows no exceptions to the pattern; Rita Mae Brown's *Rubyfruit Jungle* [1973] finally did for lesbian writing what Vidal's novel did for gay fiction, at least as far as popular, mass-distributed books are concerned.)

The second question that I wish to raise concerns the abiding presence of the frame of reference that I have been sketching up to this point. I have left quite a few threads dangling (and deliberately so, since I have no intention of providing a master narrative of historiographic totality). Yet it should be evident that both in terms of American society as a whole and Chicano/Chicana society in particular, especially as regards cultural production during a time marked by the emergence of "minority voices," scholars needed to undertake a major effort to free themselves from the hegemonic influence of Anglo categories of thought (see Sommers 1979). There is no denying the presence of a uniquely subaltern voice in much of the minority writing that emerges beginning in the 1960s. But the problematics of whether or not the subaltern can even speak qua subaltern is manifested in the inevitable incorporation, often quite unconscious, of the dominant ideology even as the subaltern sets out to mark itself off from this ideology. What I am attempting to get at is to what extent it is legitimate to speak of the homoerotic in Chicano/Chicana society and of its supposed reflexes in Chicano/Chicana writing. Concomitantly, it means that one must question how to begin speaking about the homoerotic as a component of Chicano/Chicana social and personal experience.

To be sure, there is no denying the existence of homoerotic desire among Chicanos and Chicanas. The question, however, is not whether this desire exists as part of a universal human experience (a configuration itself not without tremendous theoretical problems). Rather, the question is in what ways this desire becomes an ideologeme of Chicano/Chicana social life, in what ways it becomes a part of cultural production, and, finally, in what ways it becomes part of a critical analysis of that production. Let us agree that homoerotic desire exists among Chicanos and Chicanas, as part of either a universal human experience or specific sociocultural circumstances—which may or may not include the impact of Anglo society, whether deleterious (corruption by the depraved alien) or beneficent (the importation of the concept of the enhanced rights of human desire), with the latter itself questionable in a debate on the impact of the project of modernity on traditional ways of life. The conceptual difficulty arises, it seems to me, from the ways in which a discourse about homosexuality, about homoeroticism, and lesbian and gay liberation derives from a project of modernity that may be fundamentally at odds with traditional Chicano/Chicana life. This does not mean that Chicano/Chicana life cannot assimilate or recodify the project of modernity—or, today, its postmodern ramifications. It means that the discourse we are invoking emerges, both for those involved in cultural production and for those involved in the critical history of it, from ideological spheres outside that life. Now, one might assume that this creates some false antagonisms, as though Chicano/Chicana writers are unable to deal with homoeroticism in their characters without reference to the dominant Anglo medico-legal discourse in the first instance or subsequently to lesbian and gay liberation movements. But a challenge to the still scant bibliography and critical theory on the subject would counter this assumption.

What I would like to discern is the possibility of depictions of homoerotic desire in Chicano/Chicana literature that transcend the hegemonic models of Anglo authors and the Anglo critical establishment, such that we can sense, if not a definitive separation from prevailing creative and interpretive languages, at least substantive alternatives to it. Let me pose the question of whether there are representations of homoerotic desire (and here I am continuing, rather lamentably, to presuppose the already given of homoerotic desire and its epistemological labeling) that can be examined without reference to the Anglo academic bibliography on the subject. I would like to discuss the cases of three writers, who I believe model for us the difficulties, if not the inadequacies, of the Anglo vocabulary on the subject.

II

My first example is the writer Cherríe Moraga, a California Chicana lesbian whose writing is prominently marked by code-switching. Moraga, along with Gloria Anzaldúa, is a veritable foremother of Chicana lesbian writing. An enormously rich bibliography is now available on Chicana lesbian culture, beginning in 1981 with

This Bridge Called My Back: Writings by Radical Women of Color, edited by Moraga and Anzaldúa, and in 1983 with Moraga's *Loving in the War Years: lo que nunca pasó por sus labios* (Loving in the War Years: What Never Passed Her Lips) and continuing with recent collections like Juanita Ramos's *Compañeras: Latina Lesbians* (1987) and Carla Trujillo's *Chicana Lesbians: The Girls Our Mothers Warned Us About* (1991). There is much to consider in Moraga's exposition in *Loving in the War Years* and later in *Giving up the Ghost* (1986) about the confirmation of a Chicana feminist lesbian identity. The confirmation of this identity necessarily brings with it an examination of its correlations with Anglo and international lesbianism, especially as regards the privileging in Chicana culture of woman's identification with her mother (see, for example, Moraga's "La güera" [The Fair-skinned Blonde, or Anglo]), as a site of resistance against both Hispanic machismo and the problematic aspects of Anglo feminism.

But what I would most like to focus on with regard to Moraga, however, is the intersection between Moraga's Chicana lesbianism and the relationship between Spanish and English that is established through bilingual code-switching.[2] The bilingualism of Corky and Marisa—characters in *Giving up the Ghost* who represent different cultural and linguistic inscriptions of the same female subject— revolves around multiple differences. On the one hand, it concerns the relative predominance of a sphere ascribed to Anglo culture vis-à-vis one associated with Mexican/Chicano culture. For example, Corky, like any young person steeped in North American society, has no choice but immersion in the popular cultural themes of that society. Commercial slogans and jingles, TV shows, everyday clothes, all affirm a commitment to a specific dominant society, even when such a commitment implies that one might live the same racist discrimination of which she is a victim. Such is the case of playing cowboys and Indians when one is Indian (that is, Indian/Chicano in a direct sense, or subaltern in a generalized sense), and assuming the dominant role of the cowboy:

> CORKY [. . .]
> *when I was a little kid I usta love the movies*
> *every saturday you could find me there*
> *my eyeballs glued to the screen*
> *then during the week my friend Trudy and me*
> *we'd make up our own movies*
> *one of our favorites was this cowboy one*
> *where we'd be out in the desert*
> *'n' we'd capture these chicks 'n' hold 'em up*
> *for ransom*

we'd string 'em up 'n'
make 'em take their clothes off
jus' pretend a'course but it useta make me feel
real tough
strip
we'd say to the wall
all cool-like

(Giving up the Ghost, 5)

Corky's projected domination is joined with her lesbian posture, with an underlying, complicated mediation between a lesbianism that imitates the paradigmatic role of the rapist cowboy and a lesbianism that participates in a feminine Mexican/Chicano world in which mutual affection between women functions as a bastion against masculine domination.

Moraga has written eloquently in *Loving in the War Years,* her autobiography, of how she had to discover that being a lesbian of color need not imply assimilation to models that duplicate the binomial power game of the dominant society; rather, what she learned was that it was about forging bonds with a community of women, beginning with her own mother. In this sense, being a lesbian does not mean that the reader must assume that one of the feminine/masculine exaggerated roles of the heterosexual world is based on the primacy of genital sexuality and male sexual agency. Instead, lesbianism means to serve as a way of understanding the multiple dimensions of participation in a community of women, dominated first of all by compulsive heterosexuality and second by a racism as violent as the paradigmatic macho.

The text elaborates a homology in which white identity, masculinism, and the English language are counterposed to Chicano identity, feminism, and the Spanish language. The resulting hegemony yields a cultural semiosis that goes beyond the anatomic protuberances of the participants (and one necessarily recalls here the brilliant work of the French thinker Monique Wittig, for whom a lesbian discourse is that cultural feminist discourse that has gone beyond the dichotomy between men and women). Thus, the semiotic that operates between Corky and Marisa is the counterpart of the assimilation of an Anglo world, and the acceptance of a Chicana identity that implies, because of its specific sociohistorical coordinates, a self-conscious resistance to Anglo/white/heterosexual pressures to assimilate. This is why the subsequent dialogue between Marisa and Amalia represents the formulation of a lesbian continuity that constitutes the only true way in which the Chicano woman nourishes herself, providing herself with an identity able to save her from so-ciocultural annihilation. Lesbianism—a contestatory social attitude and also an ethos for transcending certain dichotomic traps of An-glo society—emerges as the semantic axis of Marisa and Amalia's play. It is not one option among many other sexual choices, just as code-switching is not an option either among many other linguistic choices, but rather the only valid one, the only one that confers a valid identity, the only one that makes possible the full participa-tion of women in the world, both the world inherited by them and the one they are forging in their daily communal existence.

III

It was not easy for early Chicano literary criticism to in-corporate Rechy's writing into the first versions of a canon. First (al-though he is fully Mexican on both sides, and Rechy really is his fa-ther's name), there was the issue of his non-Hispanic name. Also, the notoriety of his inaugural novels—which were among the first ex-plicit writings about "the homosexual lifestyle" in the United States in the 1960s—as well as their urban and nonbarrio settings (despite his main characters' Hispanic names), made him seem irrelevant given the sociohistorical priorities of the day. Moreover, after the elo-quent erotic ideologies contained in *The Sexual Outlaw* (1977; rev. ed. 1985) and *Rushes* (1979), Rechy turned away from specifically homo-erotic depictions to explore other narrative formulas. Of his three most recent novels, *Bodies and Souls* (1983), *Marilyn's Daughter* (1988), and *The Miraculous Day of Amalia Gómez* (1991), only the latter has a specifically Chicano/Chicana theme, although *Bodies and Souls* con-tains segments on East Los Angeles (in fact, the mother of Manny Gómez, a character in *Bodies and Souls,* is the Amalia Gómez of *The Miraculous Day*).

The proposition that I wish to make about Rechy's fiction in this period concerns not his turning away from gay or Chicano themes but his effort to depict a "queer take" on the world. For example, *Marilyn's Daughter,* which deals with the putative illegitimate daugh-ter of Marilyn Monroe—hardly a gay or Chicano theme—represents a woman's attempt to uncover the truth of her birth, to establish definitively her roots, her identity, her "real person." Only when she is able to understand that her self is the consequence of what she constructs out of life's experiential pieces—whether it be a name, a family, a sense of community, a sexuality—can the woman under-stand that whether or not she is Monroe's daughter is of absolutely no consequence, and that her problems of discerning who she is would not be resolved by such knowledge. It seems to me that what Rechy is attempting to configure here is the importance of identity construction and, more specifically, a concept of identity construction whose dimensions include sexuality, ethnicity, and even language: we are given certain elements, life-forming experiences over which we have no control, but what we do with them is the consequence of our subsequent, ongoing interaction with our identity.

Sexual preference is not a blank slate, but nor is it an unerasable program. One can say that the concept of the native speaker is psycho- and sociolinguistically a tenuous concept. But this fact does not allow us, conversely, to assert that language competence is only the result of conscious effort. Linguistic competence and sexual preference are extremely complex processes, not unimpeachable givens or effects of biological and social destiny but projects of construction. In Rechy's other two recent novels, *Bodies and Souls* and *The Miraculous Day of Amalia Gómez,* a spatial movement that becomes a psychological displacement is involved, and in both cases there is a moment of epiphany, of discovering not what one is but what one has become, be it the case of the wandering pilgrims in the former novel or the Chicana matriarch in the latter. Rechy's view of social instability, not as the curse of a degraded world but as part of lived experience that is constantly renewing itself, is eminently queer insofar as it refutes the fixed, frozen, or immutable (and, therefore, dead-end) categories of straight ideology.

IV

Francisco X. Alarcón is a third-generation Chicano born in 1954 in Wilmington, California. Currently residing in San Francisco, Alarcón studied in both California and Mexico as a child. He pursued doctoral studies in Latin American literature at Stanford, and held a Fulbright Fellowship at the Colegio de México in Mexico City. Alarcón is considered one of the most original poets in Chicano literature; certainly, he is of paramount importance in the development of a Chicano homoerotic writing, as exemplified by his 1991 *De amor oscuro / Of Dark Love* (which is modeled on *Sonetos de amor oscuro,* the gay poetry of Federico García Lorca written in 1935 and 1936 shortly before his murder, but not published until 1984). In addition to an extensive poetic production that began in the mid-1980s, Alarcón has engaged in intensive barrio activism and worked as a gay advocate.

Alarcón's writing is marked by a complex poetic voice. Although his poems might appear simple at first glance, the texts' attempts to access meanings and feelings of considerable density quickly become evident. The division of the relatively brief texts into relatively short strophes, with a highly condensed poetic line, lends the texts their deceptive simplicity. In a certain sense, Alarcón evokes one facet of an entwined classism and racism: Chicano lived experience must be simple in nature, the experience of a simple folk with simple souls, unmarked by the "deep" reactions of the more sophisticated, worldly individual (which is the self-image of the disdainful Anglo). To be sure, all lived human experience is profound, but what is relevant here is that life within the parameters of classism, racism, and, in the case of Alarcón, homophobia, is much more pathetic and tragic than that of the presumed masters. To set forth the specific resonances of Chicano daily life—not a privileged or special life, but an everyday life—is the goal of the poems.

Alarcón's *Body in Flames / Cuerpo en llamas* (1990) contains forty poems distributed between five sections. The first three sections have eleven poems each and the fourth has six poems, while the fifth consists of a single poem. The first three sections deal with the primary references of Chicano culture and heritage; topics relating to marginality; and, in an eloquent juxtaposition to the second topic, regenerative love. The fourth part evokes themes of death and spirituality, while the fifth is titled, in a way that looks toward the future, "Carta a América / Letter to America." Several of the poems that make up this collection appeared in earlier books by Alarcón, giving the impression that his texts circulate freely from one collection to another.

Alarcón's poetry is especially attractive in its focus on details of barrio life and a collective Chicano memory. "En un barrio de Los Angeles" ("In a Neighborhood in Los Angeles") opens with the lines "el español / lo aprendí / de mi abuela" ("I learned / Spanish / from my grandmother"), which immediately establishes a central correlation between Spanish and the grandmother, two primary values of Chicano (indeed, all Hispanic) life. Language is crucial to the individual's identity: it constitutes the network of meanings by means of which s/he comes into contact with and interprets the world; it marks the frontiers between one's own language community and the community of others (and the social variations of one's own dialect are marked off from those of others' dialects); and it is a cultural medium through which individuals have access to unending generations of poetry, songs, folktales, and sayings, as well as, of course, a whole tradition of written literature. Moreover, the grandmother is an icon of family and community tradition, a figure of how human beings reproduce themselves from one generation to the next and how culture is passed down from generation to generation. Significantly, in Spanish the word for language is feminine, and Alarcón associates the learning of Spanish with a profoundly felt feminine space that is created by his grandmother when he is left in her care as his parents go off to work in the fish canneries.

In the bilingual poem "I Used to Be Much Much Darker," Alarcón employs the image of skin color to characterize the degree of his physical and emotional proximity to Chicano life: when his life was closely tied to the barrio, he was much, much darker, but "maybe [now] I'm too / far up north" to be as dark as he once was. This focus on mundane details of the body and lived space, spoken in such a way as to evoke deep psychological and sentimental reactions to Chicano life, is one of the brilliant features of Alarcón's poetry.

The homoerotic dimensions of Alarcón's poetry are evident in this collection in a text in the second part, "El otro día encontré a García Lorca / The Other Day I Ran into García Lorca." In the case of men, the Chicano community generally views homoeroticism as a violation of a salutary, assertive masculinity that serves as a necessary bulwark to the corruptions of the dominant, exploitative Anglo society; in the case of women, homosexuality is viewed as a violation of an allegiance to the chaste womanhood of the Virgin of Guadalupe. These perspectives overlook the strong male-male bonding that occurs among men in Mexican and Mexican-American society, and the virtually exclusively woman's world of the cult of Mary. As I have already affirmed, these patterns of homosociality are not necessarily homosexual. Rather, they provide a significant barrio alternative to the predatory heterosexism Chicano society often associates with the Anglo world.

Alarcón's poetry figures a society in which same-sex bonding unleashes profound, refreshing sources of affection and love that are a balm for the alleged dehumanization inflicted by the Anglo world. Certainly, Alarcón envisions sexual acts: he speaks of being kissed on the mouth by García Lorca, which prefigures other forms of intimate bodily contact. But what is more significant than the legitimation of homosexual love are the heightened emotions of Chicano life. In Chicano life there can be no embarrassment attached to feeling, expressing, and recounting interpersonal intimacies that are banned, and are, indeed, meaningless in the dominant society. Finally, the very title of the collection unleashes provocative images of the materiality of the body, which violates taboos in traditional Mexican society against both men's and women's display of the body.

Alarcón's poetry is unabashedly sentimental. The phenomenon of sentimentality cuts two ways. On the one hand, it can be a cheaply bought emotion that distracts from the harsh realities of life: cry crocodile tears and you avoid facing up to the real suffering at hand. Mainstream liberals are often quick to "feel sorry" for the marginal and the oppressed—hoping, if only unconsciously, that their sentiments will suffice, rather than working toward an alternate arrangement of social reality in which the suffering of some will not provoke the easy laments of others who are implicated in the very structures of power that bring about suffering in the first place.

But there is another side to sentimentality. It can be a therapeutic response to suffering, a recovery of and insistence on deeply felt human emotions in the face of social structures that refuse to acknowledge the legitimacy of those emotions. The denial of human sentimentality in order to promote the "serious work" of life—i.e., exploitation—is ultimately a denial of basic humanity. A poetry that stimulates this sentimentality, that promotes unrestrained and uncontainable feeling, that praises what the severe, no-nonsense ethos views as uncontrollable and threatening—even if the threat comes from unabashed homoeroticism—is necessarily beneficial to the health of the reader.

Alarcón, in the typical fashion of unified poetry collections, constructs a mosaic of topics that encourage and stimulate emotional, sentimental response in the reader. Some texts focus on icons of barrio life, the trappings and fixtures that provide immediate tie-ins for the reader: elements of language, Chicano decor, and the sounds and smells of the barrio. Other texts seem more arcane, and the reader might question how these references relate to Chicano life. However, literature, and particularly poetry, are typically marked by the effort to make connections that may not be readily apparent, and to posit networks of meanings that stretch the readers' imaginations with regard to the nature of their shared experiences. Alarcón's ability to accomplish this in a seemingly effortless queer-marked language, with a markedly colloquial and accessible vocabulary, is ultimately an expression of intense poetic value.

V

My goal here has been to address some of the theoretical questions that emerge from and perhaps even take precedence over the sort of history of Chicano/Chicana cultural production and homoeroticism one might like to see written. The issue is not whether there is homoerotic writing among Chicanos and Chicanas: those who need to defend a straight or heterosexist ideology, whether from a fundamentalist Judeo-Christian point of view or from a revolutionary socialist one that submerges individual needs in a united movement front, can hardly deny the bibliographic evidence. Nor is the issue whether or not the existing production addresses a panorama of homoerotic interests as defined separately and collectively by gay men and lesbian women.

What is important is the degree to which the literary and cultural scholar's critical eye will be able to discern, with appropriate differentiation and subtlety, the aspects of Chicano/Chicana homoeroticism that coincide with an agenda defined from within Chicano/Chicana culture (and retaining for the moment an undertheorized concept of the "within" of culture), and the aspects that constitute homologies with general American and international priorities. The establishment of such homologies is not meant to confirm the queer dimensions of Chicano/Chicana culture. Quite the contrary: it is proposed that there will be substantial differences, and that those differences will be of most interest to the scholar. Certainly, there is nothing to keep writers sensitive to their subalternity from seeking correspondences with the hegemonic cultural discourse: by this time, it is hoped, we are beyond telling writers and artists what they should do to be acceptable. All I am striving for here is an understanding of differences within a program of cultural production, and an interpretive apparatus sufficiently powerful to recognize and to account for these differences (albeit not as part of a technology of discovery).

For this reason three examples of Chicano/Chicana writing have been emphasized. These examples represent challenges for interpretation based only on seeing the homoerotic as it has been identified by the dominant critical discourse. There is no non-Chicana writer whose work shows the same intersection between sexual identity, cultural identity, and linguistic identity that Cherríe Moraga shows. And if he were a questionable Chicano writer in the first place, John Rechy's move away from explicit homoerotic themes would now render him a questionable gay writer—that is, unless one can make an interpretive investment in the queer perspective that, it has been suggested, characterizes his particularly unique novelistic domain. In any event, critical thinking along the lines sketched here provides a way to avoid writing Chicano/Chicana homoeroticism as nothing more than an importation of Anglo social priorities, as well as a means of transcending the insufficiently nuanced option of seeing Chicano/Chicana homoeroticism only when it coincides with the master narrative text of an undifferentiated American literature.

6 | Montes Huidobro's *Exilio* and the Representation of Gay Identity

ROMÁN. Si habláramos todos con el corazón en la mano . . .
MIGUEL. No se puede hablar con el corazón en la mano . . .
[. . .] La gente que lo dice todo, que no se queda con nada
por dentro, acaba rehabilitada en las granjas agrícolas . . .
sembrando malanga . . . en las cárceles . . . en los paredones
de fusilamiento . . . con la boca abierta llena de moscas en las
cunetas de las carreteras.

MONTES HUIDOBRO, *EXILIO*

Of the many unresolved issues of the Cuban revolu-
tion, perhaps none is more tragic than the role of gays and lesbians
in the post-1959 society (Young 1981). There may no longer be organized programs of rehabilitative persecution (e.g., the forced labor
of the infamous Unidad Militar de Ayuda a la Producción [Military
Unit in Support of Production]) and there may now be fragmentary
manifestations of homoerotic experience in current cultural production (e.g., the fiction of Senel Paz).[1] Nevertheless, there remains the
unavoidable historical fact of the programmatic, relentless destruction in the early 1960s of any manifestation of gay life. The recent
publication of Reinaldo Arenas's autobiography, *Antes que anochezca*
(1992; *Before Night Falls*), has brought this whole sordid story to the
forefront again, challenging readers to accept the validity of not only
Arenas's sexual preferences but the ethos of his concerted promiscu-
ity, and underscoring how the left in its many guises has yet to work
out any totally acceptable appreciation of the rights of lesbian and
gay individuals.

Unquestionably, the reason why the issue of gay and lesbian rights in Cuba has remained unresolved is the continuing impossibility for gays (henceforth used to include lesbians) to find any legitimation within the three dominant ideologies that have determined Cuban social policy. In recent years an international liberation movement has focused special attention on the dreadful irony of homophobic persecution in both right-wing military dictatorships and socialist regimes (such that Julio Cortázar made a plea to the Sandinistas in *Nicaragua tan violentamente dulce* [1984; Nicaragua So Violently Sweet] not to repeat Castro's error [12–14]). For if Catholicism, in both its official and populist versions, has been a mighty fortress of homophobia (quite understandable on many grounds as part of the defense of a totally masculinist institution), and continually renews its exclusion of homoerotic desire, then Hispanic machismo, which derives only part of its ideological capital from Catholicism, must necessarily defend a variety of masculine supremacy that excludes the gender-role transformations that are integral, if not thoroughly coextensive, with gay identity. Cogent arguments have been made as to how machismo can accommodate homoeroticism—indeed, how part of its definition may even require it. Yet any homoeroticism contained within machismo functions primarily to validate the latter, by being the despised Other against which machismo measures itself (see Dollimore 1991; Sedgwick 1990). Finally, the inability of dogmatic Marxism to see in gay culture anything other than one of bourgeois capitalism's many diseased faces, and its failure to distinguish between homosexuality (particularly as it was viewed and consumed by the foreign tourist in Havana) as part of the corrupt market system and gay identity as a dimension of personal liberation, provided a potent substratum for the homophobia of the Castro revolution, which itself had its origins in one of the great subsystems of machismo, the armed forces.

These are not three separate ideologies, however, but rather primary reference points that combine in various ways to exclude gays, as Arenas makes abundantly clear in an oeuvre dedicated to the analysis of Cuban homophobia. Thus, Catholicism and machismo are wed in the exile community's rejection of gays, which is why the persecution of gays in the 1960s was quite literally the only aspect of the Castro regime's policies that the community did not attack with sustained vigor. But machismo and the homophobia of dogmatic Marxism combined fatally to make that policy inevitable, and it was carried out with a grim determination that made the homophobic campaigns of all the right-wing military dictatorships in Latin America in the last thirty years pale by comparison (see Young 1981; and Néstor Almendros's now-legendary documentary film *Conducta impropia* [1984; Improper Conduct]).

Arenas's writing has circulated extensively in the United States in Spanish and English, and much was made of the triangulation between Castro, AIDS, and Arenas's decision to commit suicide that was suggested in his final note to the world. To the best of my knowledge, however, no Cuban writer from the exile community in the United States had included a gay character as a significant feature of his work until Matías Montes Huidobro's *Exilio* (1988; Exile). A professor of Spanish at the University Hawaii, Montes Huidobro is probably the most important Cuban playwright working in the United States. *Exilio* is one of a number of successes he has had in the Latino theater in the United States. Composed of the classical three acts, *Exilio* focuses on five Cubans at three different stages in their shared fortunes: exile in New York in 1958 and political activism against the Batista regime; the return in 1963 to Cuba and the traumatic institutional realignments inherent to revolution (in this case antihomosexual cultural policy and the witch hunt against gays); and back in New York in approximately 1983, with the group divided between those who have returned to exile in the United States because of their opposition to Castro and those who make a triumphant visit to New York as members of the official party apparatus. The play centers on the characters of two heterosexual couples and a gay man; the five are linked by the involvement of one husband with the other couple and the gay man in the theater. Indeed, Montes Huidobro's play is built around metatheatrical conceits. These include life as a stage, social institutions as theatrical embodiments, theater as privileged cultural production for the modeling of social life, theater as a domain of refuge for the individual seeking alternate realities, and theater as the epitome of individuals' enactment of their personal lives, which includes the dramatic as a rhetorical strategy of interpersonal communication.

Whereas the five are joined in 1958 in the common goal of Cuban liberation (quaffing symbolic *cubalibres,* one of many theatrical signs the dramatist gleefully makes use of), back in Cuba in 1963 their solidarity crumbles. One couple identifies with Castro's policies: Miguel becomes an official poet of the Revolution (the play is filled with roman à clef allusions to real-life literati) and his wife, Beba, becomes a high functionary; in the second act, Beba arrives to take over the job of director of the Teatro Nacional previously held by Román, their comrade-in-arms in the 1958 exile. Román's wife, Victoria, is a famous actress, and along with Miguel, her husband Román, and the playwright Rubén, they had long collaborated in using art as a form of political protest. However, when Beba, who is the only one without a theater background, arrives to displace Román as director, she also confirms the rumor that Rubén will be detained as a homosexual and sent to one of the rehabilitation camps, whose goal is to make socialist agents out of exponents of the putatively seamiest side of bourgeois capitalism. Beba announces the party line:

> En primer lugar, no es de Rubén de quien estamos discutiendo. Estamos hablando de la necesidad que tiene la Revolución de darle una solución a problemas que emergen a consecuencia de la burguesía, entre los cuales se encuentra el homosexualismo; y un homosexual no puede representar a la Revolución debidamente. (58–59)[2]

Although José A. Escarpanter's rather unfocused prologue alludes in passing to Rubén's role in the play as a synecdoche for the "ataque al poder castrista" (7; attack on Castro's power), he leaves the impression that the play is basically about exile. Certainly, exile is the basic mise-en-scène of each act, and the life of Rubén, Román, and Victoria in New York in 1983, along with the visit of Beba and Miguel as self-satisfied spokespersons for the regime, underscores the profound divide in contemporary Cuban culture of which exile is the sign. Yet I would propose that *Exilio* is really about queerness, understanding this term as the antithesis of, the antagonist to the masculinist, straight, compulsorily heterosexist patriarchy embodied in the play by the dominant, if absent, figure of Fidel Castro—the personal embodiment, as Beba and Miguel recite endlessly, of the revolution. This is despite Beba's assertion that "El inconveniente que tienen ustedes es que todo acaba en el plano personal" (58; The problem for you is that everything always ends up on a personal plane). Certainly gay identity is a category of queerness, but it is not its principal defining feature, since "queer" means nonstraight, and gay (or lesbian) is only one way of being nonstraight.

Indeed, Rubén's sexual identity is never an issue in the play—that is, in terms of how he interprets it, with whom he has relations (in any register of the word), and what might be his personal history. Rubén's sexuality, however, is an axis for other developments in the play. In this sense, the play makes use of the concept of the "third man out" or the "tercero en discordia," in the sense that Rubén functions as a semantic shifter between the two straight couples. Although the first act includes some standard, grossly homophobic remarks uttered by Miguel, Rubén's imminent arrest in the second act brings out the ugly side of revolutionary culture, especially as it is correlated structurally with the displacement of Román by Beba as director of the Teatro Nacional. In the third act, Rubén arranges for Beba and Miguel to be received by Román and Victoria, as part of some delirious plan to assassinate them in order to free himself of the nightmares of his imprisonment (Rubén's liberation from the rehabilitation system and his return to the United States is never explained, but perhaps Montes Huidobro counts on his audience's familiarity with Arenas's personal story; in any case, this is further evidence of the play's lack of concern with the details of Rubén's experience and its use of him as a structural shifter). Rubén's plan goes awry, and the ensuing confusion gives way to a confrontation between Beba and Miguel that exposes the moral corruption of their existence. As the final curtain falls, Victoria and Román, rid of their troublesome guests, reaffirm the domestic tranquility of their exile.

It should be clear that even as Rubén articulates the horrors of the persecution he suffered at the hands of Castro's agents of social morality—albeit principally in terms of the devastating psychological impact it had on him and not the lived details as such—his performance in the last act mediates between the thoroughgoing corruption of Beba and Miguel and the space of personal fulfillment and tranquility now inhabited by Román and Victoria (it is significant that Victoria has left the theater, as a way of ridding herself of the pain of the past). Where Rubén is incidental to the first act but a structural correlative of the second, in the third act he provokes the confrontation between the two couples in order to reveal the differences that have occurred in the twenty-five-year historical period depicted in the play.

The often incidental appearance of Rubén and the outrageousness (gay hysteria?) of his behavior in the third act, followed by his disappearance before the final curtain, ought not to distract one from the fundamental role he has been assigned in the play as its "odd" character. While one might wish Montes Huidobro had focused more on his personal story, the fact that he does not lends validity, in a perverse sort of way, to Beba's further assertion in Act Two that "Aquí no se trata de problemas individuales" (59; We're not dealing with personal problems here). *Exilio*, in fact, is not about individual problems, precisely because it confirms the split in contemporary Cuban culture noted above. What is significant is that it does so through the figure of Rubén, rather than with the more-customary romantic device of a divided family. The narrative genre of the romance is profoundly patriarchal, and therefore profoundly heterosexual, and its use in so much of the literature of the Cuban exile helps to explain why, again with the eloquent exception of Arenas's novels (e.g., *Otra vez el mar* [1982; *Farewell to the Sea*], *Viaje a la Habana: novela en tres viajes* [1990; Trip to Havana: A Novel in Three Trips]), queerness in general and gayness specifically remain untreated.

But by making use of the figure of Rubén, Montes Huidobro deftly and innovatively introduces a gay character into the corpus of Cuban exile cultural production. In addition, he suggests—to those who continue to subscribe to the combined Catholic/machista ideology of sexual and cultural straightness—the disquieting double proposition that homophobia in Cuban society transcends the temporal pre-Castro/post-Castro divide and the spatial Miami/Havana divide, and that Rubén's queerness is one potent site for the deconstruction of the revolutionary lie. One will recall that it is Rubén's apparent attempt to stage an assassination of Beba that leads to their confrontation. It may not be a definitive anagnorisis in the traditional, tragic sense, but it certainly involves the smashing of Beba's posture as a commissar of the revolution:

> MIGUEL. Eres Beba, Beba *darling.* A mí no me vas a confundir con tus juegos, con tus artimañas. Es demasiado tarde, porque de sobra sé quien eres tú. Y en la embajada lo sabe todo el mundo. Esta es una misión que me han encomendado, que tengo que cumplir. ¡Idiota! ¡Estúpida! ¡Yo [y no Rubén] te voy a matar! Has caído en desgracia y yo estoy aquí para eliminarte. (99)[3]

Miguel continues in this vein, insisting that he has been charged with eliminating Beba, and the two leave with her conviction that she will never return to Cuba alive. There is no reason to invest any truth value in this exchange, however, because what matters is not what is said but that the exchange takes place as the consequence of Rubén's provocation:

> RUBÉN. [. . .] Pero si yo me acuerdo, como si fuera una película que acabara de ver . . . Cuando nos llevaban en las guaguas a los campos de concentración, a las cámaras de gas . . . Rehabilitados para que no hiciéramos lo que queríamos hacer . . . Fumigados . . . Enterrados hasta el cuello, con aquella miel derretida en la cabeza para que las hormigas bravas vinieran a comernos vivos . . . como te comerían a ti, Beba *darling,* como te comerán a ti . . . (97)[4]

Rubén emerges here as the conscience of those who have suffered not only the abuses of power perpetrated by the revolutionary gov-

ernment but also the major structural features such as the rehabilitation camps. In this sense his experience is a global metonymy
of sociopolitical horrors, as much as Beba represents the agency of
those horrors. If one can entertain the proposition that Beba is, in the
language of Mary Daly, a token torturer (1978, 96), a woman who
becomes an agent of patriarchal oppression (and who ultimately becomes a victim herself), opposition to her can only be expressed effectively in the queer figure of Rubén, whose queerness represents,
more than simply sexual liberation, freedom from any form of structural oppression. It is significant that Rubén carries Miguel along
with him—Miguel, who in the first act had dismissed him as "Rubén
maricón" (30)—and it will be Miguel rather than Rubén who kills
Beba. Discord has been sown in the belly of the monster, which is
why Rubén can depart with some measure of peace at the play's end,
and Victoria and Román can await the final curtain secure in the
tranquility of their exile.

The issue that emerges in Montes Huidobro's *Exilio,* much more
important than the subject of exile (which is necessarily an obsessive
theme in contemporary Cuban cultural production outside Cuba), is
the nature of Rubén's sexual status. The dignifying of gay individuals has generally meant respect for their standing as a minority: historical, cultural, and, obviously, sexual (and it has been important
to define this sexuality in terms other than strictly genital involvement). But minority politics, important though they are, cannot
form the basis of Montes Huidobro's play, which in no way purports
to be the defense of a gay individual, his psychological biography, his
erotic choices, his social standing. Rather, the figure of Rubén serves
as a point of entrance into the domain of queerness: the refusal to
accept the patriarchal straight and its numerous, expanding, con-
centric circles of social behavior. Even if one does not wish to make a
categoric argument for how, ultimately, the Castro experience has
meant the reaffirmation of patriarchal hegemony through a personalist, Stalinized dictatorship grounded in an unquestioned ideology
of machismo, one cannot come away from *Exilio* without having to
consider the full implications of Rubén as the agent, no matter how
minimally, of the assault on the Bebas.

The Representation of the Body in the Poetry of Alejandra Pizarnik

nadie me conoce yo hablo mi cuerpo

PIZARNIK, "LOS PEQUEÑOS CANTOS," *TEXTOS DE SOMBRA Y ÚLTIMOS POEMAS*

Visión enlutada, desgarrada, de un jardín con estatuas rotas. Al filo de la madrugada los huesos te dolían. Tú te desgarras. Te lo prevengo y te lo previne. Tú te desarmas. Te lo digo, te lo dije. Tú te desnudas. Te desposees. Te desunes.

PIZARNIK, "EXTRACCIÓN DE LA PIEDRA DE LOCURA," *EXTRACCIÓN DE LA PIEDRA DE LOCURA*

I

An interest in the representation of the body in contemporary culture implies a series of interlocking concerns: an attention to a presumably ever-expanding scientific (or, perhaps now, counterscientific) knowledge about the structure and function of the components of the body, including different systematic ways of classifying those components; the relationship between one's body and one's perceptions of it, ranging from inner spiritual feelings to various forms of self-contemplation; the ideological issues associated with classifying bodies in terms of sex, race, or other metonymic features; the uses of the body, whether instrumental (e.g., as the site of political statements, as in public protests, or as the site of political repression, as in torture) or reflexive (e.g., for sexual pleasure or artistic expression, as in display texts like theater or dance); the politicization of the body as a metonym for social issues, as in the case of explicit signs of sexual preference; and, finally, the preoccupation with the limits of the body—the extent to which the body is autonomous, self-contained, or perceptually independent, and the degree to which any of its aspects must be defined in relationship to an individualized or collectivized other (e.g., both linguistic functions and sexuality—even masturbation—involve imaginings of others).[1] Many of these considerations may be viewed as various facets of a single imperative: the need to engage in a sustained practice of rethinking the body in counterpoint to any ideology that would hold it as already defined (see Benstock 1991, Chapter 2, "Signifying the Body Feminine;" Turner 1984; Featherstone, Hepworth, and Turner 1991; Goldstein 1991).

"Thinking through the body," as Gallop's superbly ambiguous trope (1988) states (with "through" read either as a locative preposition or as a verbal particle), entails grounding and regrounding human experience in a body that is problematized, both as part of a materialist questioning of the Western primacy of immanence and as part of current sociocultural priorities regarding threats to the integrity and the very survival of the body. This may not necessarily mean that the body (rather than, say, some other putative dimension of human experience like the mind or the spirit, or a particular emotional phenomenon such as love or adventure) has assumed an obsessive centrality in contemporary culture, especially in whatever is judged to be its vanguard sectors. But it does mean that when the body is either thematized or utilized as a semiotic field of reference and symbolization, it is likely to be treated as problematical rather than as a signifying given. Clearly, this involves more than simply re-viewing the body from different perspectives or discovering new vistas of the body (e.g., the recent thematization of the genitals, especially in photography). Rather, it requires interrogating the very bases on which any definition of the body is proffered. Thus, for example, simply to refocus a gaze on the female body is insufficient; one must begin with questioning both the definition of the female body and the legitimacy of artistic representations of this body.

Perhaps speaking of the need to deconstruct the body is too facile a characterization of this position. Yet, to a large extent, it does mean disassembling certain givens, particularly those relating to essentialist characterizations and to the implication that there is an already known about the body which presumes that the body's position in society is fixed prior to birth and maturation. Likewise, it refers to the difficulties of holding in place any understanding of the body constructed from the site of an individual consciousness, no matter whether that construction is the consequence of internalizing cultural givens or of forging an eccentric knowledge in counterpoint to cultural givens. Whereas perhaps former considerations of threats to the body's survival centered on a hostile environment, the consciousness at issue here involves something the ideological menace to which an individual's corporally based self-construction is subject—something like the bell-jar motif bequeathed to contemporary literature by the poet Sylvia Plath, or the eponymous yellow-wallpaper sign of Charlotte Perkins Gilman's 1892 short story.

II

In the twenty-five years since her suicide, the Argentine poet Alejandra Pizarnik (1936–1972) has emerged as a crucial figure in contemporary Latin American feminist writing. The cultural consciousness associated with her person and her literary production includes major strains of Western marginalization, with the inflections specific to Argentine society. Pizarnik was a woman, a Jew, the daughter of an immigrant-refugee family, a lesbian, a clinically certified schizophrenic who spent her last years institutionalized (she took her life while at home on a weekend pass), a suicide (in a country where suicide is still a capital offense), and a poet. The enormous critical interest that her work has stimulated, both during the periods of military dictatorship in Argentina (1966–1973, 1976–1983), when much of it circulated clandestinely, and during the post-1983 period, when a previously suppressed and fragmented cultural production may now be subjected to intense sociopolitical interpretations, has allowed it to be read within multiple and divergent interpretive registers. Nevertheless, there is a critical consensus that Pizarnik's poetry (both in traditional verse form and in nonmetrical prose microtexts) is indisputably important.

My previous work on Pizarnik has centered on the eleven prose vignettes that make up *La condesa sangrienta* (1971a; *The Bloody Countess,* published in Manguel 1986), which deals with the figure of Erzébet Báthory, a sixteenth-century Hungarian noblewoman accused of the torture and death of over six hundred girls in rituals apparently intended to provide her with eternal youth and beauty. I have examined Pizarnik's interpretations of the lesbian dimensions of Báthory's rituals in *Gay and Lesbian Themes in Latin America* (1991a). A separate essay, part of an examination of literary versions of violence and power during the Argentine military dictatorships, takes up the question of how *La condesa sangrienta* can be read as an allegory of patriarchal power, with Báthory constituting one of Mary Daly's token torturers. This understanding of the text both explains how the Countess was able to pursue her sadistic rituals with relative impunity and why Pizarnik's treatment of her has provoked so much interest in the context of analyzing the neofascist ideology of the Argentine dictatorships (Foster 1995b; Daly 1978, 96).[2]

The present essay analyzes Pizarnik's poetry with respect to her representation of the female body. One may rightly expect to encounter in Pizarnik's work many of the strategies employed to deconstruct the male technologies of gender in men's poetry on women. Indeed, it is not necessary to read far in Pizarnik's poetry to discover procedures for the defamiliarization of the standard commonplaces of womanly allure: the intensely ironic, even sarcastic reformulation of the tropes of description and evocation, and the displacement of the poetic tradition of the female poetic voice by the appropriation of male diction, with all of the disconcerting ambiguities such an appropriation implies. These strategies, in various combinations, characterize a contemporary feminist tradition in poetry from a "medusian" perspective, to trope Hélène Cixous's famous proposition.

Yet what I would like to focus on here, in an attempt to refine the analysis of the aforementioned strategies in Pizarnik's work, is the cluster of tropes relating to the human body. Pizarnik wrote at a time when lesbian identity could not be forthrightly articulated. (Indeed, it has only been in the past ten years that Argentine literature can pride itself on an explicitly lesbian/gay cultural project.) As a consequence, her poetry, written in Spanish, a language whose gender markers are consistently overt (see Read 1990), is characterized both by an evasiveness as to the gender identity of the poetic voice and its addressee, and by the adoption of a conventional, normalized female/male discourse of love. One question concerns whether it is appropriate to assume Pizarnik was making concessions to social circumscriptions on erotic expressiveness. A second question is whether or not, beyond such a concession, one can identify a poetic encodement of the human body—its physical contours, its experienced sensations, and its linguistic projections—that validates the importance attributed to Pizarnik in terms of the various categories of marginalization mentioned above (see the studies in *Body Guards* [Epstein and Straub 1991] on issues of gender ambiguity). Formulated precisely, the question is, Is Pizarnik's putative importance for a lesbian identity borne out by a rhetoric of poetic expression that undermines hegemonic heterosexism? Or might there be a specific Talmudic understanding of the woman's body as the site of corrupting uncleanliness?

A much more challenging question, considered within the context of Deleuze and Guattari's revindication of schizophrenia (1983), is whether or not what was judged to be Pizarnik's ultimately suicidal mental illness does not, in fact, offer significant insight into a restructuring of sexual experience, anchored in her texts in a particular mental and physical sense of the body. An investigation of these questions, along with others that will arise in the close scrutiny of Pizarnik's poetry, will provide the basis for a characterization of her production beyond the stylistic descriptions and the untheorized inventory of feminist and psychoanalytical themes that have been the basis of most of the criticism to date (Fagundo 1990, 451).

III

One approach to the representation of the body in Pizarnik's poetry would be to inventory the vocabulary of her texts. Although it may be thinly contextualized in terms of theory, such an approach is indeed revealing. To begin with Pizarnik's first collection, *La tierra más ajena* (1955; The Farthest Land) (and depending on which criterion of lexical classification is used), almost eighty separate references to the body occur in the twenty-eight poems. Approximately twelve are reflexive, self-characterizations of the poetic voice, while over sixty are linked to second- and third-person deixis. There is a concentration of references to the face, with ten references to *ojos* (eyes), five to *labios* (lips), four to *manos* (hands) (plus two to *uñas* [fingernails] and three to *dedos* [fingers]), three to *dientes* (teeth). In addition, the references to nonfacial items—including three references to *pechos* (breasts), one reference to *vello* ([pubic] hair), one to *arterias* (arteries), and two to *piel* (skin)—establish topographical points of reference that will recur insistently throughout her writing. *Las aventuras perdidas* (1958; The Lost Adventures), which consists of only twenty-two texts, some of them no more than five or ten lines long, contains fifty corporal references. Over a fifth of them are devoted to *sangre* (blood), with additional references to *herida* (wound), *venas* (veins), *corazón, huesos, cadáveres* (heart, bones, cadavers), and *uñas*.

Pizarnik's key cycle of prose poems, *Extracción de la piedra de locura* (1968; Extraction of the Stone of Madness), contains over fifty allusions to body parts, with a characteristic concentration on items like *huesos, corazón* (sixteen references), *sangre* (blood), and *sexo* (sex), as well as the predominance of the generic word *cuerpo* (body), which appears sixteen times. The texts in this collection are notable for what becomes Pizarnik's metapoetical emphasis, and there are, as a consequence, clusters of images relating to *voz* (voice), including *labios; mano,* including *gestos* (gestures); *ojos,* including *visión* (vision) and *mirada* (look, sight); and *lengua* (tongue). These items have a metapoetic function to the extent that they refer to a process of poetic participation or assimilation, composition, and communication (including the two functions of transmission and reception). By the eleven vignettes of *La condesa sangrienta,* there is no longer much sense in even tabulating pertinent lexical items, and references that fall within the semantic orbit of the key word in the book's title are so evident they might as well be in boldface type: *sangre* alone occurs nine times in the eleven vignettes, and *ojos,* the basis for the voyeuristic element of the text I have described elsewhere (Foster 1991a, 100), appears eight times, along with one occurrence of *mirada.*

Pizarnik's ten principal collections contain almost six hundred references to the body. It is notable that, despite the presumed I-based character of poetry, approximately 450 of Pizarnik's references are in the second and third person; some of these references, to be sure, may involve the doubling of the poetic voice. The items that predominate, each occurring in at least five percent of the total references, are *corazón, cuerpo, huesos, manos, ojos* (occurring in almost ten percent of the total references), *sangre,* and *voz.* This inventory does not take into consideration the possibility of a synonymy in series like *voz, lengua, respiración, soplo, boca, dientes, garganta* (voice, tongue, breathing, puff of breath, mouth, teeth, throat)—without exhausting the list—with respect to the metapoetic dimension of Pizarnik's poetry. One could contemplate a similar concatenation of terms beginning with a prime like *sangre* (approximately forty occurrences) or *manos,* both of which exercise crucial functions in the sadomasochistic features of these compositions, whether literal (*La condesa sangrienta*) or figurative (patriarchal authoritarianism).

IV

However, such an inventory is inadequate. An inventory of vocabulary items is basically meaningless in that it divorces lexemes from both their syntactic and poetic context, assuming that they possess an intrinsic meaning, when poetry is precisely the verbal discourse with which we most associate the principle that meaning is a function of an overall textual structure. That structure may not be totalizing (although it is presumed to be totalizing by a certain tradition), but it is determinant to a greater extent than nonpoetic discourse. Therefore, it is unreasonable to expect to find much significance in the high incidence of occurrence in Pizarnik's poetry of lexical items such as *cuerpo* or *ojos*.

But there is another issue regarding the vocabulary of Pizarnik's poetry that only tangentially concerns the extent to which individual words may be interpreted outside their place in the poetic discourse, and the extent to which they may be classified and homologized extratextually as well. This second issue involves the much touted surrealistic nature of Pizarnik's writing. I leave aside any discussion here as to the exact quality of surrealism in her texts—whether these texts correspond to any surrealistic movement (which would certainly be a retarded one at the time of Pizarnik's major production, from the mid-1950s to the mid-1970s); whether it is a matter of an Argentine neosurrealism, stimulated by a number of possible factors and involving several possible groupings of participants in terms of reviews, presses, or personal affinities (Sola 1961); or whether it is sui generis, the consequence of Pizarnik's specific way of encoding experience, influenced by an already permanently established surrealistic option in Western culture. Personally, I incline toward the latter proposition, on the basis of the interpretations proposed in the following sections of this essay (see also Lasarte 1983). However, at this juncture I am simply stating that I wish to sidestep the question of the precise nature of Pizarnik's affiliation with surrealism.

What I do wish to underscore, however, and which directly relates to an inventory of corporal references in her poetry, is the need to gauge how processes associated with a surrealist aesthetic expand considerably the dimensions of such an inventory. Were we dealing with nonpoetic discourse written in a neutral, automatized, or non-self-referential language, it would be enough to chart the occurrences of words like *cuerpo, manos, lengua,* and *ojos,* since there would be little disagreement that such items refer to body parts. Furthermore, there could be little controversy over what other words to look for or which ones would, given the sociocultural coordinates of Pizarnik's texts, be more likely to occur than others (e.g., *cejas* [eyebrows] over *pelitos* [pubic hairs]; *boca* over *vagina* [vagina] or any one of its scatological, colloquial variants; *cara* [face] over *trasero* [backside]; or even *senos* [breasts] over *tetillas* [nipples]). And from these facts one could assert that Pizarnik is not writing a specifically erotic, less a pornographic, poetry (whatever the distinction between the two might be), despite the unusually high incidence of anatomical references for an Argentine poet, and, moreover, for a woman (Argentine women poets in recent years have been more willing to ignore taboos about the use of colloquial, even scatalogical, language to refer to the body. One thinks immediately of Susana Thénon's *Ova completa* [1987], whose pseudoclassical title is even funnier than the gross expression which it evokes, "complete female gametes," along with echoes of "complete works" [*obras completas, opera completa*] as well as a putative feminine form of the common masculinist expression in Spanish and Portuguese referring to a full scrotum and meaning "I'm fed up").

Processes like hypostasis, personification, anthropomorphization, and metonymy are figures of poetic diction that expand the limits of the neutral inventory of corporal references. Moreover, if one considers the corporal to be present in more than just an inventory of nouns, and to be equally represented in predicate functions like verbs, adjectives, and adverbs, Pizarnik's representation of the body assumes dominant proportions. For example:

> por un minuto de vida breve
> única de ojos abiertos
> por un minuto de ver
> en el cerebro flores pequeñas
> danzando como palabras en la boca de un mud

> (*El árbol de Diana*, 15)[3]

Three neutral lexical items refer to the body here: *ojos, cerebro,* and *boca* (I will throughout this discussion be using "neutral" to refer to an everyday, nonpoetic lexicon, the kind of vocabulary that would appear in an illustrated dictionary's topographical representation of the body—as in, for example, *The Oxford-Duden Pictorial Spanish-English Dictionary* [1985]). In addition, there are two neutral verbs, *ver* and *danzar.* In this context, the introduction of a lexical item like *flores* and the anthropomorphization involved in presenting *flores* as the subject of *danzar* homologizes the term *flores* as an anatomical referent. In the poetic universe of this text, *flores* assumes a meaning function equivalent to that of the real body parts. It then becomes a question of understanding what bodily experience is to be understood from such an incorporation of *flores* into the semantic realm of the body.

An excellent example of the processes I am describing is to be found in "La noche" (The Night), where the personification of the night establishes a corporeal presence which not only matches that of the poet, but in a certain sense outstrips it:

Poco sé de la noche
pero la noche parece saber de mí,
y más aún, me asiste como si me quisiera,
me cubre la conciencia con sus estrellas.

. . . .

Pero sucede que oigo a la noche llorar en mis huesos.
Su lágrima inmensa delira y grita que algo se fue para
    siempre.
Alguna vez volveremos a ser.

(*Las aventuras perdidas,* 44)[4]

The personification of the night is accompanied by the assignment of physical attributes that enable it to be seen as a person, including the physical agency implied by verbs like *cubrir, llorar, gritar,* and *irse* (I am assuming that *delirar* does not involve corporal instrumentality). The fundamental irony of the poem is expressed in the opening and closing propositions, although it is more explicit in the first, which says that the night knows more of one than vice versa. The consequence of this circumstance is the point of the poem: that the night is able to engage in a superior agency vis-à-vis the poet, who describes herself as the patient of the bodily incursions of the night, which penetrates to the very marrow of her bones. The real bodily presence of the poet is overwhelmed by the corporality of the night—which is customarily understood as, if not an abstraction, a diffuse rather than concretely agentive presence.

The final stanza may thus be read as an affirmation of the poet's own sense of diffuseness, of the disintegration and even intangibility of the body that is frequently associated with Pizarnik's poetry as a dimension of the recurrent themes of death and suicide, and as preliminary versions of the psychotic fragmentation of the self that sustains the appeal to death and suicide (I should specify that I agree with Thorpe Running [1985] that one ought not read Pizarnik's poetry in terms of the master trope of suicide, as somehow validating a subsequent biographical fact [see also DiAntonio 1987]). The current absence of being implied by the poet's declaration of coming to be once again is not made in the context of the articulated embodied presence of the night, but as a coda to the poem, with all the emphasis that such a placement enjoys: the night is overwhelming, as it has been described, but the poet does not exist. In the case of "La noche," the invocation of the night via a complex personification is correlated with the immateriality of the poet's own body.

The resulting correlation is less the foregrounded deployment of surrealistic motifs (and there is an undeniably Lorquian quality to many of Pizarnik's poems), than it is the juxtaposition of the loss of the human body's physical presence and integrity with the over-determined embodiment of a range of phenomena—abstract, inani-mate, intangible, external—that impinge in a threatening, even de-structive way on the body. A similar process may be found in "El miedo," also from *Las aventuras perdidas* (Forbidden Adventures), where the verse "el miedo con sombrero negro" (46; fear wearing a black hat) involves a metonymy implying that fear possesses a head. It may also be seen in the lines from "La luz caída de la noche" (The Fallen Light of Night; also from *Las aventuras perdidas*), "yo no sé del sermón / del brazo de hiedra / pero quiero ser del pájaro enamorado / que arrastra a las muchachas" (48; I do not know of the sermon / of the arm of ivy / but I want to belong to the bird in love / who carries girls off), in which human attributes—and in the first case a direct bodily referent—are again correlates of the poet's self-description in destabilizing terms: "mi delirio" (my delirium), "el mandar de la nada" (the command of nothingness), "Mi sangre rabiosa" (My rabid blood).

The foregoing provide a few illustrations of the correlation of hy-postasized entities with the poet's sense of bodily disintegration and denormalization. The hypostasized entities, as part of the process of personification or anthropomorphization, are introduced as existing materially via reference to specific body parts, instruments of the aggressive agency, or reference to metonymies of body parts, either nouns or predicates, that confirm a physical presence. Examples of this correlation occur throughout Pizarnik's poetry, and confirm the special status given in her poetry to the evocation of the bodily— vis-à-vis herself and vis-à-vis the forces she confronts—and to the rhetorical figures which contribute to that correlation. Although Pi-zarnik's poetry extends over almost twenty years, it is remarkably consistent in its sustained utilization of this correlation.

Although there are elaborate images of death, disintegration and destruction, and suicide throughout Pizarnik's poetry, the interrela-tionship between madness and death, frequently through direct sui-cidal statements, abounds in the texts written during the last five years of her life. It is also during this period that she turns to prose compositions, some of which have narrative dimensions, like the eleven vignettes that make up *La condesa sangrienta*, but the bulk of which are readily identifiable as prose poems. "Continuidad"

(Continuity), taken from *Extracción de la piedra de locura,* exemplifies Pizarnik's continued use of specific figures in her evocation of the antagonistic elements:

> No nombrar las cosas por sus nombres. Las cosas tienen bordes dentados, vegetación lujuriosa. Pero quién habla en la habitación llena de ojos. Quién dentellea con una boca de papel. Nombres que vienen, sombras con máscaras. Cúrame del vacío—dije. (La luz se amaba en mi oscuridad. Supe que ya no había cuando me encontré diciendo: soy yo.) Cúrame—dije. (35)[5]

In this excerpt there is a triple evocation of the facial components of the antagonists, who, although they cannot be called by their proper names—in violation of the principle of poetic discourse whereby the privilege and the power of poetry lies in the ability to name things in a manner impossible in conventional language—are metonymized in personified terms via a master metonymy of the face. It would seem clear that here Pizarnik is speaking about writing, especially with the figure "boca de papel," an image that alludes to the topos of the *flatuus poeticus.* And one could refer to many statements clustered around interconnected verbs like breathing, speaking, crying, and shrieking, as in the utterance from "Ojos primitivos" (Primitive Eyes) in *El infierno musical* (1971b): "Escribo contra el miedo. Contra el viento con garras que se aloja en mi respiración" (I write against fear. Against the wind with claws that resides in my breathing). Moreover, if the facial components of poetry assume threatening forms despite being unnamable, in an allusion to the metonymy of the counterface they are masked shades (i.e., a mask is something that only the face can wear, and even if the face is not present, the mask refers back to the face, just as the poem, as a metaphor of disguise, refers back to the poet even when the latter is absent).

The poem is overlain by the two imperatives, "Cúrame," whose vocatives are unnamed; the verb is only one of numerous indirect and direct references to the psychiatric process present in Pizarnik's final poetic compositions. Note the short composition that is in direct contradiction to the command in "Continuidad":

> Manos crispadas me confinan al exilio.
> Ayúdame a no pedir ayuda.
> Me quieren anochecer, me van a morir.
> Ayúdame a no pedir ayuda.

> (*Extracción de la piedra de locura,* 20)[6]

But in "Continuidad" the imperative "Cúrame" is linked to the "vacío," presumably another metaphor for the poetic text, whose meaning depends in part on the absence implied by the mask, just as the cure demanded depends for its meaning on the terrifying nature of the unnamable things whose eyes, teeth, and mouth the mask is molded to. The semantic primes of Pizarnik's texts present here—the problematics if not the impossibility of poetic discourse, the threatening unnamable, the allusion to (mostly psychiatric) sickness—are once again built around a haunting allusion to metonymic, personified body parts.

V

For all of the recurring images in Pizarnik's poetry relating to the body—along one semantic axis insistently charting the breakup of the body and the disintegration of a fragile yet profound psychic domain, and along another detailing the parameters of a frustrated poetic discourse—it is not enough to simply describe the multiple variants of these images, complex though they may be. I am claiming that throughout Pizarnik's poetry images of the body enter into figurative configurations dominated by forms of metynomic personification, which extend references to classifiable anatomical points to include not only predicates associated with such references but also articles—hats, masks, clothes. These articles are their conventional complements and extensions, which is, to be sure, also a metonymic process.

This dominant discourse practice maps Pizarnik's sense of horror in her physical and emotional interaction with a threatening universe (whether generally existential or specifically social, in the ways in which writing is an intertext of determinant historical signs). It remains to be seen how it assumes a more integral function in her major poems, not as a dominant semiotic feature but as the organizing principle, the primary vehicle of meaning. "Poema para el padre" (Poem for the Father), which Pizarnik wrote less than a year before her suicide, may serve as an example here:

> Y fue entonces
> que con la lengua muerta y fría en la boca
> cantó la canción que no le dejaron cantar
> en este mundo de jardines obscenos y de sombras
> que venían a deshora a recordarle
> cantos de su tiempo de muchacho
> en el que no podía cantar la canción que quería cantar

la canción que no le dejaron cantar
sino através de sus ojos azules ausentes
de su boca ausente
de su voz ausente.
Entonces, desde la torre más alta de la ausencia
su canto resonó en la opacidad de lo ocultado
en la extensión silenciosa
llena de oquedades movedizas como las palabras que
    escribo.

(*Textos de sombra y últimos poemas,* 51) [7]

Unlike Sylvia Plath's famous poem to her father, "Daddy," which offers a stunningly brutal characterization of the phallocentric order, Pizarnik here writes for and in the place of the father. Although it is important to note in feminist writing the appearances of images of the father and of the phallic as it relates to other men, few of Pizarnik's poems actually deal with masculine figures. (To be sure, the phallic may also be characterized in terms of the phallocentric mother—the "Mommy dearest" motif—and Erzébet Báthory, the Bloody Countess, is clearly a figure of masculinist power). This is partly a function of the I-centered dimension of her expression, and the focus of so many of her texts on a characterization of her own specific emotional states. Moreover when the Other is present, it is most typically as a personification of hostile and threatening forces, as I have outlined above, and not as another person, whether man or woman, phallic or otherwise.

In the case of "Poema para el padre," Pizarnik's incarnation of her father centers on his never being able to speak in his own voice, never being able to bring forth his own song. In this sense it is quite different from the expected feminist denunciation of her father's triumphantly repressive voice. Pizarnik seems to be describing a man who was himself the victim of the phallocentric denial of voice to the other. The reader immediately recalls Pizarnik's Jewish immigrant origins during the Holocaust, an autobiographical allusion that is not otherwise present in her writing (see DiAntonio [1987] and Friedman [1987] on Pizarnik's Jewish identity). But, then, this autobiographical dimension may be more present than would otherwise seem to be the case, if one wishes to argue that the generalized sense of horror and immolation in her poetry can be read as an overwhelming reference to the Jewish experience of the Holocaust and its repercussions on one consciousness, whose ultimate suicide, insistently foreshadowed in her poems, ends up belying any idea that she is a survivor. Finally, the fact that Pizarnik was writing at a time when

Argentina was living under a military tyranny of explicit neofascist and antisemitic dimensions cannot be overlooked (as, unfortunately, it has been in virtually every critical study).

Pizarnik's father is dead at the time of the poem marked by the deictic "entonces"—literally dead, from an autobiographic point of view in 1971, and dead in terms of "la lengua muerta y fría en la boca" (which may also be taken as a reference to a language, perhaps as sociolect, that was spoken by the father and eliminated by the Holocaust or, if the language were an ideolect, done away with by whatever general extermination the poet has in mind). The "[no] A, sino B" structure of the poem, whereby the father's song cannot be sung "en este mundo de jardines obscenos y de sombras" but can be sung "desde la torre más alta de la ausencia," is metonymized, in terms of the mouth whose tongue is the source of poetic expression, the eyes that contemplate the exterior world, and the voice that projects the song back out into the world from which it came (to the extent that he is repeating "cantos de su tiempo de muchacho"). What is truly remarkable about this poetic text is that, in spite of so many inscriptions of emotional and physical fragmentation in other poems by Pizarnik, along with an abundance of images of violence and death, "Poema para el padre" is essentially integrative, based on the recovery of the function of the dead tongue and the efficacious production of the absent anatomical features that give shape to the restored song.

The images of the poem's final lines contain a number of apparently overdetermined references to the counterproductivity of poetic discourse—the opaque, the occult, the silence, and the shifting empty spaces. Yet these images ultimately refer to a fullness of expression obtained through the daughterly agency of the surrogate father, that is quite the contrary of the failure of expression alluded to elsewhere in Pizarnik's poetry. Furthermore, if the daughter is speaking on behalf of the father (which is why the poem is entitled "para el padre" and not "del padre" or "por el padre"), she cannot be said to be revalidating a phallocentric, patriarchal discourse (I am overlooking the discourse politics involved in anyone attempting to speak for any other person, especially one judged by the speaker to require someone else's voice). The point is that her father's voice is the voice of the oppressed, the marginal, and the silenced, and she is engaging in a process of revoicing it. This process of revoicing depends on the recovery and reintegration of the bodily instruments of the father that had disappeared with his death. And it is the memory of that death that brings the song back, just as the circumstances of suffering and death had brought the songs of collective memory to the father's consciousness. And it is this restored song that ultimately echoes in the words of the poet that close the poem.

From a feminist point of view, Pizarnik suggests a significant alternative dimension to the phallocentric voice: the circumstance of the father figure whose own repressive destruction can, even in the larger context of the daughter's vertiginous mental decline (recall that the poem is written less than a year before her suicide), be contravened through the agency of her poem. This is hardly a revindication of phallocentricism, since the anatomical points of regency of the father underscore his own victimization at the hands of the masters "que no [lo] dejaron cantar." Finally, though the daughter may be unable to stop her own disintegration at the hands of other masters in other "jardines obscenos," so horrifyingly chronicled in the texts that frame "Poema para el padre," she is able to envision the power of reconstituting the material voice of her father and speaking for herself.

It would, of course, be a vain undertaking to canvass Pizarnik's texts seeking parallels to this last-minute homage to the silenced father. One must accept that it is a dramatic exception to her otherwise unmuted mapping of the body's destruction by presumably the same forces that silenced her father's speech. (See, however, the late prose poem "Los muertos y la lluvia" [The Dead and the Rain], in *Textos de sombra y últimos poemas* [1985; Texts of Shadow and Other Poems], which speaks of her father in the context of the Holocaust: "la tumba sagrada de mi ilícita infancia" [31; the sacred tomb of my illicit infancy]). The phallocentric silencing by a direct menace to the body is the basis of a sequence of fragments taken from one of Pizarnik's most important compositions, the title poem of *Extracción de la piedra de locura,* which is dedicated to her mother:

> Rápido, tu voz más oculta. Se transmuta, te transmite. Tanto
> que hacer y yo me deshago. Te excomulgan de ti. Sufro, luego
> no sé. En el sueño el rey moría de amor por mí. Aquí, pequeña
> mendiga, te inmunizan. (Y aún tienes cara de niña; varios
> años más y no les caerás en gracia ni a los perros.)
> Mi cuerpo se abría al conocimiento de mi estar
> y de mi ser confusos y difusos
> mi cuerpo vibraba y respiraba
> según un canto ahora olvidado
> yo no era aún la fugitiva de la música
> yo sabía el lugar del tiempo
> y el tiempo del lugar

> en el amor yo me abría
> y ritmaba los viejos gestos de la amante
> heredera de la visión
> de un jardín prohibido
> La que soñó, la que fue soñada. Paisajes prodigiosos para la
> infancia más fiel. A falta de eso—que no es mucho—, la voz
> que injuria tiene razón.
> La tenebrosa luminosidad de los sueños ahogados. Agua
> dolorosa. (56–57)[8]

It is important to note that the sequence quoted probably does not constitute an example in Pizarnik's writing of explicit same-sex markers in a vocative context. Rather, the sequence seems to shift between a direct reflexive characterization and the characterization of the self via a disengaged second-person vocative ("Se transmuta, te transmite"). The fact that a disengaged personal referent is involved is likely most apparent in the deprecatory parenthetical statement. In any case, at most what is involved is a mirrored doubling of the poetic voice (compare the comments on this aspect of Pizarnik's poetry in Molloy 1991, 119).

The poem turns on the hyperbolic description of both "mi estar y de mi ser" as confused and dispersed, which involves something like a hypostasis of any attributes associated with *estar*—since, by definition, they cannot, in the realm of everyday language, constitute material attributes. The iterative references to destruction are accompanied by specific verbs that refer to acts of agents of power (which, with the exception of the dreamland "rey," are unnamed): "Te excomulgan," "te inmunizan" (which can be construed as a phenomenon of dissolution, provided that the immunization is against something that will save her, like love or poetry), "prohibido," "injuria," "ahogados" (which may or may not be agentive). In this context, "la que fue soñada" may even be construed as referring to the object of an act of power, especially to the extent that if the threatening other dreams you, you cannot properly dream yourself, and the other determines your being (both *ser* and *estar*)[9] contrary to how you would integratively determine yourself. Even if the self-knowledge of the indented verses signals a confused, diffuse body, it corresponds to the as-yet-unforgotten, still-not-fugitive song—if not a song of bodily integrity, at least one's own. This condition of the body contrasts with the loss characterized subsequently as "los sueños ahogados."

Aside from the conventional reference to the love-struck king, this sequence of "Extracción de la piedra de locura" does not specify the speaking other who is the constantly evoked source of loss and destruction. Significantly, in the paragraph preceding the sequence quoted above, the poet has already announced her own confusion with those who speak (for) her. She would like not to speak against them, but she must. Still another metonymization of the poet's act of speaking occurs here, in the form of a catachrestic reference to a body part:

> Cada hora, cada día, yo quisiera no tener que hablar. Figuras de cera los otros y sobre todo yo, que soy más otra que ellos. Nada pretendo en este poema si no es desanudar mi garganta. (284)[10]

VI

The final text that I would like to examine is "Tragedia" (Tragedy), one of Pizarnik's later prose poems. In it Pizarnik does turn to an explicit same-sex identity, in a context in which, rather than a dialogue with the personified other, concrete bodies are, despite their repersonification as dolls, being specified:

> Con el rumor de los ojos de las muñecas movidos por el viento tan fuerte que los hacía abrirse y cerrarse un poco. Yo estaba en el pequeño jardín triangular y tomaba el té con mis muñecas y con la muerte. ¿Y quién es esa dama vestida de azul de cara azul y nariz azul y labios azules y dientes azules y senos azules con pezones dorados? Es mi maestra de canto. ¿Y quién es esa dama de terciopelos rojos que tiene cara de pie y emite partículas de sonidos y apoya sus dedos sobre rectángulos de nácar blancos que descienden y se oyen sonidos, los mismos sonidos? Es mi profesora de piano y estoy segura de que debajo de sus terciopelos rojos no tiene nada, está desnuda con su cara de pie y así ha de pasear los domingos en un gran triciclo rojo apretando el asiento con las piernas cada vez más apretadas como pinzas hasta que el triciclo se le introduce adentro y nunca más se lo ve. (*Textos de sombra y últimos poemas*, 39–40)[11]

Although this text does not involve a comprehensive typology of the female body, almost half of the lexical items are references to the body, either principal nouns or their associated predicates. And, although unlike the immediately preceding text in the same collection, "Violario" (38–39), in which the poet speaks of the attempt by an old woman at a wake (*velorio*) to rape her (*violar*), with specific allusion to the French lesbian poets Renée Vivien and Nathalie Clifford Barney (see Jay 1988), "Tragedia" does not overtly evoke sexuality. However, any discussion of the poem must begin with the identification of two obviously important women who are repersonified as dolls at a tea party. Moreover, the text is almost unique in Pizarnik's writing for its concatenation, rather than dispersion, of the references to the body, unified in one place by the adjective *azul*. *Azul*, so significant in Latin American poetry since modernism and Rubén Darío's eponymous collection (1888), is a positive qualifier of psychic transcendence: the bodies of these female dolls, rather than being the site of dismemberment, now suddenly attest to a privileged feminine experience, confirmed by the ritual of the tea party.[12]

The fact that the context is a tea party underscores another unique, salient characteristic of this composition and its description of a special feminine space: its uncharacteristic humor. This humor is evoked by the nice-little-girl gentility of the tea party; the specification of the women as the girl's teachers of singing and piano (which is also a marker of feminine gentility); the presence of death (which, surprisingly, seems to have no role in this ritual); the absurdly grotesque penetration of the piano teacher by her bicycle (the consequence of her obeying the patriarchal injunction that women keep their legs tightly pressed together—or is it, rather, a hilarious reference to the vagina dentata, capable of devouring a bicycle seat?); and the resulting inappropriateness of the title. In the universe of Pizarnik's poetry, being penetrated by an inanimate bicycle seat as the result of the pressure of one's own legs is hardly a momentous tragedy, not when compared to the terrible violations of the female body that recur throughout her texts, perpetrated by agents of sinister, destructive forces. In a text describing communion with the female body, even if this communion takes place in a childish garden party and the women have been repersonified as dolls, the conjunction of elements describing the body move from integrative to puckishly absurd.

"Tragedia" may not be characteristic of Pizarnik's evocation of the body in general. Nor does it go as far as other later texts of hers, in which a turgid eroticism clearly involves same-sex confluences, and where it would be almost willful on the part of the critic not to perceive dimensions of a lesbian sexuality (e.g., "Las uniones posibles" [Possible Unions], "A tiempo y no" [On Time and Not], "Una traición mística" [A Mystic Betrayal], "Niña entre azucenas" [A Girl among the Lilies], and "La muerte y la muchacha [Schubert]" [Death and the Girl (Schubert)]—all included in *Textos de sombra y otros poemas*).

"Tragedia" is certainly a singular composition in which a poetic universe of same-sex identity is marked by essentially positive, humorous specifications of the body.

Critics have been generally unwilling to deal with the lesbian dimension of Pizarnik's personal experience, although there are scattered references to her sexual identity. While I have examined the sexual needs of Erzébet Báthory (Foster 1991a, 97–102), there is no reason to believe that Pizarnik's own preferences were aligned with those of the Bloody Countess. Indeed, as I have already stated, it is arguable that she saw the Hungarian noblewoman as a figure of the most violent abuse of power, and therefore of a whole with those whom she identifies as "los dueños del silencio" (the owners of the silence; from "Anillos de ceniza" [Rings of Ash], in *Obras completas* [1990], 247) and whom her poetry attempts to countermand. Even Piña, in the only extensive biography of the poet available (1991), finds no need to discuss Pizarnik's sexual life, as though this most intimate aspect of life, even in the case of so dramatically confessional a poet as Pizarnik, were of scant consequence. Fagundo's encyclopedia entry (1990) is no different in this regard.

It must be noted, however, that Pizarnik's poetry reveals little interest in romantic or sentimental motifs. And even the erotic has little prominence in her work, despite this work's overwhelming image of a woman's tragic writing from her own profoundly experienced body. While *La condesa sangrienta* does narrate a complex erotic undertaking, it is Báthory's body that is at issue—and, I repeat, there are eloquent reasons to insist on a disengagement between the narrator and her protagonist, whatever the productively morbid fascination the latter exercises on her. Furthermore, it is only in the epigrammatic compositions of *Los trabajos y las noches* (1965) where Pizarnik speaks sustainedly to another in anything like amatory terms. Also, one should not expect to find in Pizarnik a duplication of the parameters—romantic or sentimental—of the male erotic obsession; this caveat extends also to a feminine version of male homosexual desire.

Indeed, it could be argued that one important dimension of lesbianism resides not in any necessary use of same-sex markers but in the eschewal of heterosexual linguistic and semantic conventions, which imply a restrictive definition of the erotic (see various essays in Abel 1992; Moi [1985] also discusses this topic in her survey of feminist literary theory). Yet there is no denying the marked reflexivity of the poet's voice. For example, in "En tu aniversario" (On Your Birthday) Pizarnik says, "Recibe este amor que te pido" (Receive this love that I request from you) (*Obras completas,* 238). The conjoining of the two verbs depends on a restriction, which is violated, concerning the source of complement. This violation underscores the recurring mapping in her poetry of the inability to transcend herself, which is presumably what an experience with the other—emotional, sentimental, sexual, erotic—involves.

Pizarnik's poetry revolves around three fundamental processes that impede identification of or with the other. These three processes must be taken into account in the specification of a beloved, same-sex or otherwise. The first is the I-based nature of Pizarnik's poetry, a correlative of her presumed schizophrenia and the imperative to plumb it. Secondly, there is a utilization, as a consequence of this perception, of an extended romantic irony whereby the poetic voice doubles and redoubles itself, fragmenting and refracting (and occasionally converging) the elements of her identity via multiple mirror images (such that the poem becomes itself a higher-order, if maddeningly ineffective, mirror). And, finally, as part of the process of dismembering and assemblage, there is the extensive use of personification and metonymy. This means both that human identity is displaced into a component that does not require real-world gender markers, and that the nonhuman (i.e., anonymous, threatening forces) are anthropomorphized and, therefore, also lack real-world gender markers. In the latter case, a persuasive argument can be made that those forces are all elements of the authoritarian patriarchy, whose violence is a principal object of Pizarnik's poems. These are the "dueños del silencio," against which the nonsilence of the feminine poet strives to prevail. But the marking of those elements as masculine is, once again, fundamentally metonymic; as *La condesa sangrienta* makes abundantly clear, it is not just men who are the agents of the authoritarian patriarchy (i.e., the penis is not the phallus, to echo Lacan), a circumstance confirmed by the feminization of her father in the poem discussed above. (See Halliday 1990, 79ff., concerning the special circumstances of silence dealt with by lesbian poets; several studies in Jay and Glasgow 1990 address the question of a specifically lesbian discourse).

Yet it would be ludicrous to assert that sexual matters in a text can only be confined, or can only be legitimately discussed when confined, to overt thematics—although such a claim does, in fact, seem to prevail among scholars of García Lorca's poetry.[13] While willful critical discretion has been a factor in the avoidance of lesbian features in Pizarnik's poetry, with the exception of the text analyzed above, which was published posthumously, her poems reveal only scant same-sex markers. Also, in some cases, such markers may be a function of the doubling of the poetic I in her discourse. Where les-bianism does, however, become an issue beyond the explicit descrip-tion of homoerotic affiliation is in the special sense of the body that is transmitted by Pizarnik's texts. If it is true that lesbianism involves much more than female-female genital coupling and, indeed, that coupling in the "psychopathia sexualis" sense of the word may not even be involved (Faderman 1981; Rich 1986; Wittig 1975), then we might begin to understand the imperative that interpretive analysis seek other ways of framing the question.

Rich's concept of the lesbian continuum may not be particularly applicable to Pizarnik's poetry, inasmuch as the latter is hardly in-terested in constructing relationships in the face of the burden of having to detail so painfully the destruction of the body and its self-consciousness. Nevertheless, it is directly pertinent, in that it situ-ates lesbianism somewhere other than in genital sexuality (which becomes, then, only intermittently incidental to a lesbian con-sciousness), and establishes a chain of signifiers that leads back from the experience of a feminine social integration to the process that impedes it in the physical and psychological destruction of the hu-man subject under the sway of the patriarchal authority:

> Una noche en el circo recobré un lenguaje perdido en el mo-mento que los jinetes con antorchas en la mano galopaban en ronda feroz sobre corceles negros. Ni en mis sueños de dicha existirá un coro de ángeles que suministre algo semejante a los sonidos calientes para mi corazón de los cascos contra las arenas. ("Piedra fundamental," *El infierno musica*, 16)[14]

Pizarnik may at times feel herself an accomplice of the forces antag-onistic to her, as evident in the line "aquello que me es adverso desde mí" (that which was adverse because of myself; in "Piedra funda-mental," *El infierno musical*, 14). But it does not take a lengthy read-ing of Mary Daly and others to grasp that the victims can, in a ter-rible irony, be their own worst victimizers, and that it is an act of cruel responsibility toward those who speak their own physical and psychological oppression to see them as desocialized and au-tonomous agents of their own destruction, when the condition of social withdrawal, egomania, and identity displacement must all be read as symptoms rather than causes of their alienation. The an-tithesis that is repeated throughout her texts regarding the function of poetry as an antidote, a bulwark, or a reprieve from both the deafening roar of the destructive forces and the silence of a self-sufficient oppression brings with it the inevitable recognition of the fragility of the poet's effort:

> algo en mí no se abandona a la cascada de cenizas que me arrasa dentro de mí con ella que es yo, conmigo que soy ella y que soy yo, indeciblemente distinta de ella.
>   En el silencio mismo (no en el mismo silencio) tragar noche, una noche inmensa inmersa en el sigilo de los pasos perdidos.
> No puedo hablar para nada decir.
> Por eso nos perdemos, yo y el poema. ("Piedra fundamental,"
> *El infierno musica,* 14)[15]

It is for this reason that none of the facets of the integrity of a feminine identity—along whatever continuum one wishes to postulate, from a sort of greeting-card happiness (rejected in María Luisa Bombal's famous formulation that life was a lot easier when she realized she did not have to be happy) to the form of woman's interdependency in Rich's and Wittig's archetypal lesbianism—remain an elusive goal in Pizarnik's literature, whether cast in terms of her own poetic I or in terms of Erzébet Báthory's hermetic, sadistic, gynocentric realm at Csejthe Castle, which constitutes its own perverse lesbian fantasy.

One can then approach the dismemberment of the body in Pizarnik's poetry, which is manifested in an impressive lexical density of corporal references and in the metonymic processes confirming the body, by drawing on a corporalization of the diverse realms that impinge on the body, through judicious reference to feminist theorizing concerning the status of the self under the weight of authoritarian oppression. It is not just a free-floating patriarchal violence that constantly threatens the feminine, as evoked in the multiple shadings of the master trope of rape, but also the diverse and interlocking institutionalizations present in Pizarnik's writing: militaristic tyranny (located in the Hapsburgs in *La condesa sangrienta*), the psychiatric establishment, the sociopolitical process that silenced her father, and even an authoritarian poetic discourse that her poems must break down in order to overcome the threat of repression. (Perhaps academic criticism has to a certain extent subjected her to such repression; see an early poem like "Poema a mi papel" from *La tierra más lejana,* 20; see also the following lines from a 1971 poem: "En esta noche, en este mundo" (In this night, in this world), "la lengua natal castra / la lengua es un órgano de conocimiento / del fracaso de todo poema" (the native tongue castrates / the tongue is an organ of knowledge / about the failure of every poem) [*Textos de sombra y últimos poemas,* 63]). As Judith Roof (1991) has written:

> Th[e] relation between writing and the [body] presumes, of course, that the ultimately autoerotic and self-circular process by which this writing is generated comes from experience of the body that occurs in a prerepresentational state. How else does the body escape the appropriation and marking a propertied, patriarchal system? Somehow the woman's relation to her body, even if that relation is an analogy, must precede the discourses that alienate the woman from her body, discourses that supercede an originary language to which the woman has access via her body. (132)

Furthermore, Sylvia Molloy (1991), in introductory comments concerning the representation of the body by a group of Latin American women writers that explicitly includes Pizarnik, writes that:

> I prefer [rather than emphasizing synecdoches of woman in texts by male poets] to call attention instead to signs of physical fragmentation of the female body in texts written by women and to observe what use they make of that physical fragmentation in their attempt to represent woman. In such cases the dismemberment of the female body by a woman writer, the erotic component, and by extension, the fetishizing impulse, becomes much more complex in nature. For, unless the case can be made for a narcissistic fetishization of fragments of the self or for a lesbian fetishization of fragments of the other, the fragmented female body, in poems written by women, is not primarily engaged in an exclusively erotic transaction. It is basically involved in a textual transaction where mutilation and fragmentation are cleverly used not to subdue the other but to portray the self.
>
> But not only the body is creatively dismembered in women's texts. Voice, woman's voice—hard to find, agonizing to enunciate—speaks too in fragments, is composed of shards. (117–118)

VII

Thus, to study the representation of the body in Pizarnik and to pursue the complex images of suffering, displacement, and dismemberment—all with overtones of death, and later ones revealing a growing concentration of references to suicide—necessarily involves more than either the compilation of a corporal lexicon for her texts or the examination of localized processes inscribed with a generalized rhetoric of metonymic animation, anthropomorphization, personification, and hypostasis. In order to accurately gauge the impact of Pizarnik's stunningly terrifying writing and its place in contemporary Argentine poetry (whether associated with feminism or not), it is imperative to see the figuration of the body as deeply imbricated with a coherent, sustained examination in her texts of the implacable forces that systematically dismember the individual on every level of her being (see Halliday 1990 concerning motifs of physical destruction in lesbian poetry and discursive strategies to countermand them). The body is not incidental to the map of schizophrenic disintegration that is commonly described in psychoanalytical readings of her poetry. Rather, it is an integral corollary of the all-encompassing repercussions on the individual of a social systematics, one now amply charted by feminist theory, that is the exclusive object of examination in Pizarnik's writing: "¿Quién inventó la tumba como símbolo y realidad de lo que es obvio?" (Who invented the tomb as a symbol and reality of what is obvious?; "Las uniones posibles," in *Textos de sombra y últimos poemas* [1972], 19).[16]

The Crisis of Masculinity in Argentine Fiction, 1940–1960

In this chapter I wish to examine the representations—both explicit and implicit—of a crisis in masculinity in Argentine fiction during the period 1940–1960. This crisis in masculinity is multidimensional, involving the role of men in society, society as patriarchy, the disruptive challenge of women's lives, issues of sexual identity and erotic preference, and the discontinuities between public models and private lives.

In 1946 Juan Domingo Perón assumed the presidency of Argentina, in the company of his wife, Eva Duarte de Perón, known historically as Evita. Evita died of cancer at the age of thirty-three in 1952, and Perón continued to govern Argentina until he was overthrown by a military coup in 1955. After twenty years in exile, Perón returned to Argentina in 1973, and through a complicated electoral process resumed the presidency in 1974. Upon his death in that year, his vice president and third wife, María Estela, became president, thereby fulfilling a goal that many had attributed to Evita. María Estela was overthrown by the military in 1976, ending thirty years of direct domination of Argentina politics by Perón and his legacy. (The current president of Argentina, Carlos Menem, is a member of the political party Perón created, but he has essentially rewritten the founder's institutional legacy.)

A significant dimension of Perón's cultural influence was as a paradigm of authoritarian masculinity. Perón was reputedly impotent (at least, he is not known to have fathered any children). But he synthesized a masculinist heritage for Argentina, which derived from the all-male enterprise of the Spanish conquest and from the period of nation building. The latter was underwritten by a military establishment that has always considered itself the final arbiter of national life, and has thought itself endowed with the right, as one general turned president by fiat reputedly understood it, to annul the constitution in order to save it (General Juan Carlos Onganía, as interpreted by Gunther 1968, 227). Perón embodied the image of the male as general, as president, and as "Father of the Nation" in a series of complex, interlocking political and social ideologies that confirmed a specific dynamic of being a man, a specific model for the exercise of paternalistic authority, and a specific interpretation of daily life that privileged male rights and responsibilities.

This model generally exemplifies the hegemonic Western patriarchy. In the context, however, of an Argentina that has accorded primacy to military authoritarianism (Argentines, who until recently were subject to universal male conscription, pride themselves on being *hijos del rigor* [sons (and daughters) of discipline]), the period of Peronismo—which began during the latter part of the Great Depression and involved covert participation in World War II on the side of the Axis powers, and ended with a military takeover of the government—involved a profound restructuring of Argentine. On the one hand, model social programs effectively accorded a measure of welfare protection and political power to subaltern groups; yet, by contrast, there were increasingly harsh measures to repress dissident opinion, particularly when such opinion was expressed in the intellectual and creative sectors of society. On the other hand, Evita was successful in obtaining the vote for women in 1947 and in providing a model herself for the effective direct participation of women in public life. Feminism in any of its postwar manifestations, however, had no place in the Peronista state, and women's issues that did not fit the agenda of the state were systematically stifled. Finally, although an enormous reorganization of Argentine society took place during the late 1940s and the 1950s, no systematic rethinking of the patriarchy was possible during that period. This is reflected in the systematic reendorsement of reactionary Catholic morality in ways that severely proscribed an attempt to engage in public discourse about sexual and gender roles. Military governments since 1955 have reaffirmed such proscriptions, with the result that it has only been during the past ten years of constitutional democracy that Argentina has seen the legalization of divorce and tentative steps toward gay rights (although there has been no support for women's reproductive rights).

Drawing on the theoretical premise that fiction involves an interpretive reading of the social text (a major postulate in contemporary literary historiography), this chapter will examine major texts published in the 1940s and 1950s regarding Argentine social life and its historical contexts. Principal authors of the period who dealt with issues of gender and sexual dissidence (if not directly with homoeroticism) include David Viñas, who wrote several novels on militarism and authoritarianism; Beatriz Guido, who provided a feminist reading of authoritarianism; Silvina Bullrich, the first Argentine writer to engage in a first-stage feminism, which involved the depiction of women's oppression; Adolfo Bioy Casares, whose novels in his own name and in conjunction with Borges examined problematical dimensions of dislocated male protagonists; Horacio Verbitsky, a chronicler of shifts in the daily life of lower-class individuals during the period, including Buenos Aires's important Jewish community, which had mixed fortunes under Perón; and Manuel Mujica Láinez, who produced the first truly queer reading of Argentine culture. Attention must also be paid to important essayists who provide a different cultural inflection to the interpretation of a society in transition, specifically the leftist sociologist Juan José Sebreli and the conservative grande dame of Argentine letters, Victoria Ocampo. Of interest also are Perón's political writings and Evita's extremely influential autobiography, *La razón de mi vida* (1951; *Evita by Evita*, 1980).

Two of these texts will be examined here with regard to how they establish principles for the production of meaning, toward a specific representation and interpretation of social life as it is modeled by the characters in the novel and the life experiences they enact. Specifically, I am concerned with depictions of male authoritarianism and its responses to threats, social circumstances that serve to confirm or enhance it, events in the lives of characters that exemplify the inadequacies of the patriarchal model, and the fictional characters' reactions to the limitations of a masculinist society. These novels will be read against the hypermasculinity of Juan Domingo Perón as a public figure and the entire social apparatus evoked by this figure. Critical principles are drawn from neoideological theories of fictional meaning, from feminism (especially the strands that investigate the impact of patriarchy on men), and from queer theory (in its scrutiny of the internal contradictions of the structures of compulsory heterosexuality).

Blindness and Insight in Silvina Bullrich's *Bodas de cristal*

Por encima de todo un matrimonio es eso: un inmenso secreto que se llama intimidad.

BULLRICH, *BODAS DE CRISTAL*

Sabía que lo que estaba ocurriendo ocurría a expensas mías, que yo era víctima de algo [. . .].

BULLRICH, *BODAS DE CRISTAL*

Published in 1951, Silvina Bullrich's *Bodas de cristal* (Crystal Wedding Anniversary) established a solid readership for her novels; published also in French, it gave her the international cachet that has always been important for confirming the importance of Latin American writers at home. Bullrich was the first Argentine writer to effectively analyze the institution of matrimony. Her decision to write in the first person, several decades before there was any theoretically based feminist principle concerning the need to discover one's own voice, countered the practice, still preponderantly pursued in the male-dominated Latin American novel of the period, of the third-person omniscient authorial voice; Eduardo Mallea, who at the time was at the height of his literary prestige, wrote no novels in the first person, and it is difficult to recall any important Argentine novel of this period of psychological realism, social realism, and neorealism who wrote in the first person. Not until Manuel Mujica Láinez's *Bomarzo* (1962), a novel that now lends itself to a queer reading, was there a major Argentine novel in the first person. Borges, of course, frequently used the first person in his short fiction of the period. But even Marta Lynch's *La señora Ordóñez* (1967; Mrs. Ordóñez)—the other principal novel of feminist consciousness prior to the period of a concerted feminist production in Argentina, which was a response to military tyranny beginning in the late 1960s, and certainly took its cue from Bullrich—is written from the point of view of an omniscient author.

Bullrich's divergence from the practice of authorial omniscience—*Bodas* alternates segments written from the female protagonist's point of view with third-person narratives—privileges the Wife's attempts to analyze the circumstances of her marriage in a way that was totally innovative for the Argentine novel of the period. The entire text of the novel is anchored in the morning after the fifteenth-anniversary celebration of the couple. Waking before her husband, the Wife props herself up, contemplates the sleeping body of her husband, and undertakes a long interior monologue in which she evaluates in unflattering terms his performance as a husband. Although the sexual dimension is never stated explicitly, except to refer to occasions when he rejects her attempts to elicit his affection, her analysis begins with the contemplation of his body, and her commentary is relentlessly materialistic in its grounding in words and deeds rather than emotional states. Bullrich seems early to have repudiated the horizons of the feminine mystique, in that she has never prized the ideal of a unique feminist psychology promoted by the patriarchy. At the same time she is valued by one strand of feminism that attempts to privilege feminine difference.

Bullrich implicitly endorses in all her writing the dominant strain of liberal feminism that was already well established in Argentina, which values equal opportunity for women at the expense of promoting any notion of radical sexual difference rooted in social, historical, and cultural difference. The abiding strength of liberal feminism in Argentina, and the concomitant undernourishment of radical feminist analysis, may explain why there has yet to emerge in Argentina any tradition of a lesbian-marked narrative (despite important work by writers like Reina Roffé). And the writings of all the authors, beginning with Bullrich, who have been identified as feminist are resolutely grounded in heterosexism, as much as they may criticize the injustices of the patriarchy.

Thus it seems to me inaccurate to characterize Bullrich's narrative as feminist in any significant sense of the word: it is only feminist as part of a historical record of writings by women that represent the beginnings of a questioning of the masculine prerogative. Consequently, Bullrich's Wife is never able to forge any discourse other than that of an ill-defined victimization. Within the confines of the lament of the victim, she must limit herself to the chronicling of indignities and microstrategies—such as a repugnance for her attempt to have an erotic fling with a male friend, who she sees as only repeating the outrages of her husband—for resisting being always the victim. Since *Bodas* does not create a feminist discourse either in the form of an analysis of the patriarchy or in the form of a model, through an act of representative contestation, of feminist liberation, it must be read in other terms. Those other terms can be found in the context of a deconstructive opposition to the prerogatives of male power. By providing a founding text for a tradition that opens up the possibility of a fundamental problem with a society organized around an established, congealed program of male power, Bullrich's novel is important to any examination of the fissures in that program. Even if such a depiction does not constitute a femininist interpretation in any detailed way, it does look toward the revision of the patriarchy by feminism and other agendas of social dissidence.

The program of male power that is figured in *Bodas* corresponds in general terms to the stereotype of the Latin American macho. In *Bodas* and in subsequent novels, Bullrich offers little in terms of alternatives to that stereotype (it is interesting to speculate about what *Bodas* might have looked like if the Wife's universe had included, if not a "gay" friend, at least someone drawn from the worlds on the margins of the central masculinist enterprise). This stereotype includes the following oblique characterization, provided as an indirect interior monologue by one of the husband's many female lovers:

> Tan vanidoso, tan ignorante de lo que había ocurrido en ella, de su larga pena de tantos años, de su desamparo, de la soledad que él le había proporcionado, y de esa protección que ahora la envolvía. Luis, monótono en sus métodos de conquista, seguro de sus encantos, de su dominio físico. Luis, que envejecía sin haber madurado. Un pobre hombre. Infinitamente pobre en su afán de ser mezquino en sus dones. (87)[1]

This characterization complements his wife's contemplation of his sleeping body at her side, on the first morning of the sixteenth year of their marriage:

> Sin embargo está aquí, a mi lado, entre las sábanas de hilo un poco gastadas y no del todo frescas porque ya llevan tres días de puestas. Es mi marido. Cuando lo conocí tenía treinta años. Y hoy, por primera vez, tengo la impresión de que acaso sé muy poco de él. Allí, en esos treinta años, en esa gran laguna de treinta años sin mí, podían dormir estancadas, resucitar de pronto, las justificaciones de sus actos imperdonables. (88)[2]

The lover's pitying tone and the Wife's indulgent patience is joined by the recorded comments of other women in Luis's life. (The metonymic reference to the slightly worn, not-quite-fresh bedsheets is a lovely rhetorical touch.) The multiplicity of perspectives provides a supertriangulation of his profound limitations as a human being, limitations that are integral to his status as an Argentine man. Chapter 20 of the novel exemplifies the European sophistication of Argentine culture in the period following World War II, a period that saw an enormous influx of refugees, many with "interesting" pasts. A group of women, including Luis's wife and one of his lovers, are gathered in the latter's powder room during a lull in a fancy dinner party. There they discourse on the relative merits of Argentine men as husbands and lovers, including references, almost audacious for the time, to their sexual prowess. The women's bemused and mocking discussion of the pretentious masculinity of the Argentine male is as hilarious as it is telling in terms of the unique analysis Bullrich provides in her novel:

> —No hay que preocuparse—dijo la francesa mientras sacaba de su cartera un perfumero diminuto y se perfumaba detrás de la oreja—. Los hombres argentinos son como los dolores físicos: mientras están presentes no podemos pensar en otra cosa, pero después hay que hacer un esfuerzo para recordarlos. Son poco memorables. (106)[3]

It is significant that we never learn the name of Luis's wife, despite the fact that her analytical eye serves as the novel's focal point. Bullrich clearly intends for us to understand that we are dealing with a paradigmatically mediocre middle-class marriage. Thus, the generalizing thrust of her novel, so reminiscent of Mallea's repeated attempts to represent an Argentine *typus* (no matter how often he gives his characters specific names), points toward the characterization of an Argentine Everywoman. This Everywoman, in the name of all women of her class and circumstance, engages in an excrutiating scrutiny of their disappointing, perhaps even sometimes grim, matrimony. It is not that her marriage is a failure (assuming one had a reliable metric to discern such things, since the standards of the public discourse are hardly helpful here). When she has a fleeting and ultimately emotionally disastrous adventure with another man who, no doubt believing himself to be driven by the noblest virtues of male gallantry, assures her that he wants only her happiness and so stands ready to save her from her disastrous marriage, she does not even attempt to explain to him that he has failed to grasp the issue. She does not want out of her marriage, nor does she really believe that she is getting even with her husband. Quite simply, she only wants to understand what's going on, and for that she does not need another man.

What the Wife wishes to understand is how marriage really works, how the institution of matrimony justifies and reduplicates itself, how one comes to terms with (she even uses the expression "resign oneself to") its uncertainties, and how one can negotiate it without going insane or committing suicide. The Wife's horizons of social experience do not include alternatives to marriage. One of Luis's lovers is a spinster, but her discourse—the indirect discourse transcribed above—reveals that, all in all, her life with her neurotic and nagging mother is not an attractive alternative. And, although there is one very brief mention of homosexuality and an interesting allusion to a case of strong homosociality,[4] woman-woman love can have no place in Bullrich's fiction. Moreover, matrimony is the zero degree of social organization in Argentina, without even the weak dissent to it one might wish to find in American literature (there is virtually no Argentine writing on bachelors or spinsters, although Mallea's novels—and Mallea himself was a bachelor—inaugurate a shift in the demographics of civil status in the novel). As a consequence of these circumstances, *Bodas* suggests no alternative life experience for the Wife. Marriage is not viewed as a prison into which women, having no other choices except for the convent or the brothel, are cast by ironclad social custom. Rather, it is simply something to be explained. Hers are sentiments of bewilderment rather than of despair (despite occasional fits of depression over her husband's clearly explainable absences).

Thus, what the Wife scrutinizes is an institution that, because it is simply there, demands understanding in terms of its gaps and internal contradictions. But what she explains to herself, abetted by the information she has gleaned from her movement in the social circle into which she is led by her husband and his lovers (who generously include her in their social events), is the essentially fallible nature of men and how, after all, women are the stronger sex. This inversion of sexual roles, which guarantees to women the power of a superior psychological position, is what allows for the Wife to accept the realities of her matrimony. In the end she realizes the wisdom of the Frenchwoman's position cited above, and sees that—except for the foolishness of Luis's one lover, who commits suicide in response to his boredom with her—it is women who are best able to negotiate the complexities of the marriage bed. For this reason, the Wife's point of view ends up aligning itself with the self-help volumes, published in the same period, that urge women to maximize their femininity because, after all, they are in fact the stronger sex.

Hence the Wife is finally able to contemplate her husband's body with bemusement and satisfaction: "Es mi marido" (118; He's my husband). And, in place of the fundamental principle of the narrative organized around her contemplation of the sleeping man—the desire to know—she is able to begin the first day of her sixteenth year of marriage with the following conclusion:

> Mi marido, mi hombre eres tú, hoy. Llegas a mí canoso, con la frente que empieza a despoblarse, con una red de arrugas, frutos de dolores y de excesos desconocidos para mí [. . .]. No sé nada de ti. Salvo que estás aquí un poco agotado por esa vida tempestuosa que yo no conocí, pues aun cuando corrió a

mi lado eras como un arroyo que corre junto a nosotros sin que podamos adivinar su rumbo ni su lengua. Tú siempre fuiste el río, yo siempre fui la orilla. Y yo, entre todas las mujeres, te elijo a ti, entre todos los hombres. Te elijo así, un poco vencido, un poco cansado, Luis. (114–115)[5]

Coming at the end of the novel, the triumphalism of this interior declaration, which ends up by canceling out all of the distrust with which the Wife undertakes the scrutiny of her sleeping husband, and suspending all points of conflict between the two of them in favor of the transcendence of her unimpeachable social and legal status as "the Wife," also undercuts the very principle of the narrative the reader has just read. The opportunity for leisurely scrutiny that has propelled the novel is no longer valid—and this point is supported by the rhetorical figure of epiphonema that organizes the passage from which I have just partially quoted. Throughout the segment that has been elided, there are seven repetitions of the phrase "No sé (si)," and the eighth one is the complete sentence "No sé nada de ti." Clearly, there no longer is any need to know, for there is no longer anything significant to find out about the man: he is just there, and he is the Wife's husband.

In the context of this assessment of matrimony and the facile inversion of the binary hierarchy of traditional concepts of male and female sexual roles, it is difficult to understand how anyone could associate feminism of any ideological or theoretical sort with the triumphalism sustained by Bullrich's novel (see the survey of criticism in Frouman-Smith 1990). Certainly, this position presents no threat to the patriarchy. Indeed, the patriarchy and the institution of matrimony emerge strengthened from Bullrich's novel, to the extent that the narrative formula of delegitimating what had appeared to be a reasonable basis for a serious questioning of the role of the Wife only shows that there was no justification for such questioning in the first place. The antilogy that resides within the proposition of understanding that there is nothing to understand, of coming to know that there is nothing to know, ends up being the driving principle of the narrative. It leaves the opening implied proposition, that women like the Wife may have good reason to be dissatisfied with their social role, without any foundation: "Y todos esos recuerdos, esas emociones se hundieron suavemente conmigo en el sueño" (119).

One might well ask whether Bullrich's novel is engaging here in heavy-handed irony. To what extent is the Wife's speculation via first-person narrative about the legitimacy of her social role, which ends with her falling gently and contentedly to sleep in the embrace of that social role, a way of demonstrating that the dynamic of the patriarchy works with such smooth efficiency that a narrative project such as that of the Wife's is necessarily doomed to failure? There is no place outside of ideology, no place from which to establish a fulcrum point of alternative knowledge. Therefore, the resistance to an ideology from within that ideology (as the only place in which resistance is able to occur), can exist and survive counterresistance only if the ideology's internal contradictions are unable to neutralize the threat of resistance. Thus radical feminism has engaged in the minute analysis of the internal contradictions of the patriarchy and the unreconcilable aporias of compulsory heterosexuality; for it is only by exploiting such features of the hegemonic ideology that it can be successfully resisted, or that resistance can begin to take place.

Perhaps the reader who begins *Bodas* with the assumption that social conditions in Argentina in the early 1950s enabled the Wife's resistant reading of her social role is being deceived by the conditions for reading afforded by circumstances other than those of this narrative's main character. I would argue that this is the case, even if it only means that the readers occupy a social space significantly different from that of Luis's helpmate, such that they can perceive the dreadful irony of her concluding musings and her lapse into trouble-free slumber. In this sense, Bullrich's irony on one level is directed against those readers who may believe that the Wife's opening inquiry about her marriage is going to lead somewhere. Like the utterances of those women who experience spousal abuse, only to accept one more time their husbands' tearful protestations of repentance, the Wife's triumphant acceptance of the superiority of her position because of her husband's weaknesses, weaknesses that not even he is aware of ("No quiero juzgarlo con demasiada severidad" [112]), relegitimates the circumstances that she initially wanted to critique.

But even if the novelist does assume an ironic stance toward overly susceptible readers, the principal irony at work here is the one occupying the space between the suspended, canceled narrative of the Wife and the larger narrative framework of the novel. In this space, the reader is asked to appreciate how efficiently the patriarchy functions to engender the Wife's willingness to accept things as they are. To be sure, this space is only inviting, only providing an opportunity for meaning, if the reader can accept grounds of resistance for Bullrich that do not exist for the Wife. Such grounds, of course, are provided by our cultural disposition to attribute to narrative fiction an opportunity for resistance that we might not find readily available in daily lived experience. Although narrative fiction is not outside the controlling ideological framework of our daily life, its existence is predicated on the assumption that it can efficiently exploit, through the sort of controlling irony I have identified for *Bodas,* the internal contradictions of the social text that might not otherwise be apparent or utilizable. The first-person narrative in *Bodas*—which constitutes, in an immediate sense, an attribution of uniquely privileged access to interior mentalities—generates the potential for irony that allows the reader to understand how the Wife can never, despite her preliminary efforts, understand the efficient system of which she is a functioning constituent. For this reason the epinaphora of "No sé" is a forced attribution on the part of the authorial narrator, since it is a level of understanding disconsonant with the nonunderstanding that she finally accepts as desirable.

From this point of view, Bullrich's novel reveals two levels of critical analysis of the patriarchy. On one level, there is the Wife's depiction of a man utterly unconscious of himself, a man who has begun to undergo the ravages of declining maturity (best expressed in the harsh judgment, that after the age of eighteen, it is all downhill for men), and whose essential weakness allows for the superior strength of women. The Frenchwoman's assertion that men are as inconsequential as passing aches and pains is supplemented by the Wife's perception that her husband is nothing more than a meaningful absence, nothing more eventful than the humdrum monuments (patriarchal ones, of course) of the cityscape:

> Y en verdad, ¿cómo puedo yo olvidarlo si lo tengo siempre aquí, a mi lado, o si tengo a mi lado el evidente vacío de su ausencia? [. . .] Para mí Luis es tan memorable como la estatua de San Martín, la Recoleta, el monumento de los Españoles; todos mis recuerdos se agolpan alrededor de él. (107)[6]

In an earlier passage, the power of the masculine is reduced to that of a bumbling monster:

> Y una de esas mañanas pensé que Luis no era más que un Frankestein [sic] hermoso, un monstruo que extendía su gran mano para acariciar a una niña y la mataba a pesar de él, sólo por la leve y acaso bien intencionada presión de sus dedos de hierro que no podían percibir los latidos de agonía. (93–94)[7]

To be sure, one must also see things from the point of view of the little girl who is the victim of the monster's caress. In fact, the metaphor here seems to be more reminiscent of the sexual symbolism of King Kong than it is of Frankenstein's monster. But the intent is in any case unmistakable: Men intend no harm, no matter what the consequences of their caresses may be.

Although this perception does nothing to diminish the violence that derives from the power assigned by the patriarchy to the masculine, it does undermine the idea of fully empowered men who consciously and efficiently execute a social program in which women are systematically, deliberately deprived of power. One would certainly want to argue that the effects are the same for both the little girl and the woman, and undoubtedly they are. Yet men as unthinking monsters do much to undermine the self-sufficient masculinity on which the paradigm of the Argentine macho is predicated: "—Ningún hombre que se crea obligado a infinidad de aventuras mediocres puede ser apasionado. ¡Se diluyen tanto!" (105).[8] Luis is reduced to a pathetic figure who is ultimately abandoned by all of the women he seduces (abandonments that include one woman's grandiloquent gesture of the suicide), ridiculed by others, and finally viewed as an errant but lovable boy-child by his wife. This is hardly the stuff of the mythology of the Latin Lover on which a major example of masculinist Argentine popular culture like the tango is predicated, in which the crocodile tears of the abused male in the tango serve all the better to reinforce the moral superiority of the male.

However, a much more effective critical take on the patriarchy is implied by the irony of Bullrich's narrative, to the extent that any opportunity for women like the paradigmatic Wife to scrutinize the conditions of her matrimony will ultimately be neutralized by the patriarchy, at least on the level of lived experience (i.e., excluding the opportunities afforded by narrative fiction). The ironic modeling of the patriarchy as including efficient mechanisms for neutralizing dissent contradicts the the Wife's rationale for believing that she can afford to be indulgent toward her husband. If the Wife's manner of acquiescing to the advantages of her situation is alarming, it is because the patriarchy need not convince the Wife that she should refrain from dissent. All it needs to do is systematically undercut the premises on which she has sought to construct a critique, which it can do without any need to be viewed as a hypostatized force or to appeal to the intervention of designated agents (e.g., as in other texts like Tennessee Williams's *Suddenly Last Summer* [1958], where the medical doctor, as an agent of the patriarchy, performs a frontal lobotomy on a woman with an all-too-inquiring mind). Rather, the routine functioning of the patriarchy suffices to calm the Wife's doubts, as the normal flow of daily events convince her that there is no better alternative to her matrimony and that this is as good as it's ever going to get. Pretending to be asleep when her husband finally awakens, she asks him "¿Qué día hace?" (What's the day like?), and she has no reason to contradict him when he replies "Un lindo día" (117; It's pretty out).

The image of the patriarchy as a default system administered by pitifully weak and doltish men that nevertheless works reasonably well—such that from the inside there is no effective way to criticize it—does not support the idea of a social dynamic that is the result of qualified and assertive leaders' dedicated efforts at social engineering. Mallea's "invisible Argentine" is deprived of the opportunity to exercise such a role, which the author unquestionably views as necessary to the re-creation of a valid society, representatives of an alternative position such as the fascist right equally value the role of the decisive leader (see Stabb 159–169). Both Mallea in his cultural elitism and the proponents of authoritarian rule saw their respective heroic figures as stymied by capitalism's zealous denisons, for whom profit rather than spiritual values was the driving force of civilization. But in this scenario, at least, one active agent is pitted against another. In the social universe of Bullrich's novel, the patriarchy represented by Luis is passive, yet—despite the temptation to view it as a pathetic embodiment of masculinity—therefore even more effective, because its very blandness forecloses any opportunity for a systematic critique from within. As a final irony, that a novel like Bullrich's offers the only available space for critique (which, in the 1950s at least, could be safely ignored except by a certain cultural elite, and not necessarily the same elite as that of Mallea, who served for many years as director of the literary supplement of the prestigious Buenos Aires daily *La nación*), is perhaps the best indication of patriarchy's bland efficacy.

David Viñas and the Masculine Fall

—Somos fieros por dentro.
—Todos somos fieros por dentro, don Antonio.
—Sí; pero se limpian solos.
—La mujer se había incorporado y lo iba desvistiendo como a un chico amarillento que habla de cualquier cosa, repitiendo frases que ella había oído alguna vez y que sonaban a fórmula mágica, imposible de modificarse en el menor detalle:
—No tengo vergüenza, te aseguro que no, Isabel; sino un malestar—decía—, algo que siento en la piel y me impide que

nadie me vea en mis cosas, en mis cosas íntimas, en eso que
uno no muestra a nadie porque solamente le pertenece a uno.
No me gusta que me toquen, que me anden sobando—levantó
el brazo para que Isbael pudiera quitarle la camisa—. ¡Ni al
peluquero aguanto! (David Viñas, *Cayó sobre su rostro*)[9]

David Viñas published his first novel, *Cayó sobre su rostro* (He Fell on
His Face) in 1955. General Juan Domingo Perón, reelected in 1950 as
president—of the Argentine people—and for many as savior—was
deposed in September 1955, after several months of intense opposition to his regime by a coalition of conservative forces that included
his onetime staunch supporters, the Church and the military. Perón's
second term had seen a marked decline in his exercise of power, attributed by many to the disappearance of Eva Durate de Perón, who
died in 1952. In a retroactive interpretation, both Peronistas and the
opposition would include those who firmly believed that she had
given political meaning and coherency to his government, and that
her death—especially the manner in which it lent itself to the construction of martyrdom and to subsequent popular and official can-
onizations—revealed the emptiness at the heart of Perón's own ideology, which always vascillated between indigenous fascism and
legitimate populist reform.

The years between Evita's death and Perón's overthrow were
marked by economic crisis and scandal. The diminishing returns of
blocking any social, political, and economic crises with hard cur-
rency reserves, combined with what seemed to be an inescapable
morass of ethical fraud that could no longer be covered over by
plaza-filling demagoguery, were accentuated by ugly rumors regarding Perón's lapse into the dirty-old-man syndrome, which reputedly
involved not only encounters with minors but also the utilization of
official programs (some established by his dead and deified wife) as
virtual pimping agencies. Whether or not these rumors, strategically
highlighted by allegations of the General's impotence and the sexual irregularity of his wife's past as well as their matrimonial alliance,
had even a shred of truth about them is irrelevant. For perceptions,
both passively and actively enhanced, fueled opposition efforts from
both the socialist left and the conservative right to bring Perón down,
in a massive discreditation of Peronismo and the cult of the macho
caudillo (strongman, or political boss) on which his power was built.

Unquestionably, the caudillo had been an abiding feature of Argentine social and political life. Some will argue that Carlos Menem,
down to the synecdoche of the luxuriant sideburns that he affected
in the early years of his first term as president (which began in 1989),

is a mostly contemporary, neoliberal, multinationalist encarnation of this venerable *typus* of Argentine history. Originally local warlords, caudillos were key figures in the reorganization of the Argentine territories after the separation from Spain. Working within a feudal liege-lord kind of system—which was also influenced by the substratum of the indigenous chieftain, especially in the provinces outside the immediate radius of the nascent Creole oligarchy—the caudillos cemented political control over what were to become the provincial governments, and ensured a hierarchy of power that ultimately benefited the primus inter pares of the Buenos Aires establishment. As an integral part of the national political scene, caudillos who exercised too much authority found that their fiefdoms were subject to "intervention" by the central government, in a process of checks and balances that served both local authorities and an increasingly powerful metropolis. Juan Manuel de Rosas, during his dictatorship that assumed national proportions in the mid-nineteenth century, never abandoned the fiction that he was simply the governor of the Province of Buenos Aires, supported by the rest of the provincial governors in his role of intermediary between the country as a whole and European powers.

The caudillo system has always sustained a personalist form of political power in Argentina. While this system may have been attenuated over the years by shifting government ideologies—the fiction of constitutionalism, militarization in the name of national security, and the efficiency of centralized neoliberalism (one more confirmation of the legendary wisdom that "Dios está en todos lados, pero atiende en Buenos Aires" [God is everywhere, but he only holds office hours in Buenos Aires])—it has remained valid because it works both to consolidate centralized control from Buenos Aires and to ensure a measure of hierarchical power in the provincial microcosms. By the same token, the caudillo system has been historically reduplicated down to the humblest local level, where the ability of the dominant governmental establishment to get things down, despite whatever vicissitudes of human nature or the official system, has depended almost wholly on the efficient functioning of the caudillo system.

It may not be a completely accurate account of political history to describe Perón as a kind of caudillo, whose rise to power was driven by the alliances forged with a vast network of subaltern caudillos that included even the smallest townships. "Para un peronista, no hay nada mejor que otro peronista" (There is nothing better for a Peronista than another Peronista) expresses the all-encompassing homosocial logic of the system of *verticalidad* (hierarchy), the Party's inviolable network of personalist dependencies and male allegiances in which individual subjective identity is dictated by one's position and in which the dominant identity, that of the powerful man, is the consequence of mutually reinforcing, overdetermined networks of social confirmations. When the son of the caudillo in Viñas's novel urges his father to abandon the backwater of Cañuelas and to partake of Buenos Aires's sophistication, the father's paradigmatic response is:

> Allá [en Buenos Aires] sería millonario, muy rico; aquí, en cambio, vivo bien y la gente sabe que vivo o que estoy enfermo, y se comentan mis cosas ¿me entendés? [Allá] la gente se conoce. Aquí, en cambio, me conocen. (137)[10]

Cayó sobre su rostro is the first in a lengthy inventory of novels and other literary works by David Viñas that undertake a detailed interpretation of Argentine social history, always within complex parameters and always relating to issues of gender identity. It is the story of Antonio Vera, a legendary Argentine caudillo from the province of Buenos Aires whose years coincide with the Rosas dictatorship, the expedition into the desert against the indigenous population that resisted the fencing in of the Pampas for cattle grazing, and the rise of the Liberal state with the male-dominated generation of 1880. *Cayó,* which is divided into fifteen alternating chapters entitled "El día del juicio" (the day of judgment; the narrative present) and "Los años" (the years; the narrative past), provides a sketch of the life and times of a traditional caudillo. The narrative present is organized around the last days in Vera's life, while the narrative past is a series of flashbacks in which Vera recalls the major stations of the cross, so to speak, in his life's story. There is nothing remarkable about these flashbacks, and the fact that they are keyed to the relentless monotony of provincial life only serves to confirm the typicality of Vera as an old-time caudillo. Nor is there anything remarkable about the events of the narrative present, at least as regards the fame and fortune of the patriarchy's workaday soldiers like Vera.

The novel opens with Vera attempting to collect on a debt owed to him by one of his ragtag tenement farmers. Unsuccessful in his mission, he faces the wrath of the family's young son, who is less outraged over the implacability of the due dates of the economic system than he is over the insistence by Vera that, when they do get the money together, it be delivered to him personally by the boy's mother, with the clear implication that late payment fees will be extracted from her person. The boy's angry movements startle Vera's horse, and he is thrown to the ground. Choosing to blame the unreliability of his mount rather than the successful aggressions of the boy, Vera rides away from his tenants, mustering all the dignity that a man of his now-reduced stature can muster. Yet the affront to his person—caused less by the nonpayment of the debt (since caudillos can afford gestures of patronizing generosity) than by the boy's open defiance of Vera's *droit de seigneur*—inaugurates a chain of events that will end in Vera's ignominious death in the arms of a prostitute.

Vera's falling on his face is a narrative hypogram that organizes the novel into an exposition of the emptiness of the figure of the caudillo, an emptiness underscored less by his failure to fulfill a crucial role in the social pact of the patriarchy than by the utter triviality of the role left to him to play. While it is true that one can find a number of social roles in Argentine society that do not differ substantially from the roles of Western society as a whole, the caudillo is, if not unique to Argentina, certainly a historically significant, major principle of the social organization of the patriarchy throughout Argentine history, and most specifically during the early period of national organization covered by the dates of Vera's story. I have written elsewhere of how the paternal/caudillo figure in María Luisa Bemberg's *Camila* (1984), a major contemporary feminist film, is cast in an allegorical mode: Camila's avenging father is a paradigm of the exercise of patriarchal authority and of the consequences of a violation of that authority (Foster 1992b, 14–26). This figure of the patriarchy, which resonates internally with the arbiters of the current state and externally with a historical projection beyond the mid-nineteenth-century time frame of the movie, models the overwhelming and implacable Law of the Father that infiltrates every corner of society.

But while Bemberg's film—as well as many other feminist texts in recent Argentine cultural production (e.g., the novels of Marta Lynch, the theater of Griselda Gambaro, and the poetry of Alejandra Pizarnik)—involves fairly intense representations of the Law of the Father and, therefore, invites detailed allegorical readings as regards Argentine social history, Viñas's novel is characterized by the plain ordinariness of Vera and the virtual insignificance of the activities that have made up his life. Viñas will strive for a more evidently allegorical mode in later novels, for example, *Los dueños de la tierra* (1958; The Owners of the Land), *Los hombres de a caballo* (1967b; The Men on Horseback), and *Cuerpo a cuerpo* (1979; Body to Body). The first, which concerns a labor uprising that leads to terrible, violent reprisals, served as the basis for Héctor Olivera's 1974 film *Rebelión en Patagonia* (Rebellion in Patagonia); the second deals with the military mentality; and the third ties the military mentality specifically to the "Dirty War" against subversion in the late 1970s that led to the disappearance and execution of at least ten thousand individuals, among them some of Viñas's own children. Indeed, Viñas's writings, both literary and sociohistorical, have, throughout the almost fifty years of his career, focused primarily on authoritarianism and related issues such as the military mentality, law and order, the figure of the father, and the performance of masculinity.

Underscoring the violence of the patriarchy, Viñas has eloquently charted in his novels the correlation between a specific image of masculinity, the consequence of that image, the spiritual life of the individual who seeks to sustain and maintain it, and the structure of enforcement that it requires. Long before feminist writers in Argentina had taken up the theme of the rape of woman by man as a strategy for enforcing masculine primacy, Viñas, taking his cue from Esteban Echeverría's *El matadero* (1871 [written ca. 1839–1840]; *The Slaughterhouse*)—the founding text of Argentine fiction—had reported on the rape of man by man as an instrument for brutally enforcing the male order. Whereas a woman is raped by a man for having been perceived to challenge male supremacy, a man is raped by a man not only for the same reason but also, and more significantly, as punishment for failing to realize standards of masculinity (a failure that is, of course, an implied challenge to masculine supremacy). Gender performance entails a perpetual engagement with the overdetermined enactments of masculinity required to stave off assaults, including literal and figurative rapes, that are the cost of inadequate enactments in speech, dress, body language, interpersonal comportment, affective object choice, and sexual behavior (both direct and implied). In the all-male world of *Los hombres de a caballo,* the demands of gender performance are omnipresent, and the hierarchy of institutional and parainstitutional power is established on the basis of an ongoing assessment of each man by all others in the social group, with passing and failing evaluations handed out accordingly and rewards and punishments for each grade applied unremittingly. Thus an adequate reading of the novel must establish a truly staggering inventory of the many faces of male-male rape in what otherwise appears to be masculine business as usual.

To return to *Cayó,* the essential trivialness of Vera's life (in which the only outstanding event seems to have been seeing one of his comrades-in-arms killed by hostile Indians in the infamous military expedition of liquidation in 1869) contrasts with other inquiries by the novelist into the pattern of masculine supremacy. (Curiously,

Viñas has often been attacked for the machismo of his literature, which seems to be more a case of the messenger being blamed for the message, as though a critical analysis of machismo were somehow a confirmation of its legitimacy; anecdotes regarding Viñas's personal life are irrelevant here.) But, of course, the exercise of the patriarchy involves much more than the rape of political prisoners by the agents of military authority. It involves the daily application of a host of criteria of the social order that legitimate, in an unbroken web that envelops all social subjectivities without distinction in one hege-monic and hierarchical organization, the patriarchy as natural and God-given. Men like Vera are the undistinguished tokens of this hegemony, and it is precisely in their lack of distinction, in their ordinariness, and in the inconsequentiality of their daily existence that one can best see the thorough naturalization of that hegemony.

In the case of Viñas's novel, an inventory of the allusions to situ-ations in which a normalized masculinity is enacted is not what is at issue. What we contemplate is simply the basic norm of Vera's conduct, and for that matter, of the conduct of all of the charac-ters of the novel: not only are the men and women all involved in unmarked enactments of the patriarchy, but even the circumstan-tial "deviant," a gay man who is first a barber and then a factotum in the local brothel, functions to reproduce the male-female para-digm in the now-indulgent, now-rough treatment accorded such exceptions-that-prove-the-rule in the one large provincial family. In any event, the strict parameters within which the town faggot must—indeed, is forced to—conduct himself reiterates in a con-trolled and marked way the principles of gender difference. As a consequence, there is never any questioning, on the level of narra-tive exposition, of gender difference, never any doubt as to the gen-ders to which the various characters are assigned, and never any question as to how they will interact with each other. Indeed, the immediate way in which the young boy in the novel's opening chap-ter grasps why Vera insists that his mother bring the arrears payment by in person underscores how quickly social participants (primarily as a matter of survival) understand how the sexual dynamic works.

It is important to stress that there is never any direct, overt chal-lenge to Vera's masculinity or to his stature as a caudillo. Despite their son's momentary rebelliousness (precisely because he realizes that Vera will in effect have his way with his mother), the parents are re-signed to the legitimacy of Vera's claim to the money owed him and to the sexual surcharge for the payment in arrears. Vera's son, while he has become a citizen of the Buenos Aires metropolis (thanks to the cultural pretensions of his mother, who is now dead), makes only a passing gesture toward separating his father from his milieu, and only in order to afford his father the wider sphere of influence in the capital. Gervasio, the homosexual barber who is now a brothel hanger-on, pleads with Vera not to call him by his nickname, Pechuga. Yet their dialogue reveals how Gervasio is resigned to Vera's use of the name as an almost affectionate denomination and how, in any event, Vera pays no heed to his protestations. In the course of the novel, Vera also deals with his housekeeper, Isabel, from whom he obtains compliance in the specification of a new routine. He deals with a brothel prostitute, who is exemplarily compliant and industrious in fulfilling her obligations. Finally, Vera recalls his dead wife with pride. Her soft blond beauty and her cultural aspirations honor him as a man worthy of winning such a woman, and while many of his recollections of her are tinged with a mixture of uncertainty because of her difference and sexual stereotyping (for example, he thinks of her as "Una fofa vaca blanca rubia y sagrada" [a bloated white pale sacred cow; 59]), her uniqueness is a prize appropriate to his masculine social power.

Wherein, then, does there lie any "crisis" for Vera, if not in his confidence in his position and the virtually universal acquiescence he elicits from others? I would propose that it lies in his growing sense of old age and the fragility of his body. In this sense the confrontation between him and the young son of his tenant farmers becomes significant, beyond the boy's objection to the presumed sexual abuse of his mother, since it also constitutes a confrontation between an old man and a boy. As Vera departed after his humiliating fall from the horse in front of the family, "[se repetía] a cada rato: 'Estoy viejo, estoy viejo'" ([he repeated] at every moment, "I'm old, I'm old"; 29). Throughout the rest of that day and the following one, which would be the last day of his life, Vera can be seen fighting the signs of his old age: the accumulation of a lifetime of painful memories (beginning with the death of his comrade), the loneliness resulting from his wife's death and the absence of his son, the aches and pains of his body and the appeal to his housekeeper Isabel to provide him with company as he eats and with the warmth of her body as he shivers in bed, and a concern over diminishing sexual prowess. His visit to the brothel is a way of asserting his stature as a man: "Y él se empezó a mover: *eso* era una prueba. La única en la que se podía comprobar" (131).[11]

The title of Viñas's novel clearly alludes to the Edenic Fall, though not in any direct religious sense (which one would hardly expect to find in a novel by David Viñas), nor in any specifically social or existential sense. The latter would apply were *Cayó sobre su rostro* about the patriarchy as a social institution, with an accompanying consideration of how social institutions are affected by fissures or ruptures in that system through the "fall" of one of its key agents—as in, for example, the detailed representation of the death of the protagonist in Carlos Fuentes's *La muerte de Artemio Cruz* (1962; *The Death of Artemio Cruz*). Rather, as I have insisted, Vera's role is not so much to enact the patriarchy, with an exposition of the accompanying problematics of that enactment, than it is to figure the patriarchy in a static way. Thus, Vera's fall is a personal drama. But it only interests the reader to the extent that what Vera figures interests a society driven by the ethos of the caudillo, and in particular a society in the specific period in which the novel was written (which leaves one to speculate as to what type of novel Viñas might have produced had he written a more directly historical novel dealing with Perón, a project that might not have been politically possible given the political climate of the day—it will not be until thirty years later, with Tomás Eloy Martínez's *La novela de Perón* (1985; *The Perón Novel*), that such a novel is written—and which certainly would not have fit with the larger issues of concern to Viñas as both a novelist and cultural critic).

Yet however much Vera's fall is a personal drama, it would be incorrect to read it in humanistic/existential terms as the decline of the body of Everyman, understood as an embodiment of universal mankind. As much as Vera's story is a trivial one, the sociopolitical dimensions are never very far from it, in that it ultimately captures a fundamental historical type of the Argentine patriarchy:

> Vicente no quería enfrentarse a su padre, pero le irritaba ese invariable tono de mando, de "haga esto y no discuta", cierta puerilidad de cosa aprendida y repetida que había en todas sus opiniones, de grosería, de machismo exhibido constantemente y de estrechez considerada rectitud, conducta, estilo. Él había ido a verlo para cumplir con un compromiso . . . (138)[12]

Vera's fall through and into the decrepitude of the body has three principal representations in the novel. The first is his fall from the horse because of the aggressive reactions of the son of his tenant farmers:

> Y por un momento se sintió en el suelo, ahí tirado, a los pies de esa mujer y de esos dos hombres, que no podían compren-

der que él estuviera caído, en la tierra, sin atreverse a acer-
carse, sin pedirle disculpas o (a lo mejor) ofrecerle un vaso de
agua o cualquier cosa. (15)[13]

The interpretive phrasing of the narrator in "no podían comprender
que él estuviera caído" surely cannot refer to their inability to perceive that he has fallen. Rather, this verbal construction implies a
sense of incredulity that such a thing could be happening, a mute
stupefaction in the face of the impossible becoming actual. Such a
fall, with its dimensions of public humiliation, is inconceivable for a
man of Vera's authority.

After his fall Vera, rather than expressly feeling anger toward the
boy, attempts to justify the mishap by blaming it on the horse. At
the same time he remembers a similar incident in the past in which
Vera's horse did not bolt, but instead trampled the young man who
had attempted to force Vera to dismount. The novel's controlling
narrative strategy emerges in the chapter "Los años," which follows
the description of the incident with the horse. The latter occurs in the
chapter "El día del juicio" (which echoes the biblical theme of the
Fall). In "Los años," Vera recalls the period of the Expedición al De-
sierto (1869) and the subsequent electoral campaign of its leader,
Julio A. Roca, who ended up serving as president between 1870 and
1876 (a period in which the central government's control over the
Pampas was consolidated, in large part through the caudillo system).
Vera recalls the support for Roca because " 'Es macho, Roca, muy macho' " (18; Roca's a macho, a real macho), while at the same time
evoking the incident of his comrade's death while he, in a cowardly
fashion, remained in hiding. Evidently, Roca served as the model for
an entire generation, a standard against which to measure oneself
and even to overcome bad memories of youthful cowardice, because,
as one of his other companions tells him, "[Roca se] los va a coger a
todos, Vera" (21; [Roca's] going to fuck all of them, Vera). In this context, Vera's initial fall, prompted by the aggressiveness of the young
male with whom he enters into a fleeting homosocial competition
for control over access to the body of the mother, is a sudden and
startling retraction from the position of the macho.

Vera's second fall comes in the context of his complex relationship with Isabel, who has become a spousal substitute for his dead
wife. Although it is never made explicitly clear, it would seem that
she is also the mother of a son by him. This son is eventually introduced by Vera into his household as a playmate for his legitimate
son; he eventually becomes a wild buck who seems to haunt Vera in

the background of his consciousness, perhaps as a feral counterpart to his legitimate son who, in the wake of his mother's influence, has become an urban sophisticate. Vera surprises Isabel by demanding that they eat together at the same table, but she only accepts if she is able to nag him about his sloppy table manners. In turn, he complains to her about her son's irregular habits, accuses her of stealing his clothes to give to her son, and protests that she is not as clean as he would want the woman who shares his bed to be:

> —¿Le molesta que no sea señora, don Antonio?
> —¿A mí?—el índice titubeaba—. ¡Qué me va a importar que no seas señora, vos!
> —Es que usted es un señor ¿no, don Antonio?
> —Y vos qué sabés lo que es un señor—ahora golpeó las cacerolas colgadas en sus ganchos, que resonaron en la cocina inmensa—. ¿Ves?—y de nuevo golpeó las cacerolas como divertido con el ruido—. ¿Ves? ¡De esto sabés vos!—y batió más fuerte—. ¡De cacerolas, sabés vos, de cacerolas!
> —¿Y eso qué tiene que hacer con Gervasio, don Antonio?
> —¿Cómo qué tiene que hacer?—el viejo se tambaleaba, indeciso, ablandado—. ¡Si es lo único que conoce, Isabel! ¡Cacerolas!
> —Es hijo mío, don Antonio.
> —¡Hijo de puta . . . de puta vieja!
> —*Mío,* don Antonio.
> —¡Claro que sí! ¡Claro que es tu hijo! ¡De cacero . . . !—y se fue desmoronando despacio sobre la mesa, con las manos delante de la cara. (56)[14]

There is a clear subtext to this exchange: it concerns the man-woman relationship between Vera and Isabel and Gervasio as a signifying shifter of that relationship where *mío/tu* is articulated, but *nuestro* (our) is unable to be spoken. The inability for the truth of the possessive shifter to be spoken has directly related to the unresolved question-and-answer exchange between Vera and Isabel as to whether or not she is a lady and whether or not it matters to Vera, who is a *señor* (not exactly a gentleman, but a man with a social status). Sexuality, paternity, and social hierarchy are all bound up in this exchange, in the middle of which Vera collapses face down on the table in front of Isabel. The chapters that follow this second fall deal with Vera's relationship with his wife and son, and Gervasio's entrance into the family unit as a playmate for Vicente. They deal also with Isabel's ministrations to the prostrate Vera—her attempt to get him into bed, to cleanse/expropriate his body as a sign of her solidified authority in the domestic space—and with Vera's attempt to have her join him in bed to keep him warm. Vera's frailty and disorientation are evident in this sequence in which Isabel, while waiting on him and kneeling at his feet, comes to control his body, the body of a dying man:

> —¡Quiero escupir, Isabel! ¡Escupir, escupir!
> —Ahora sí, don Antonio—ya estaba ahí arrodillada entre sus piernas, sosteniendo esa palangana que iba a resultar muy chica para todo lo que pugnaba por saltar de su boca, del fondo del pecho, de los intestinos retorcidos, de todas sus entrañas dadas vueltas. [. . .]
> —Eso le pasa por no cuidarse, don Antonio. (64–65)[15]

Vera's third fall is the final one. The next day, having recovered from the spell that occurs with Isabel, Vera decides to visit the local brothel. Along the way he is advised that Guastavino has been victimized by Gervasio and his friends. Their humiliation of Guastavino and a friend, in which they make them strip and dance, constitutes the form of rape referred to above that is part of the system of gender surveillance and maintenance. At the brothel, Vera insists on getting to the heart of the matter with an embarrassed and evasive Guastavino/Pechuga, less out of a concern for the sexual deviant than as part of his disgust with Gervasio's behavior. Dissatisfied with Guastavino's explanations, which deny the caudillo full control over his sphere of influence, Vera decides to avail himself of the brothel's services: "Y era tan lamentable su condición [la de Guastavino] que Vera no pudo menos de sentirse superior. La primera en saludarlo fue doña Hortensa [the brothel's madam] . . ." (112).[16]

The brothel has always served in Latin America as a sphere for the confirmation of masculinity. Organized to allow for the supposed unfettered and unmediated display of male prowess, the economy of the brothel is designed to remove any element—modesty, timidity, insecurity, impotence, and socially unacceptable desire—that might impede the individual's fully successful, multiply determined displacement of the sexual performance that is the primary metonym of masculinity. Such a display occurs not only before the prostitute, whose major function may be less the execution of pleasure than the fulsome approval of her customer, but also before other prostitutes, before the madam (unquestionably a paradigm of the Lacanian concept of woman as phallus, as the confirmer of the male order), and before other customers, themselves tokens of the phallic social order. While the free-floating microcosm of the brothel may serve to encourage lubricity and to provide alternate ways of extracting money from the client, it also constitutes an extract of the male world in which each client is displaying his worldliness before the others and vying for their approval. Witness this exchange in the brothel:

> Y todos se rieron anegándose en esa súbita diversión, pero al final no fue nada más que un chapoteo, y se quedaron en silencio esperando que Vera dijera algo—"¡vamos!" "estoy harto de ustedes y váyanse al diablo", pero él los hizo esperar consciente de su dominio, practicando una venganza juguetona que se prolongó hasta que Hortensia y Corti y la misma Catalina con su frente alta de pensador se parecieron un poco.
> —¿Leticia?
> La patrona alargó el cuello, señalando. (114)[17]

The implication here is that Vera, after the public humiliation of falling from his horse and the more private one of passing out in front of Isabel and then being helped to bed as though he were a child, needed to avail himself of the services of the brothel less to placate his sexual appetite than to confirm before the others his male superiority as a caudillo. Only when he has asserted himself, controlling the conversation, does he get around to asking for one of the girls: his major business is the practice of his "venganza juguetona"; Leticia is perhaps an afterthought.

Once with Leticia, Vera appears to be more interested in continuing to find out about Gervasio's humiliation of Pechuga. One of the major features of Viñas's narrative structure is an elliptic shift in the telling of events, such that an action may be first insinuated and later confirmed after the inclusion of intervening material; frequently what is narrated directly is not the action itself but its effects, leaving the reader to piece together exactly what happened between the foreshadowing and the "after a while." In this case, Viñas does not directly relate what happens after Vera mounts Leticia. After an intervening chapter, however, in the pattern of the alternation between past and present events that I have said characterizes the organization of *Cayó*, Leticia emerges naked and screaming from her room, and the reader begins to piece together the fact that Vera has died while having sex with her. This is Vera's final fall, and it is literally face down on the body of the prostitute, a prime social instrument of the confirmation of his virility. Dying in the act of asserting metonymically his masculinity, Vera suffers a culminating indignity to his male power. Since death is integral to the human condition and dying in a proper manner is integral to male control over the world (typically in the Hispanic world, in one's own bed and surrounded by one's family, and not on a prostitute's mattress, much less on a prostitute), what drains Vera of his authority is not death itself, but the manner of his dying, with his nakedness exposed for all to see:

> Y ahí se quedaron los dos contemplando ese gran cuerpo echado boca abajo, sin nada obsceno en su magnífica desnudez de cetáceo. (144)[18]
>
> Y los dos se volcaron en esa faena [de darle vuelta] con las frentes fruncidas, doloridos, tan doloridos como antes la mujer, con pudor de ese cuerpo que se volvía pesadamente, con los miembros, todos los miembros lacios, con respeto de ese hombre viejo que los había mandado y que en ese momento giraba como un pez entre sus brazos . . .
>
> El sirviente [Pechuga] salió marcando un paso de baile y los otros se quedaron mirando ese cuerpo tendido boca arriba, tan blanco y tan paralelo a este techo blanco, las dos mujeres y el hombre con una actitud de término de tarea, la vieja avanzando pasito a pasito como para verificar algún detalle ínfimo: la forma del ombligo, el color de la piel o el tamaño del sexo. (145)[19]

This last taking-the-measure of Vera's sex at the moment of his death is his last attempt to signify his place in the order of masculine power, and perhaps the lack of further reference to it signals the fact that the caudillo's phallic marker is no longer of consequence.

Indeed, the subsequent need to dress him and get him out of the brothel is a gesture of contradictory social content. On the one hand, it signifies the need to transfer his body to the social space, his home, that will confirm his now purely symbolic stature. In according him the dignity of his station, the brothel denizens are paying obeisance to the social structure of which he has been a dominant spokesman. Appearances must be observed as part of the ever-and-always enactment of social ideology which exists only through such sustaining enactments. However, the need to dress Vera and get him out of the brothel underscores his sudden failure, his sudden collapse as a man, in the symbolically public space of the brothel. With "todos los miembros lacios," Vera has ceased to perform as is expected of the male. No longer able to assert his authority through ritualized sexual performance, Vera is an acute embarrassment to the establishment, and what has happened must be kept a tight secret.

The act of dressing Vera in order to return him properly to the external world served so contradictorily by the brothel (the contradiction does not lie in how it is not supposed to exist, but in its function as the most public confirmation of the virility of the patriarchal agents), is the antonym of Isabel's undressing of him as a child the night before. Both acts are of a whole with the diminishing of Vera's masculinity. In the first instance, he is too weak (or too drunk) to undress himself, and he is infantilized by Isabel's expert ministrations. In the second instance, in death he is in no position to don the garments that both conceal the categorical signs of his maleness and serve as its conventional external markers. Neither nakedness nor clothing is a natural sign, to the extent that they are assigned meaning by the social. But they acquire meaning in different spaces (brothel, external world) as confirming markers of a successful, proper, and decent masculinity. In their communal (re)dressing of Vera, the brothel functionaries are reassembling his public figure, but it is one that cannot have more than a perfunctory meaning. Ironically, Pechuga saves Vera's linen undershirt for himself as a souvenir: "El sirviente contempló devotamente la camiseta de hilo . . ." (150).[20]

One could argue that there is something rather nostalgic about *Cayó sobre su rostro*. After all, the old caudillo system Viñas is writing about disappeared with the rupture in traditional personalist politics produced by the 1930s military coup, which overthrew the last of the great caudillo presidents, Hipólito Yrigoyen. Certainly, it is no coincidence that Viñas begins his novels focusing on the legendary forces of masculine power at the end of the Perón regime, which encourages the reader to discern an identification between Vera and Perón (I will not attempt to make much of the superficial similarity of their names, but it is worth noting that Perón was himself from the interior, and military service gave him the entree into Buenos Aires and presidential politics). It has often been remarked that Perón represented a continuation of the power and style of the personalist caudillo—although one could argue that Evita, also from the provinces and herself an illegitimate daughter of a landowning caudillo, understood and practiced them both better than he did. Nevertheless, the professional militarization of executive power that came with the 1930 coup, which Perón supported and of which he was a direct beneficiary even as a democratically elected president, significantly changed the display of masculine authority. Menem may have flirted in recent years with the persona of the provincial caudillo (e.g., with his Facundo-like sideburns during his early years in office), but he is now thoroughly the uptown business executive of the neoliberal order.

The Peronista period of the late 1940s and 1950s is, however, surely a period of enormously significant political transition in Argentina, in that its populism breaks with the highly directed democracy controlled by the landed oligarchy since the 1880s, while at the same time reconfirming certain national myths inspired by national socialism which Perón reinterpreted as a third-way Justicialismo. Peronista populism reactivated certain Creole archetypes, including that of the caudillo—perhaps not so much in the person of Perón himself, but in that of the Peronista delegates outside the metropolitan center. This would explain why such figures would have interested pro-Peronista writers at the time (see writers discussed in Goldar 1971), as well as anti-Peronistas like Viñas, if only to deconstruct their authority.

Should it be argued that Vera's series of falls speak less to a crisis of masculinity than to the "natural" aging process, it would underestimate how the construction and enforcement of masculinity depends, on a day-to-day basis, on apparently insignificant details. But these details, as anyone knows who has experienced the high social cost of deviating from them, if only momentarily and transitorily, are the very stuff of the insistent performativity required to keep masculinity in place. Masculinity is a process of continual display, and in order to make it clear, it requires a constant pattern of overdetermining its meaning—always talking and walking, so to speak, like a man. Any fissure in the texture of meaning threatens the dynamic as a whole, and for this reason there is a point to be made about political meaning in Viñas's novel:

> En otras palabras: que toda la gente lo miraba, le seguía los movimientos; era un espectáculo, y en un espectáculo el público se ríe o llora porque no tiene otra posibilidad. (41)[21]

otes

Preface

1. The authors included are Oscar Zeta Acosta (Mexican-American); Moisés Agosto (Puerto Rico); Magali Alabau (Cuba); Francisco X. Alarcón (Mexican-American); Albalucía Angel (Colombia); Gloria Anzaldúa (Mexican-American); Carlos Arcidiácono (Argentina); Reinaldo Arenas (Cuba); Rafael Arévalo Martínez (Guatemala); Bernardo Arias Trujillo (Colombia); Rane Arroyo (Puerto Rico); Walmir Ayala (Brazil); Aluísio Azevedo (Brazil); José Balza (Venezuela); Porfirio Barba Jacob (Colombia); Miguel Barbachano Ponce (Mexico); Sabina Berman (Mexico); José Bianco (Argentina); José Joaquín Blanco (Mexico); Abigael Bohórquez (Mexico); Jorge Luis Borges (Argentina); José Maria Borghello (Argentina); Marta Brunet (Chile); Silvina Bullrich (Argentina); José Rafael Calva (Mexico); Adolfo Caminha (Brazil); Nancy Cárdenas (Mexico); Lúcio Cardoso (Brazil); Julián del Casal (Cuba); Denise Chávez (Mexican-American); Isaac Chocrón (Venezuela); Copi [pseud. of Raúl Damonte] (Argentina-France); Gerardo Cornejo Murrieta (Mexico); Carlos Correas (Argentina); Gasparino Damata (Brazil); Herbert Daniel (Brazil); Marcos Denevi (Argentina); Augusto D'Halmar (Chile); Alina Diaconú (Argentina); José Diez-Canseco (Peru); José Donoso (Chile); Jorge Eduardo Eielson (Peru); Marco Antonio Ettedgui (Venezuela); Víctor Fernández-Fragoso (Puerto Rico); Hugo Foguet (Argentina); Fernando Gabeira (Brazil); Griselda Gambaro (Argentina); Magali García Ramis (Puerto Rico); Enrique Giordano (Chile); Witold Gombrowicz (Poland/Argentina); Eduardo Gudiño Kieffer (Argentina); Ricardo Güiraldes (Argentina); Pablo Gumiel (Bolivia); José Hernández (Argentina); Juan José Hernández (Argentina); Sor Juana Inés de la Cruz (Mexico); Sara Levi Calderón (Mexico); José Lezama Lima (Cuba); Jaime Manrique Artila (Colombia); Abniel Marat (Puerto Rico); Nemir Matos-Cintrón (Puerto Rico); Glauco Mattoso (Brazil); William Manuel Mena-Santiago (Puerto Rico); Gabriela Mistral (Chile); Nicholasa Mohr (Nuyorican); Sylvia Molloy (Argentina); Carlos Monsiváis (Mexico); Luis Montaño (Mexico); Carmen de Monteflores (Puerto Rico); Carlos Montenegro (Cuba); Mayra Montero (Cuba); Cherríe Moraga (Mexican-American); César Moro (Peru); Manuel Mujica Láinez (Argentina); Elías Miguel Muñoz (Cuba); Francisco Nájera (Guatemala); Elías Nandino (Mexico); Michael

Nava (Mexican-American); Frances Negrón (Puerto Rico); Salvador Novo (Mexico); Achy Obejas (Cuba); Carlos Olmos (Mexico); Sheila Ortiz Taylor (Mexican-American); Senel Paz (Cuba); Renato Pellegrini (Argentina); Terri de la Peña (Mexican-American); Darcy Penteado (Brazil); Cristina Peri Rossi (Uruguay); Néstor Perlongher (Argentina-Brazil); Virgilio Piñera (Cuba); Alejandra Pizarnik (Argentina); Estela Portillo-Trambley (Mexican-American); Manuel Puig (Argentina); Manuel Ramos Otero (Puerto Rico); John Rechy (Mexican-American); Oswaldo Reynoso (Peru); Julio Ramón Ribeyro (Peru); João do Rio (Brazil); Cassandra Rios (Brazil); Mireya Robles (Cuba); Nelson Rodrigues (Brazil); Carlos Rodríguez-Matos (Puerto Rico); Rafael Rodríguez-Matos (Puerto Rico); Reina Roffé (Argentina); Rosamaría Roffiel (Mexico); João Guimarães Rosa (Brazil); Evelio Rosero Diago (Colombia); Jaime Saenz (Bolivia); Floyd Salas (Mexican American); Luis Rafael Sánchez (Puerto Rico); Alberto Sandoval-Sánchez (Puerto Rico); Vera Sant'Anna (Brazil); Silviano Santiago (Brazil); Severo Sarduy (Cuba); Ernesto Schóo (Argentina); Iván Silén (Puerto Rico); Lygia Fagundes Telles (Brazil); Piri Thomas (Brazil); Marta Traba (Argentina); Luz María Umpierre (Puerto Rico); Roberto Valero (Cuba); Fernando Vallejo (Colombia); Eleodoro Vargas Vicuña (Peru); Varo, Carlos (Puerto Rico); Xavier Villaurrutia (Mexico); David Viñas (Argentina); Mauricio Wácquez (Chile); J. Rodolfo Wilcock (Argentina); Luis Zapata (Mexico).

2. In particular I have in mind the freewheeling sexuality of *Olofe's Razor*.

3. I have written on lesbianism in Pizarnik's work in two separate essays: in *Gay and Lesbian Themes* (Foster 1991), concerning her prose piece *La condesa sangrienta,* and in *Violence in Argentine Literature* (Foster 1995). See also Susana Chávez-Silvermann (1995) and Daniel Altamiranda's excellent entry in *Latin American Writers on Gay and Lesbian Themes* (Foster, ed., 1994).

Chapter 1

Epigraph translation: Something is disorderly
Disorderly in the new world order

1. This essay is adapted from Foster 1995a.

2. The novel's title is based on a hypothetical feminine form of the Spanish word for "love": *amor.* In the novel, Amora is the name of the protagonist.

3. Without going into too much detail, Rich's proposition is that lesbianism is not a question of yes or no: one is neither categorically lesbian nor categorically straight. Rather, issues of sexual identity, homoerotic feelings and behavior, and gender solidarity extend along a continuum, with different individuals situating themselves at different points along that continuum. For Rich, a lesbian is any woman who defines her life in terms of other women— not necessarily one who acts, feels, self-identifies, or engages in sex in a specific categorical way, or who enunciates herself as a lesbian in essentialist terms.

4. *Mujeres* means "women" in Spanish.

5. Yet it may be possible to employ a reading strategy whereby the female protagonist of the documentary narrative *Hasta no verte, Jesús mío* (1969; Un-

til We Meet Again) transcends patriarchal authority. Her relationship with the author/narrator becomes sexually problematic in ways that challenge heterosexist feminist interpretations.

6. The book's publication by Planeta, one of the major publishing houses in Argentina at this time and part of an international consortium, lends the book all of the legitimacy and mainstreaming that comes from being widely distributed and prominently displayed.

7. "Gay" is used here to refer only to male writers. For a preliminary canon of authors of a lesbian-marked Latin American literature, see Martínez's groundbreaking study (1996).

8. Sánchez has written elsewhere about the need to counter the overwhelming decency of Puerto Rican society with a poetics of *lo soez* (the dirty).

9. Piñera also authored important dramatic texts.

Chapter 2

Epigraph translation: A decent woman is one who rides roughshod over machos.

1. If Evita were still alive, she'd be a dyke.

2. If Evita were still alive, she'd be a Montonera (a member of the urban guerrilla group of the late 1960s and early 1970s that took its name from a group of pro-Independence irregulars who were active in the mountains of rural Argentina during the early nineteenth century).

3. Eva Perón appears briefly in the second part of Jaime Chavarri's movie *Las cosas del querer* (1995), where she is depicted as having rescued the Spanish flamenco singer and dancer Miguel Molina in a scandal involving public indecency (i.e., homosexuality). Although Miguel Molina, who died recently, did end up in Argentina after being "encouraged" to leave Franco's Spain, it seems unlikely that Evita was ever his benefactress in any run-in with the law. But, historical accuracy aside, the important thing is that the film attributes this role to her.

Perhaps the best-known connection between Eva Perón and the Buenos Aires gay demimonde was Paco Jamandreu, Evita's principal dress designer in Argentina. He speaks of his personal relationship with her in *Evita fuera del balcón* (1981). His personal memoirs, *La cabeza contra el suelo* (1975), which present a frank discussion of his homosexuality, contain numerous references to her. The only reference to Eva's knowledge of Jamandreu's personal life occurs in a passage describing her sighting of him in the street at three in the morning. Directing her chauffeur to stop the car, she confronts him: "—Mirá que no cambiás! ¡Las tres de la mañana! ¡Yirando!" (80; You never change! Three o'clock in the morning! Working the streets!).

However, in *Evita fuera del balcón*, Jamandreu speaks of Evita's reaction to an inaugural party held in 1945 in his new design study. The morning after the party, Eva Duarte, still only one actress among many competing for attention, calls to thank him for his invitation: "Muy linda tu fiesta, pendejo!

150

Progresás, eh! Todo muy lindo, encantadora la gente. [. . .] Pero cuanta mariquita, querido! No te fayó una, eh? Bueno, son la sal de la vida, ahora me doy cuenta que yo me estoy metiendo demasiado en el vinagre de la vida. Voy a empezar a salir más. Cuando hagas otro party invítame" (no pag.; Your party was great, kiddo! You're making progress, no! Everything was very lovely, and the people where charming. . . . But what a lot of fags, darling! They were sure all there, right? Of course, they are the salt of life, and I can see I'm really beginning to get into the thick of things. I'm going to start going out more. Next time you have a party, be sure to invite me). No matter how much Jamandreu may be exaggerating Evita's interest in his circle of friends, one can assume his admiration for her has kept him from outright fabrication.

Little material is currently available on the history of homosexuality in Argentina. Although Guy (1991) makes some references to it, she is principally interested in the record for women (she refers briefly to Eva Perón's alleged experiences as a prostitute, and only in passing to the relationship between prostitutes and Evita's work for women's rights in the creation of a broad base of Peronista loyalists [207–208]). Jorge Salessi has begun to construct such a history in several recent articles (1991, 1995).

In another dimension, a South African transvestite and political commentator, Evita Bezuidenhout, has assumed a persona built around the figure of Eva Perón. I have not been able to obtain a copy of his book, *A Part Hate, a Part Love: The Legend of Evita Bezuidenhout* (ca. 1994).

4. Homosexuals have best understood the historical yoking of love and death. They have all imagined themselves fornicating madly with Evita. They suck her, they resuscitate her, they bury her, they idolize her. They are She, She to the point of extenuation.

5. Posse serves as Menem's ambassador to the Czech Republic.

6. Note also should be taken of the recent play *Eva y Victoria* by Mónica Ottino, directed by Oscar Barney Finn; the Victoria of the title is Victoria Ocampo, Eva Perón's paradigmatic nemesis. One intriguing interpretation of the play is that, in the second act, when the model of personal antagonism of the first act is overcome, a homosocial female bonding takes place that, within the Adrienne Rich tradition, could be called lesbian.

7. It can be assumed that Posse was familiar with Copi's work. The first Argentine monograph on Copi was published by César Aira in 1991, although Posse does not cite this work in his bibliography.

8. The Argentine novelist Ernesto Schóó published a very informative note on Copi in 1995 in which he discusses Copi's homosexuality; he makes no mention, however, of Copi's play about Eva Perón.

9. This is undoubtedly a reference to one of the founding fictional texts of Argentine literature, Esteban Echeverría's short story "El matadero" (which was written around 1840 but not published until 1874, after his death). Noted for its images of social violence in the context of Argentina's first dictatorship, "El matadero" concludes with the death of a young man at the hands of the political opposition.

10. After assuming office in 1973, Perón immediately distanced himself

from the left, which was subsequently dismantled, first by official ostracism and then by a war of extermination: the *guerra sucia,* begun after the military's return to power in 1976.

11. Sebreli 1960 concerns one of the first individuals—Martínez Estrada— of the Argentine intellectual elite to defend the Cuban revolution. Sebreli 1964, one of the most reprinted sociology texts in Argentina, is a probing examination of the profound changes in Argentine social life wrought by the Peronista experiment.

12. It is necessary to go farther and consider in each case the role of the individual in historical events.

13. Her brief life, her spectacular conversion, her unchecked actions, the dramatic circumstances of her death have become a legend and turned her into a Romantic heroine.

14. Equally inadmissible is a variant of the anti-Peronist interpretation that depicts Eva Perón as a mere mechanical product of the machine of the state, the political apparatus, and the massive political propaganda.

15. It was a separable relationship to the extent that, although divorce was never a real possibility, widows either lost the *de* association upon the death of their spouses or became *viuda de;* the patronymics, bestowed upon them at birth, remain inseparable (certainly an ironic attribution in the case of Eva, since Duarte is her unmarried mother's name).

16. Both creation and creator, product and producer at the same time, reflected image and that which reflects, goal and source, she suffers history and at the same time she chooses it.

17. The myth of Evita as a symbolic expression of the desire for justice and equality of Argentine women and workers, in reality only halfway achieved, and at the same time as an expression of fear over the loss of their privileges on the part of the bourgeoisie, was something like a myth with a dynamic, creative, progressive character, [and] was oriented toward the future and not the past, as are regressive myths.

The characteristic of regressive myth is the eternal return to the past and the negation of historical time, of progress. The death of Eva Perón was a historical contingency, but perhaps it coincided with a necessity that its cycle was complete: we cannot imagine an Evita growing old in the inactivity of exile. Evita's death comes to coincide with the end of power for the plebeian wing of Peronismo.

It is for this reason that among the popular classes, one finds the phrase endlessly repeated in 1955: "If Evita were still alive, this would not have happened." There was the vague intuition that the fall of Peronismo owed itself more than anything to the brake applied by Perón himself on the working class, which Evita represented within the government more than Perón himself.

18. In opposition to the necrophilias of certain Peronistas who were demanding Evita's mummy in order to turn it into a magical object of mystic adoration, I would prefer that Evita's tomb remain open and that her phantom continue to upset people's consciences. Those heroes who in one way

or another die for the liberty of Latin American people have no burial; the bodies of Evita and Che [Guevara] have no rest, nor have their statues begun to be molded. To defile the taboo, to desecrate the myth, in its angelical version as much as in its diabolical one, revealing the true historical meaning of Evita and causing to come to the surface of consciousness the secret of her power, which a severe internal and external censorship requires us to hide, is one of the ways—which belongs more to the writer than to the politician—to contribute to the clarification of the conscience of the working class and Argentine women, or at least of their possible leaders, of their cadres, on whom depends that the social transformation of the country, historical change, cease to be a nostalgic myth in which the most burning hopes and dreams of a large part of the people are projected.

19. The typically petit bourgeois youthful rebellion against the conventions and taboos of family and society, the Bohemian desire to startle those who are bourgeois.

20. Since I am also unable to withdraw myself from literary influences, I identified Evita with the Sartrean bastard, that character whom society's condemnation transforms into the implacable censor of itself. The lyrical exaltation of youth, the heroic drunkenness of a young man, if he is in addition a left-wing intellectual, cannot be stopped by trivial daily facts.

Chapter 3

Epigraph translations: Are you confused because I'm telling you all this?

Because each one of us . . . must find his own filth. (Note: Do not confuse with the body.) Filth, friend, filth, the body backwards.

1. The text here plays on the anagrammatic relationship between *porco* (pig), which connotes "filth," and *corpo* (body).

2. This chapter appeared originally as Foster 1996.

3. Our point of departure is not the premise that sexuality constitutes an exclusive methodological category, nor that it is the only basis for examining personal identity. Nevertheless, given the fact that sexual oppression and repression are to be found among the multiple manifestations of the inequality between the sexes, how can we ensure that the dominant culture will be more representative of the interests of woman? In order to transform oppressive cultural definitions and categories, we must have recourse to feminine experience and attempt to understand its codes, its discourses, and its systems of signs—that is, to undertake the type of study that the analysis of the sexual imagination in feminist literary creation would make possible.

4. There is virtually no criticism available on Hilst other than brief newspaper reviews of her books. See the interview "Hilda Hilst: Um coração em segredo" (1993) for basic information.

5. My little dove, do you remember you dipped my prick in your cup of chocolate and then proceeded to suck it. Ah! Your gorgeous tongue. I am evoking all the sounds, all the tones of the landscape of those afternoons . . . cicadas, dark anuses ("cucliform" birds from among the "cuculideans" [the author is playing here on the word *cu* (butt)] . . . My God!) and the smells . . . jasmine-mango, the lemon trees . . . and your soft, elongated movements, my frenetic movements. . . . Ah! Marcel, if you will recall, experienced a whole universe in one of his madeleines.

6. I knew it was not something for people to inquire much about, that life is viable as long as it remains on the surface, in the shadings, in the water colors.

7. I suddenly felt nausea and a deep pain in my chest. I was still able to ask: is there any other life?

Yes. Millions of creatures like me. You will be one of them. It is tedious and even unacceptable, but that's the way it is.

8. I decided to write this book because throughout my life I have read so much garbage that I resolved to write my own.

9. I had the feeling that that was the most important afternoon of my life.

10. Bleeding just like a little virgin.

11. I said good-bye kissing him on the lips, the implacable fillet of those lips, a tongue that denied me nothing, teeth that sank themselves into my flesh, so that I would remember his taste on that night, so that I would remember tomorrow evening, and so that I would remember now and in the hour of my death, and for the rest of the nights I was to live without him.

12. Did that hurt her or not? She said yes. Louder, bitch, and she screamed yes, yes, yes.

13. It was an alphabet of translucent and changing letters, with arabesques, projected on a screen. I followed it letter by letter.

14. Listen, doctor, even a man of the world like you needs on occasion to be told stories.

15. I am going to use a softening cream with oil of peach pits and a very delicate perfume. You will only feel a cold playfulness at the first contact and then right away the massage will produce heat. I will begin with the cavities under the toes of the left foot. There will not be a centimeter of your skin over which my fingers will not pass.

Chapter 4

Epigraph translation: Be patriotic: have children.

1. *Compadrismo* in Latin America is the special bond between two men; a similar bond between women is called *comadrismo*. Typically, men who are bonded by *compadrismo* are the godfathers of each other's children and rely on each other for all forms of social support. In the case of women, their subaltern position provides the added dimension of a network of support against

a totally masculinist society. In all cases, this special bond creates a privileged union in a hostile world, and in this sense it goes far beyond the Anglo-American tradition of buddyism.

Chapter 5

1. It is very unfortunate that, except for some passing references in essays on culture written by women, nowhere in the four volumes of the *Handbook of Hispanic Cultures in the United States* is there any discussion of gender construction and homoeroticism in Chicano/Latino society or its cultural texts.

2. The following discussion of Cherríe Moraga's *Giving up the Ghost* is excerpted in translation from Foster 1994a.

Chapter 6

Epigraph translation:
ROMÁN. If we all talked holding our hearts in our hands . . .
MIGUEL. It's impossible to talk when you hold your heart in your hand. People who tell everything, who leave nothing to themselves, end up rehabilitated on the farms . . . sowing malanga tubers . . . in the jails . . . up against the firing walls . . . with their open mouths full of flies and lying in ditches alongside the highway.

1. Indeed, it should be noted that, at the present moment, at least in Havana, there is a full and open display of homoeroticism. Although it may be difficult to speak of anything like an organized gay culture or a privileged gay identity, it would appear that open displays of homoeroticism are no longer regarded as social or police problems in Cuba's capital, and perhaps elsewhere as well.

Note should be taken of Héctor Santiago's *El loco juego de las locas* (1995), which also deals with the Unidad Militar de Ayuda a la Producción. And with regard to the increase in gay themes in Cuban theater, mention might be made of texts by Pedro Monge-Rafuls and José Corrales. Enrique Rodríguez Mirabal's unpublished and unperformed *La vida es un carnaval* also deals with a victim of the UMAP program to make "men" out of those accused of social dissidence and sexual deviancy. I am grateful to Elena M. Martínez for information on these texts.

2. In the first place, Rubén is not who we're talking about. We're talking about the need the Revolution has to provide a solution to problems that emerge as a consequence of the bourgeoisie, which include homosexuality. And a homosexual cannot properly represent the Revolution.

3. MIGUEL. You're Beba, Beba darling. You're not going to confuse me with your games, with your wheelings and dealings. It's too late for that, because I know all too well who you are. And everybody in the embassy knows it, too. This is a mission they have assigned to me, and I've got to follow

through with it. Idiot! Stupid woman! I [and not Rubén] am going to kill you! You've fallen into disgrace, and I'm here to eliminate you.

4. RUBÉN . . . But of course I remember, as though it were a movie I'd just seen . . . When they were taking us in the busses to the concentration camps, to the gas chambers . . . Rehabilitated so we wouldn't do what we wanted to do . . . Fumigated . . . Buried up to our necks, with that honey covering our heads so that the fire ants would come and eat us alive . . . just like they'll eat you, Beba darling, just like they will eat you . . .

Chapter 7

Epigraph translations: no one knows me I speak of my body

A shrouded, rent vision, of a garden with broken statues. At the break of dawn your bones ached. You rend yourself. I'm warning you and I warned you. You disarm yourself. I'm telling you, I told you. You strip yourself naked. You dispossess yourself. You disunite yourself.

1. This essay originally appeared as Foster 1994b.

2. It must remain for another study to examine the creation of the "Pizarnik legend," that of a female *poète maudit* who has served as an abiding model for a generation of Argentine poets, especially within the context of military tyranny in Argentina and the general sense of a Babbitt-like repudiation of a Bohemian norm of poetry. Any examination of the construction of such a legend will have to take into account how much of Pizarnik's writing was published by establishment houses like the Editorial Sudamericana and Victoria Ocampo's unashamedly oligarchic little magazine *Sur* (see Piña 1991a on the image of Pizarnik as a *poète maudit;* concerning Pizarnik and *Sur,* see King 1986, 194–195). In a certain sense, Pizarnik is the Argentine counterpart to the Mexican painter Frida Kahlo, who also constitutes a powerful feminist icon of the woman's body in pain (see Chapter 1 of Schaefer-Rodríguez 1992); concomitantly, one may also speak of a "Frida Kahlo myth."

3. for one minute of a brief / unique life with eyes wide open / for a minute to see / in the brain small flowers / dancing like words in the mouth of a mute.

4. I know little of the night / but the night seems to know me, / and even more, it accompanies me as though it loved me, / it covers my consciousness with its stars /. . . . / But it happens that I hear the night cry in my bones. / Its immense tear is delirious and shouts that something has gone away forever. / We will someday be again.

5. Not to call things by their names. Things have toothlike edges, luxurious vegetation. But who speaks in the room full of eyes. Who bites down with a mouth of paper. Words that come, shadows with masks. "Cure me of the void," I said. (Light loved itself in my darkness. I knew there was no more when I found myself saying: "It is I.") "Cure me," I said.

6. Clenched hands confine me to exile. / Help me not to ask for help. / They wish to make me turn into night, they are going to make me die. / Help me not to ask for help.

7. And so it came to pass / that with his tongue dead and cold in his mouth / he sang the last song they did not allow him to sing / in this world of obscene and shadowy gardens / that came inconveniently to remind him / of the songs of his time as a boy / when he could not sing the song he wished to sing / the song they did not allow him to sing / except through his absent blue eyes / his absent mouth / his absent voice. / Then, from the highest tower of absence / his song resounded in the opacity of the hidden / in the silent extension / filled with shifting hollownesses like the words I write.

8. Quickly, your most hidden voice. It transmutes, it transmits. So much to do and I fall apart. They excommunicate you from yourself. I suffer, therefore I do not know. In the dream, the king was dying of love for me. Here, little beggar, they immunize you. (And you still have the face of a child; several years more and not even the dogs will find you amusing.) / My body opened up to the knowledge / of my confused and diffused being and existence / my body vibrated and breathed / in accord with the now forgotten song / I was not yet the fugitive from music / I knew the place of time / and the time of place / in love I opened myself / and gave rhythm to the old gestures of my lover / the heiress of the vision / of a forbidden garden / She whom I dreamt, she who was dreamt. Prodigious passages for the most faithful of infancies. Lacking this, which is not much, the voice that insults is right. / The gloomy luminousness of drowned dreams. Painful water.

9. In Spanish, *ser* is used for propositional predicates involving adjectives and nouns; *estar* is used for propositional predicates involving adverbs, typically of place and manner, and for adjectives when used in a subjective or affective fashion.

10. Every day, every hour, I would want not to have to talk. The others, figures of wax, and I more other than they. I aspire to nothing in this poem but to untie my throat.

11. With the noise of the eyes of the dolls moved by the wind which was so strong that it caused them to open and shut a little. I was in the small triangular garden drinking tea with my dolls and death. And who is that lady dressed in blue with a blue face and a blue nose and blue lips and blue teeth and blue breasts with golden nipples? She is my singing teacher. And who is that lady dressed in red velvet clothes who has a face like a foot and emits particles of sounds and rests her fingers on white mother-of-pearl rectangles that descend and you can hear sounds, the same sounds? She is my piano teacher and I am certain that beneath her red velvet clothes she is wearing nothing, she is naked with her face like a foot and thus she will take a ride on Sunday on a large red tricycle gripping the seat with her legs harder and harder like pincers until the tricycle slips inside her, never to be seen again.

12. One recalls that Lewis Carroll was one of Pizarnik's favorite authors (Piña 1991a, 222).

13. Most criticism still resolutely ignores homoeroticism in Lorca because

it appears not to be overtly thematicized in his writing—although his biographers are now willing to discuss the homosexual alliances and experiences of his actual life, since they were, after all, probably a major factor in his death by torture in the hands of the Guardia Civil (Schonberg 1956; but see the refutation in Appendix C of Gibson 1983). What is perverse about all this is that, in order not to have overt thematics that would demand an honest analysis, critics have simply ignored those compositions that do contain open traces of homosexual desire—although the reconstruction and magnificent staging of the play *El público* and studies by Binding (1985) and Sahuquillo (1986) have made that approach increasingly difficult. The fate of Lorca's contemporary Luis Cernuda is something else again, and it is only thanks to the diligent work of Carlos Monsiváis that the insistent homoerotic dimension of Mexico's Contemporáneos poets can no longer be veiled by critical silence.

14. One night in the circus I recovered a lost language in the very moment in which the horsemen carrying torches in their hands galloped fiercely around some black steeds. Not even in my dreams of happiness can there exist a chorus of angels that provide to my heart anything like the hot sounds of the hooves against the sand.

15. something in me does not abandon itself to the cascade of ashes that overwhelms me within me with her who is I, with me who is she and who is I, unspeakably distinct from her / / In the silence itself (not in the same silence) to swallow the night, an immense night immersed in the secrecy of the lost steps. / I cannot speak to say nothing. / That's why we lose ourselves, I and the poem.

16. I have avoided quoting from *Obras completas: poesía y prosas* (1990). This edition has been criticized for being incomplete, both in the absence of an extensive number of her texts and in the apparent errors introduced in transcribing many of those that are included (Piña 1991b). It would, however, appear that this edition does complete the published representation of Pizarnik's oeuvre, and in this sense it complements *Textos de sombra y últimos poemas* (1982).

Chapter 8

Epigraph translations: Above all else, a marriage is this: an immense secret called intimacy.

I knew that what was happening would happen at my expense, that I was the victim of something (. . .).

1. So vain, so ignorant of what had happened with her, in her long suffering of so many years, her abandonment, the loneliness that he had given her, and that protection that now enveloped her. Luis, monotonous in his methods of conquest, sure of his charms, of his physical dominion. Luis, who was growing old without having matured. A poor man. Infinitely poor in his tendency to be niggardly in his gifts.

2. Nevertheless, here he is, next to me, between the linen sheets that are somewhat worn and not completely fresh because they've been on the bed for three days. He is my husband. He was thirty years old when I met him. I was twenty when I met him. And today, for the first time, I have the impression that perhaps I know little about him. There, in those thirty years, in that great lacuna of thirty years without me, the justifications for his unpardonable acts could lie dormant, to be suddenly awakened.

3. "Don't worry about it," the Frenchwoman said as she withdrew from her pocketbook a small vial of perfume and dabbed herself behind the ear. "Argentine men are like fresh suffering: as long as they are still present we cannot think about anything else, but then you've got to make an effort to remember them. They are quite unmemorable."

4. Images of homosexuality—negative, to be sure—in Bullrich's fiction, especially *Mal don* (1973), are examined by Alfredo Villanueva-Collado (1991).

5. My husband, you are my man, today. You come to me grey, with your hairline receding, with a network of wrinkles, the fruit of sufferings and excesses unknown to me. . . . I know nothing about you. Except that here you are a bit worn-out by that tempestuous life I did not know, because even when you ran to my side you were like a stream that runs alongside us without our ever being able to make out its course or its language. You were always the river, and I was always the bank. And I, among all women, choose you, among all men. I choose you as you are, a little vanquished, a little worn out, Luis.

6. And, to tell the truth, how can I forget him if I always have him here, at my side, or if I have at my side the evident emptiness of his absence? . . . Luis is for me as memorable as the statue of San Martín [Argentina's major hero of the Independence], the Recoleta Cemetery, the Monument to the Spaniards. All my memories cluster around him.

7. And one of these mornings I thought that Luis was nothing but a pretty Frankenstein, a monster that put out his large hand to caress a child, only to kill her despite himself, with just the light and perhaps well-intentioned pressure of his iron fingers, unable to perceive her death throes.

8. "No man who believes himself obligated to an infinity of mediocre adventures can be passionate. They become so diluted!"

9. "We're all beasts within, Don Antonio."

"Yes, but ones that clean themselves." The woman had sat up and was undressing him like a yellowed child who talks about any old thing, repeating sentences that she had heard one time and that seemed to be like a magical formula, impossible to be modified in even the slightest detail: "I'm not ashamed, I assure you I'm not, Isabel. But it's an upset," he said, "something I feel in my skin and that keeps me from letting anyone see me in my things, in my intimate things, in that which one shows to no one because it belongs only to him. I don't like to be touched, to be pawed." He lifted his arm so Isabel could take his shirt off. "I can't even stand the barber!"

10. There [in Buenos Aires] I would be a millionaire, very rich. Here, instead, I live well and people know that I'm alive or that I'm sick, and they comment on my affairs, you understand? [There,] people are known. Here, by contrast, they know *me*.

11. And he began to move: *that* was a challenge. The only one in which he could test himself.

12. (Vicente did not want to confront his father, but that invariable tone of command bothered him, that "do this and don't argue," a certain childishness of something learned and repeated to be found in all his opinions, of uncouthness, of a machismo that was always being exhibited constantly and of a narrowness that was considered righteousness, conduct, style. He had gone to see him to fulfill an obligation. . . .)

13. And for a moment he felt himself on the ground, thrown down there, at the feet of that woman and those two men, who were unable to grasp that he had fallen, to the earth, without daring to approach him, without excusing themselves or (at least) offering him a glass of water or anything at all.

14. "Does it bother you I'm not a lady, Don Antonio?"

"Me?" His index finger wavered. "Why would I be bothered you're not a lady?"

"Well, you're a gentleman, aren't you, Don Antonio?"

"And what do you know about being a gentleman?" Now he struck against the pots hanging from their hooks, which resounded in the immense kitchen. "See?" And he again banged the pots as though entertained by the noise. "See? This is what you know," and he hit them harder. "About pots, that's what you know about, pots!"

"And what's that got to do with Gervasio, Don Antonio?"

"What do you mean, what's that got to do with him?" The old man was stumbling, unsure of himself, softened. "Why, that's the only thing you know about, Isabel! Pots!"

"He's my son, Don Antonio."

"Son of a whore. . . . Of an old whore!"

"*Mine*, Don Antonio."

"Of course he is! Of course he's your son! About pots. . . ," and he slowly collapsed on the table, with his hands over his face.

15. "I want to spit, Isabel. Spit, spit!"

"Now, Don Antonio," and there she was kneeling between his legs, holding the pan that was going to be too small for all that was struggling to come out of his mouth, from the depths of his chest, from his twisted intestines, from all his jumbled innards. . . .

"That's what happens when you don't take care of yourself, Don Antonio."

16. And [Guastavino's] condition was so lamentable that Vera couldn't help but feel superior. The first one to greet him was Doña Hortensia [the brothel's madam].

17. And they all laughed, drowning themselves in that sudden entertainment, but in the end it wasn't anything more than a splash, and they were

160

left silently waiting for Vera to say something. "Let's go!" "I'm tired of you, so go to hell." But he made them wait, conscious of his dominion, practicing a playful revenge that went on until Hortensia and Corti and Catalina herself with her high forehead of a thinker looked like each other.

"Leticia?"

The mistress stretched her neck, giving an order.

18. And there the two were left contemplating that large body face down, with nothing obscene in its whalelike nudity.

19. And the two turned themselves over to that task [of turning him over] with their foreheads furrowed, in pain, as much in pain as the woman before, ashamed of that body that turned over heavily, with its members, all its members hanging loose, with respect toward this old man who had ordered them about and who at that moment turned like a fish in their arms. . . .

The servant [Pechuga] danced out of the room and the others were left looking at that body stretched out face up, so white and so much like the white ceiling, the two women and the woman looking like their job was done, the old woman advancing one small step at a time to check on one last tiny detail: the shape of his belly button, the color of his skin, or the size of his sex.

20. The servant devoutly contemplated the linen undershirt.

21. In other words: everyone was looking at him, following his movements. He was a spectacle, and in a spectacle the audience laughs or cries because there is no other choice.

References

Abel, Elizabeth, ed. 1982. *Writing and Sexual Difference.* Chicago: University of Chicago Press.

Acevedo, Zelmar. 1985. *Homosexualidad: hacia la destrucción de los mitos.* Buenos Aires: Ediciones del Ser.

Aira, César. 1991. *Copi.* Buenos Aires: Beatriz Viterbo Editora.

Alarcón, Francisco X. 1990. *Body in Flames/Cuerpo en llamas.* San Francisco: Chronicle Books.

———. 1991. *De amor oscuro/Of Dark Love.* Santa Cruz, Calif.: Moving Parts Press.

Almaguer, Tomás. 1991. "Chicano Men: A Cartography of Homosexual Identity and Behavior." *différences* 3 (2): 75–100.

Altamiranda, Daniel. 1994. "Pizarnik, Alejandra." In *Latin American Writers on Gay and Lesbian Themes,* edited by David William Foster, 326–336. Westport, Conn.: Greenwood Press.

Alvarez Gardeazábal, Gustavo. 1986. *El divino.* Bogota: Plaza & Janés.

Amat, Nuria. 1979. "La erùtica del lenguaje en Alejandra Pizarnik y Monique Wittig." *Nueva estafeta* 12: 47–54.

Anzaldúa, Gloria. 1987. *Borderlands/La frontera: The New Mestiza.* San Francisco: Spinsters/Aunt Lute.

———, ed. 1990. *Making Face, Making Soul: Haciendo caras: Creative and Critical Perspectives by Feminists of Color.* San Francisco: Aunt Lute Books.

Arenas, Reinaldo. 1982. *Otra vez el mar.* Barcelona: Argos Vergara.

———. 1990. *Viaje a la Habana: novela en tres viajes.* Miami: Universal.

———. 1992. *Antes que anochezca: autobiografía.* Mexico City: Tusquets Editores. Translated by Dolores M. Koch under the title *Before Night Falls: A Memoir* (New York: Viking, 1993).

Attorney General's Commission on Pornography. 1986. *Final Report [Meese Report].* Washington, D.C.: Government Printing Office.

Azevedo, Aluísio. 1890. *O cortiço.* Rio de Janeiro: Garnier.

Barbachano Ponce, Miguel. 1964. *El diario de José Toledo.* Mexico City: n.p.

Benstock, Shari. 1991. *Textualizing the Feminine: On the Limits of Genre.* Norman: University of Oklahoma Press.

Berg, Charles Ramírez. 1992. *Cinema of Solitude: A Critical Study of Mexican Film, 1967–1983.* Austin: University of Texas Press.

Bergmann, Emilie L., and Paul Julian Smith, eds. 1995. *¿Entiendes? Queer Readings, Hispanic Writings*. Durham, N.C.: Duke University Press.

Binding, Paul. 1985. *Lorca: The Gay Imagination*. London: GMP.

Blanco, José Joaquín. 1980. *La paja en el ojo: ensayos de crítica*. Puebla, Mexico: ICUAP, Centro de Estudios Contemporáneos, Editorial Universidad Autónoma de Puebla.

Bow, Leslie. 1991. "Hole to Whole: Feminine Subversion and the Feminine in Cherríe Moraga's *Loving in the War Years*." *Dispositio* 41: 1–12.

Brown, Katie. 1994. "Lesbian Porn: Friend or Foe?" *Deneuve* 4 (4): 36–39.

Brown, Rita Mae. 1973. *Rubyfruit Jungle*. Plainfield, Vt.: Daughters.

Bruce-Novoa, Juan. 1979. "In Search of the Honest Outlaw, John Rechy." *Minority Voices* 3 (1): 37–45.

———. 1986. "Homosexuality and the Chicano Novel." *Confluencia: Revista hispánica de cultura y literatura* 2 (1): 69–77. Also published in Genvieve Fabre, ed., *European Perspectives on Hispanic Literature of the United States*, 98–106 (Houston: Arte Público Press, 1988).

Bullrich, Silvina. 1966. *Bodas de cristal*. In *Tres novelas*, 7–119. 2d ed. Buenos Aires: Editorial Sudamericana.

———. 1973. *Mal don*. Buenos Aires: Emecé.

Butler, Judith. 1990. *Gender Trouble: Feminism and the Subversion of Identity*. New York: Routledge.

Cabrera Infante, Guillermo. 1967. *Tres tristes tigres*. Barcelona: Seix Barral.

Califia, Pat. 1988. *Macho Sluts: Erotic Fiction*. Boston: Alyson.

———. 1993. *Sensuous Magic*. New York: Masquerade Books.

Calva, José Rafael. 1983. *Utopía gay*. Mexico City: Oasis.

Caminha, Adolfo. 1895. *Bom-Crioulo*. Rio de Janeiro: Domingos de Magalhães.

Chávez-Silvermann, Susana. 1995. "The Look That Kills: The 'Unacceptable Beauty' of Alejandra Pizarnik's *La condesa sangrienta*." In *¿Entiendes? Queer Readings, Hispanic Writings*, edited by Emilie L. Bergmann and Paul Julian Smith, 281–305. Durham, N.C.: Duke University Press.

Chocrón, Isaac. 1988. *Toda una dama*. Caracas: Alfadil.

Ciria, Alberto. 1983. *Política y cultura popular: la Argentina peronista, 1946–1955*. Buenos Aires: Ediciones de la Flor.

Cixous, Hélène. 1976. "The Laugh of the Medusa." *Signs* 1: 875–893.

Cleland, John. 1750. *Memoirs of Fanny Hill*. London: Griffiths. Originally published as *Memoirs of a Woman of Pleasure* (London: G. Fenton, 1748–1749).

Copi. 1955. *¿A dónde va Perón? De Berlín a Wall Street*. Montevideo: Ediciones de la Resistencia Revolucionaria.

———. 1976. *Plays*. Translated by Anni Lee Taylor. London: John Calder.

Cortázar, Julio. 1985 (c.1984). *Nicaragua tan violentamente dulce*. 5th ed., exp. Buenos Aires: Muchnik Editores.

Daly, Mary. 1978. *Gyn/ecology: The Metaethics of Radical Feminism*. Boston: Beacon Press.

Deleuze, Gilles, and Félix Guattari. 1983. *Anti-Oedipus: Capitalism and Schizophrenia*. Minneapolis: University of Minnesota Press.

Denser, Márcia. 1985. *O prazer é todo meu: contos eróticos femeninos.* 2d ed. Rio de Janeiro: Editora Record.

———, comp. 1982. *Muito prazer: contos.* Rio de Janeiro: Editora Record.

DiAntonio, Robert E. 1982. "On Seeing Things Darkly in the Poetry of Alejandra Pizarnik: Confessional Poetics or Aesthetic Metaphor?" *Confluencia* 2 (2): 47–52.

Dollimore, Jonathan. 1991. *Sexual Dissidence: Augustine to Wilde, Freud to Foucault.* Oxford: Clarendon Press.

Donoso, José. 1966. *El lugar sin límites.* Mexico City: Joaquín Mortiz. Published in English under the title *Hell Has No Limits,* in *Triple Cross* (New York: E. P. Dutton, 1972).

Doty, Alexander. 1993. *Making Things Perfectly Queer: Interpreting Mass Culture.* Minneapolis: University of Minnesota Press.

Dujovne Ortiz, Alicia. 1995. *Eva Perón: la biografía.* Buenos Aires: Aguilar.

Dunn, Sara. 1990. "Voyages of the Valkyries: Recent Lesbian Pornographic Writing." *Feminist Review* 34: 161–170.

Dworkin, Andrea. 1981. *Pornography: Men Possessing Women.* New York: Perigee.

Dworkin, Andrea, and Catherine A. MacKinnon. 1988. *Pornography and Civil Rights: A New Day for Women's Equality.* Minneapolis: Organizing Against Pornography.

Echeverría, Esteban. 1871. *El matadero. Revista del Río de la Plata* 1 (4): 556–585. Translated by Angel Flores under the title *The Slaughterhouse* (*Adam* 179 [1948]: 5–13).

Epstein, Julia, and Kristina Straub, eds. 1991. *Body Guards: The Cultural Politics of Gender Ambiguity.* New York: Routledge.

Esterrich, Carlos. 1994. "Mayra Montero." In *Latin American Writers on Gay and Lesbian Themes: A Bio-Critical Sourcebook,* edited by David William Foster, 251–254. Westport, Conn.: Greenwood Press.

Eva Perón. 1974. Cuadernos de Crisis, no. 7. Buenos Aires: Editorial del Noroeste.

Faderman, Lillian. 1981. *Surpassing the Love of Men: Romantic Friendship and Love between Women from the Renaissance to the Present.* New York: William Morrow.

Fagundo, Ana María. 1990. "Alejandra Pizarnik." In *Spanish American Women Writers: A Bio-Bibliographical Source Book,* edited by Diane E. Marting, 446–452. Westport, Conn.: Greenwood Press.

Featherstone, Mike, Mike Hepworth, and Bryan S. Turner, eds. 1991. *The Body: Social and Cultural Theory.* London: Sage.

Fernández Olmos, Margarite, and Lizabeth Paravisini-Gebert, eds. 1991. *El placer de la palabra: literatura erótica femenina de América Latina: antología crítica.* Mexico City: Planeta.

Foster, David William. 1984. "Algunos espejismos eróticos [*De Ausencia* de María Luisa Mendoza]." *Revista de la Universidad de México* 37: 36–38. Also published as "Espejismos eróticos: *De Ausencia,* de María Luisa Mendoza," in *Revista iberoamericana* 132–133 (1985): 657–663. Also published in *Alternative Voices in the Contemporary Latin American Narrative,* 131–136 (Columbia: University of Missouri Press, 1985).

———. 1985. "Narrative Persona in Evita Perón's *La razón de mi vida.*" In *Alternative Voices in the Contemporary Latin American Narrative,* 45–59. Columbia: University of Missouri Press.

———. 1991a. *Gay and Lesbian Themes in Latin American Literature.* Austin: University of Texas Press.

———. 1991b. "Pornography and the Feminine Erotic: Griselda Gambaro's *Lo impenetrable.*" *Monographic Review/Revista monográfica* 7: 284–296.

———. 1992a. "Consideraciones en torno a la sensibilidad gay en la narrativa de Reinaldo Arenas." *Letras* (Curitiba) 40: 45–52.

———. 1992b. *Contemporary Argentine Cinema.* Columbia: University of Missouri Press.

———. 1993. "Some Proposals for the Study of Latin American Gay Culture." In *Cultural Diversity in Latin American Literature,* 25–71. Albuquerque: University of New Mexico Press.

———. 1994a. "El lesbianismo multidimensional: conflicto lingüístico, conflicto cultural y conflicto sexual en *Giving up the Ghost: Teatro in Two Acts* de Cherríe Moraga." *XVIII Simposio de Historia y Antropología de Sonora* 2: 331–340. Hermosillo, Mexico: Instituto de Investigaciones Históricas de la Universidad de Sonora.

———. 1994b. "The Representation of the Body in the Poetry of Alejandra Pizarnik." *Hispanic Review* 62 (3): 319–347.

———. 1994c. "Luis Rafael Sánchez." In *Latin American Writers on Gay and Lesbian Themes,* edited by David William Foster, 401–404. Westport, Conn.: Greenwood Press.

———. 1995a. "Latin American Literature." In *The Gay and Lesbian Literary Heritage: A Reader's Companion to the Writers and Their Works, from Antiquity to the Present,* edited by Claude J. Summers, 425–431. New York: Henry Holt.

———. 1995b. *Violence in Argentine Literature: Cultural Responses to Tyranny.* Columbia: University of Missouri Press.

———. 1996. "The Case for Feminine Pornography in Latin America." In *Bodies and Biases: Sexualities in Hispanic Cultures and Literatures,* edited by David William Foster and Roberto Reis, 246–273. Minneapolis: University of Minnesota Press.

———, ed. 1994. *Latin American Writers on Gay and Lesbian Themes: A Bio-Critical Sourcebook.* Westport, Conn.: Greenwood Press.

Foster, Stephen Wayne. 1984. "Latin American Studies." *Cabirion and Gay Books Bulletin* 11: 2–7, 29.

Friday, Nancy. 1991. *Women on Top: How Real Life Has Changed Women's Sexual Fantasies.* New York: Simon and Schuster.

Friedman Goldberg, Florinda. 1987. "Alejandra Pizarnik: palabra y sombra." *Noah* 1 (1): 58–62.

Frouman-Smith, Erica. 1990. "Silvina Bullrich." In *Spanish American Women*

Writers: A Bio-Bibliographical Sourcebook, edited by Diane E. Marting, 72–84. Westport, Conn.: Greenwood Press.

Fry, Peter. 1982a. "Da hierarquia à igualdade: a construção histórica da homossexualidade." In *Para inglês ver: identidade e política na cultura brasileira,* 87–115. Rio de Janeiro: Zahar.

————. 1982b. "Léonie, Pompinha, Amaro e Aleixo, prostituição, homossexualidade e raça em dois romances naturalistas." In *Caminhos cruzados: linguagem, antropologia, ciências naturais,* 33–51. Sao Paulo: Brasiliense.

Fuentes, Carlos. 1962. *La muerte de Artemio Cruz.* Mexico City: Fondo de Cultura Económica.

Fuskova, Ilse, and Claudina Marek. 1994. *Amor de mujeres: el lesbianismo en la Argentina, hoy.* Buenos Aires: Planeta.

Galasso, Norberto. 1990. *De Perón a Menem: el peronismo en la encrucijada.* Buenos Aires: Ediciones del Pensamiento Nacional.

Gallop, Jane. 1988. *Thinking through the Body.* New York: Columbia University Press.

Gambaro, Griselda. 1984. *Lo impenetrable.* Buenos Aires: Torres Agüero. Translated by Evelyn Picon Garfield under the title *The Impenetrable Madam X* (Detroit: Wayne State University Press, 1991).

Geltman, Pedro. 1969. "Mito, símbolos y héroes en el peronismo."In *El peronismo,* 109–137. Buenos Aires: Carlos Pérez Editor.

Gibson, Ian. 1983. *The Assassination of Federico García Lorca.* Harmondsworth: Penguin.

Goldar, Ernesto. 1971. *El peronismo en la literatura argentina.* Buenos Aires: Editorial Freeland.

Goldstein, Laurence, ed. 1991. *The Female Body: Figures, Styles, Speculations.* Ann Arbor: University of Michigan Press.

Gregorich, Luis. 1985. *Literatura y homosexualidad y otros ensayos.* Buenos Aires: Editorial Legasa.

Gubar, Susan, and Joan Hoff. 1989. *For Adult Users Only: The Dilemma of Violent Pornography.* Bloomington: Indiana University Press.

Gunther, John. 1968. *Inside South America.* New York: Pocket Books.

Guy, Donna J. 1991. *Sex and Danger in Buenos Aires: Prostitution, Family, and Nation in Argentina.* Lincoln: University of Nebraska Press.

Halliday, Caroline. 1990. "'The Naked Majesty of God': Contemporary Lesbian Erotic Poetry." In *Lesbian and Gay Writing: An Anthology of Critical Essays,* edited by Mark Lilly, 76–108. New York: Macmillan.

Henderson, Lisa. 1992. "Lesbian Pornography: Cultural Transgression and Sexual Demystification." In *New Lesbian Criticism: Literary and Cultural Readings,* edited by Sally Munt, 173–191. New York: Harvester Wheatsheaf.

"Hilda Hilst: um coração em segredo." 1993. *Nicaolau* 51: 4–7.

Hilst, Hilda. 1986. *Com meus ohlos de cão e outras novelas.* Sao Paulo: Brasiliense.

————. 1990. *Contos d'escárnio: textos grotescos.* Sao Paulo: Edições Siciliano.

————. 1991. *Cartas de un sedutor.* Sao Paulo: Editora Paulicéia.

————.1993. *Rútilo nada: a obscena senhora D. Qadós.* Campinhas: Pontes.

Hodges, Donald C. 1976. *Argentina, 1943–1976: The National Revolution and Resistance.* Albuquerque: University of New Mexico Press.

Howes, Robert. 1985. "The Literature of Outsiders: The Literature of the Gay Community in Latin America." In *Latin American Masses and Minorities: Their Images and Realities,* edited by Dan C. Hazen, 580–591. SALALM no. 30. Madison: SALALM Secretariat, Memorial Library, University of Wisconsin.

Hunt, Lynn, ed. 1993. *The Invention of Pornography: Obscenity and the Origins of Modernity, 1500–1800.* New York: Zone Books.

Jamandreu, Paco. 1975. *La cabeza contra el suelo: memorias.* Buenos Aires: Ediciones de la Flor.

———. 1981. *Evita fuera del balcón.* Buenos Aires: Ediciones del Libro Abierto.

Jaramillo Levi, Enrique, comp. 1975. *El cuento erótico en México.* Mexico City: Editorial Diana.

Jáuregui, Carlos Luis. 1978. *La homosexualidad en la Argentina.* Buenos Aires: Ediciones Tarso.

Jay, Karla. 1988. *The Amazon and the Page: Natalie Clifford Barney and Renée Vivien.* Bloomington: Indiana University Press.

Jay, Karla, and Joanne Glasgow, eds. 1990. *Lesbian Texts and Contexts: Radical Revisions.* New York: New York University Press.

Jockl, Alejandro. 1984. *Ahora, los gay.* Buenos Aires: Ediciones de la Pluma.

Kanellos, Nicolás, and Claudio Esteva-Fabregat, eds. 1995. *Handbook of Hispanic Culture in the United States.* Houston: Arte Público Press.

Katra, William. 1980. "Eva Perón: Popular Queen of Hearts." *Latin American Digest* 14 (2): 6–7, 19–20.

———. 1981. "Eva Perón: Media Queen of the Peronista Working Class." *Revista/Review interamericana* 11: 238–251.

———. 1988. *Contorno: Literary Engagement in Post-Peronist Argentina.* Cranbury, N.J.: Fairleigh Dickinson University Press.

Kendrick, Walter. 1987. *The Secret Museum: Pornography in Modern Culture.* New York: Viking.

King, John. 1986. *Sur: A Study of the Argentine Literary Journal and Its Role in the Development of Culture, 1931–1970.* Cambridge: Cambridge University Press.

———. 1990. *Magical Reels: A History of Cinema in Latin America.* London: Verso.

Kristeva, Julia. 1986. "Stabat Mater." In *The Kristeva Reader,* edited by Toril Moi, 160–286. New York: Columbia University Press.

Láinez, Manuel Mujica. 1962. *Bomarzo.* Buenos Aires: Sudamericana.

Lasarte, Francisco. 1983. "Más allá del surrealismo: la poesía de Alejandra Pizarnik." *Revista iberoamericana* 125: 867–877.

Levi Calderón, Sara. 1990. *Dos mujeres.* Mexico City: Diana. Translated by Gina Kaufer under the title *The Two Mujeres* (San Francisco: Aunt Lute Books, 1991).

Leyland, Winston, ed. 1979. *Now the Volcano: An Anthology of Latin American Gay Literature.* Translated by Erskine Lane, Franklin D. Blanton, and Simon Karlinsky. San Francisco: Gay Sunshine Press.

———. 1983. *My Deep Dark Pain Is Love: A Collection of Latin American Gay Fiction*. San Francisco: Gay Sunshine Press.

Lezama Lima, José. 1966. *Paradiso*. Havana: Unión de Escritores y Artistas de Cuba.

Lima, Délcio Monteiro de. 1983. *Os homoeróticos*. Rio de Janeiro: Francisco Alves.

Lozano Mascarúa, Alicia. 1989. "El cine de Jaime Humberto Hermosillo." *fem* 84: 28–30.

Lumsden, Ian. 1991. *Homosexualidad: sociedad y estado en México*. Mexico City: Solediciones; Toronto: Canadian Gay Archives.

Lynch, Marta. 1967. *La señora Ordóñez*. Buenos Aires: J. Alvarez.

Machado, Luiz Carlos. 1982. *Descansa en paz, Oscar Wilde*. Rio de Janeiro: Editora Codecri.

MacKinnon, Catherine A. 1993. *Only Words*. Cambridge: Harvard University Press.

Marcuse, Herbert. 1962. *Eros and Civilization*. New York: Vintage.

———. 1968. "On Hedonism." In *Negations*, 159–200. Boston: Beacon Press.

Martin, Robert K. 1993. "Roland Barthes: Toward an 'écriture gaie'." In *Camp Grounds: Style and Homosexuality*, edited by David Bergman, 282–298. Amherst: University of Massachussets Press.

Martínez, Elena. 1996. *Latin American Lesbian Writers*. New York: Garland Publishing.

Martínez, Tomás Eloy. 1985. *La novela de Perón*. Buenos Aires: Legasa Literaria. Translated by Asa Zatz under the title *The Perón Novel* (New York: Pantheon Books, 1988).

———. 1995. *Santa Evita*. Buenos Aires: Editorial Sudamericana.

Mattoso, Glauco. 1990a. *As aventuras de Glaucomix o pedólatra*. Sao Paulo: Quadrinhos Abrin.

———. 1990b. *Manual do pedólatra amador: aventuras e leituras de um tarado por pés*. Sao Paulo: Expressão.

Mendoza, María Luisa. 1974. *De Ausencia*. Mexico City: Joaquín Mortiz.

Miller, Francesca. 1991. *Latin American Women and the Search for Social Justice*. Hanover, N.H.: University Press of New England.

Moi, Toril. 1985. *Sexual/Textual Politics: Feminist Literary Theory*. London: Methuen.

Molloy, Sylvia. 1981. *En breve cárcel*. Barcelona: Seix Barral. Translated by Daniel Balderston with the author under the title *Certificate of Absence* (Austin: University of Texas Press, 1989).

———. 1991. Introduction to Part 2: Female Textual Identities: The Strategies of Self-Figuration. In *Women's Writing in Latin America: An Anthology*, edited by Sara Castro-Klarén, Sylvia Molloy, and Beatriz Sarlo, 107–124. Boulder: Westview Press.

Monsiváis, Carlos. 1971. *Días de guardar*. 4th ed. Mexico City: Era.

———. 1977. *Amor perdido*. Mexico City: Era.

———. 1985. "Que si esto es escandaloso." In *Amor perdido*, 263–346. 9th ed. Mexico City: Era.

———. 1988. *Escenas de pudor y liviandad*. 9th ed. Mexico City: Grijalbo.

Montero, Mayra. 1991. *La última noche que pasé contigo.* Barcelona: Tusquets.
Montero, Rosa. 1993. "El misterio del deseo: así son y así viven las lesbianas en España." *El país semanal,* 31 October, 16–27.
Montes Huidobro, Matías. 1988. *Exilio.* Prologue by José A. Escarpanter. Miami: Editorial Persona.
————. 1992. "*Olofe's Razor.*" In *Cuban Theater in the United States: A Critical Anthology,* edited and translated by Luis F. González-Cruz and Francesca M. Colecchia, 43–58. Tempe, Ariz.: Bilingual Press.
Mora, Carl J. 1982. *Mexican Cinema: Reflections of a Society, 1896–1980.* Berkeley: University of California Press.
Moraga, Cherríe. 1983. *Loving in the War Years: lo que nunca pasó por sus labios.* Boston: South End Press.
————. 1986. *Giving up the Ghost.* Los Angeles: West End Press.
————. 1993. "Queer Aztlán: The Re-formation of Chicano Tribe." In *The Last Generation: Prose and Poetry,* 145–174. Boston: South End Press.
Moraga, Cherríe, and Gloria Anzaldúa, eds. 1981. *This Bridge Called My Back: Writings by Radical Women of Color.* New York: Kitchen Table: Women of Color Press.
Mott, Luiz. 1987. *O lesbianismo no Brasil.* Porto Alegre: Mercado Aberto.
————. 1988. *Escravidão, homossexualidade e demonologia.* Sao Paulo: Icone.
Murray, Stephen O., ed. 1987. *Male Homosexuality in Central and South America.* San Francisco: Instituto Obregón; New York: GAU-NY.
Naipaul, V. S. 1981. "The Return of Eva Perón." In *The Return of Eva Perón, with The Killings in Trinidad,* 99–181. New York: Vintage Books.
Núñez Noriega, Guillermo. 1994. *Sexo entre varones.* Hermosillo, Mexico: Colegio de Sonora.
Ottino, Mónica. 1990. *Evita y Victoria: Comedia patriótica en tres actos.* Buenos Aires: Grupo Latinoamericano.
The Oxford-Duden Pictorial Spanish-English Dictionary. 1985. Oxford: Clarendon Press.
Paglia, Camille. 1992. *Sex, Art, and American Culture: Essays.* New York: Vintage Books.
————. 1994. *Vamps and Tramps: New Essays.* New York: Vintage Books.
Parker, Richard G. 1990. *Bodies, Pleasures, and Passions: Sexual Culture in Contemporary Brazil.* Boston: Beacon Press.
Paz, Octavio. 1982. *Sor Juana Inés de la Cruz o las trampas de la fe.* Mexico City: Fondo de Cultura Económica.
Peña, Terri de la. 1992. *Margins.* Seattle: Seal Press.
Penteado, Darcy. 1981. *Nivaldo e Jerônimo.* Rio de Janeiro: Editora Codecri.
Pérez, Emma. 1991. "Sexuality and Discourse: Notes from a Chicana Survivor." In *Chicana Lesbians: The Girls Our Mothers Warned Us About,* edited by Carla Trujillo, 159–184. San Francisco: Aunt Lute Books.
Peri Rossi, Cristina. 1991. *Fantasías eróticas.* Madrid: Edición Temas de Hoy.
Perlongher, Néstor. 1989. "El cadáver de la nación." In *Hule,* 68–75. Buenos Aires: Ediciones Último Reino.

Perón, Evita. 1951. *La razón de mi vida*. Buenos Aires: Peuser. Published in English under the title *Evita by Evita: Eva Duarte de Perón Tells Her Own Story* (New York: Proteus, 1980).

Piña, Cristina. 1991a. *Alejandra Pizarnik*. Buenos Aires: Planeta.

———. 1991b. "La palabra herida: sobre las 'Obras completas' de Alejandra Pizarnik." *La Gaceta* (Tucumán, Argentina), 2 July, 4th section.

Pizarnik, Alejandra. 1955. *La tierra más ajena*. Buenos Aires: Botella al Mar.

———. 1956. *La última inocencia*. Buenos Aires: Poesía Buenos Aires.

———. 1958. *Las aventuras perdidas*. Buenos Aires: Altamar.

———. 1962. *Arbol de Dana*. Buenos Aires: Sur.

———. 1965. *Los trabajos y las noches*. Buenos Aires: Sudamericana.

———. 1968. *Extracción de la piedra de locura*. Buenos Aires: Sudamericana.

———. 1969. *Nombres y figuras*. Barcelona: La Esquina.

———. 1971a. *La condesa sangrienta*. Buenos Aires: Acuarius. Translated by Alberto Manguel under the title *The Bloody Countess* and published in *Other Fires: Fiction by Latin American Women* (New York: Clarkson Potter, 1986).

———. 1971b. *El infierno musical*. Buenos Aires: Siglo XXI Argentina.

———. 1971c. *Los pequeños cantos*. Caracas: Arbol de Fuego.

———. 1985. *Textos de sombra y últimos poemas*. 2d ed. Buenos Aires: Sudamericana.

———. 1987. *Alejandra Pizarnik: A Profile*. Edited by Frank GraBiano. Durago: Logbridge-Rhodes.

———. 1990. *Obras completas: poesia y prosas*. Buenos Aires: Corregidor.

Poniatowska, Elena. 1969. *Hasta no verte, Jesús mío*. Mexico City: Era.

Posse, Abel. 1994. *La pasión según Eva*. Buenos Aires: Emecé Editores.

Prieto, Adolfo. 1954. *Borges y la nueva generación*. Buenos Aires: Letras Universitarias.

Puig, Manuel. 1968. *La traición de Rita Hayworth*. Buenos Aires: J. Alvarez. Translated by Suzanne Jill Levine under the title *Betrayed by Rita Hayworth* (New York: Dutton, 1971).

———. 1976. *El beso de la mujer araña*. Barcelona: Seix Barral. Translated by Thomas Colchise under the title *Kiss of the Spider Woman* (New York: Knopf, 1979).

———. 1988. *Cae la noche tropical*. Barcelona: Seix Barral. Translated by Suzanne Jill Levine under the title *Tropical Night Falling* (New York: Simon and Schuster, 1991).

———. 1990. "El error gay." *El porteño*, September, 32–33.

Ramos, Juanita, ed. and comp. 1987. *Compañeras: Latina Lesbians (An Anthology)*. New York: Latina Lesbian History Project.

Raznovich, Diana. 1992. *Mater erótica*. Barcelona: RobinBook.

Read, Malcolm K. 1990. *Visions in Exile: The Body in Spanish Literature and Linguistics, 1500–1800*. Amsterdam: J. Benjamins.

Rechy, John. 1977. *The Sexual Outlaw*. New York: Grove Press.

———. 1979. *Rushes*. New York: Grove Press.

———. 1983. *Bodies and Souls*. New York: Carroll and Graf.

―――. 1988. *Marilyn's Daughter.* New York: Carroll and Graf.

―――. 1991. *The Miraculous Day of Amalia Gómez.* New York: Arcade.

Reinhardt, Karl J. 1981. "The Image of Gays in Chicano Prose Fiction." *Explorations in Ethnic Studies* 4 (2): 41–55.

Rich, Adrienne. 1986. "Compulsory Heterosexuality and Lesbian Existence." In *Blood, Bread, and Poetry: Selected Prose, 1979–1985,* 23–75. New York: W. W. Norton.

Rodgerson, Gillian, and Elizabeth Wilson, eds. 1991. *Pornography and Feminism: The Case against Censorship.* London: Lawrance and Wishart.

Roffiel, Rosamaría. 1989. *Amora.* Mexico City: Planeta Mexicana.

Roof, Judith. 1991. *A Lure of Knowledge: Lesbian Sexuality and Knowledge.* New York: Columbia University Press.

Ruiz Esparza, Jorge. 1990. "Homotextualidad: la diferencia y la escritura." In *Coloquio internacional: escritura y sexualidad en la literatura hispanoamericana,* 233–252. Poitiers: Université de Poitiers, Centre de Recherches Latino-Americaines.

Running, Thorpe. 1985. "The Poetry of Alejandra Pizarnik." *Chasqui* 14 (2–3): 45–55.

Russell, Diana E. H., ed. 1993. *Making Violence Sexy: Feminist Views on Pornography.* New York: Teachers College Press.

Russo, Vito. 1987. *The Celluloid Closet: Homosexuality in the Movies.* Rev. ed. New York: Harper and Row.

Sahuquillo, Angel. 1986. *Federico García Lorca y la cultura de la homosexualidad: Lorca, Dali, Cernuda, Gil-Albert, Prados y la voz silenciada del amor homosexual.* Stockholm: A. Sahuquillo Vázquez.

Salessi, Jorge. 1991. "Tango, nacionalismo y sexualidad: Buenos Aires, 1880–1914." *Hispamérica* 60: 33–53.

―――. 1995. "The Argentine Dissemination of Homosexuality, 1890–1914." In *¿Entiendes? Queer Readings, Hispanic Writings,* edited by Emilie L. Bergmann and Paul Julian Smith, 49–91. Durham, N.C.: Duke University Press.

Sánchez, Luis Rafael. 1976. *La guaracha del Macho Camacho.* Buenos Aires: Ediciones de la Flor. Translated by Gregory Rabassa under the title *Macho Camacho's Beat* (New York: Pantheon Books, 1980).

―――. 1988. *La importancia de llamarse Daniel Santos.* Hanover, N.H.: Ediciones del Norte.

Santiago, Héctor. 1995. *El loco juego de las locas.* Princeton, N.J.: Liberto/as.

Sarduy, Severo. 1972. *Cobra.* Barcelona: Sudamericana.

―――. 1978. *Maitreya.* Barcelona: Seix Barral.

―――. 1984. *Colibrí.* Barcelona: Argos Vergara.

―――. 1985. *Un testigo fugaz y disfrazado.* Barcelona: Edicions del Mall.

―――. 1987. *El Cristo de la rue Jacob.* Barcelona: Edicions del Mall.

Schaefer-Rodríguez, Claudia. 1989. "The Power of Subversive Imagination: Homosexual Utopian Discourse in Contemporary Mexican Literature." *Latin American Literary Review* 33: 29–41.

―――. 1992. *Textured Lives: Women, Art, and Representation in Modern Mexico.* Tucson: University of Arizona Press.

———. 1996. "Monobodies, Antibodies, and the Body Politic: Sara Levi Calderón's *Dos mujeres.*" In *Bodies and Biases: Sexualities in Hispanic Cultures and Literatures,* edited by David William Foster and Roberto Reis, 217–237. Minneapolis: University of Minnesota Press.

Schneider, Luis Mario. 1985. "El tema homosexual en la nueva narrativa mexicana." *Casa del tiempo* (Mexico) 49–50: 82–86.

Schonberg, Jean-Louis. 1956. *Federico García Lorca: L'homme-L'oeuvre.* Paris: Plon.

Schóó, Ernesto. 1995. "Copi: el autor de la vida es un tango." *El cronista cultural,* August 11, 1–2.

Schwartz, Kessel. 1975. "Homosexuality as a Theme in Representative Contemporary Spanish American Novels." *Kentucky Romance Quarterly* 22: 247–257.

Sebreli, Juan José. 1953. "Inocencia y culpabilidad de Roberto Arlt." *Sur* 223: 109–119.

———. 1956. "Testimonio [sobre el peronismo]." *Contorno* 7–8: 45–49.

———. 1960. *Martínez Estrada: una rebelión inútil.* Buenos Aires: Palestra.

———. 1971. *Eva Perón: ¿aventura o militante?* 4th ed., exp. Buenos Aires: Editorial La Pleyade.

———. 1979. *Buenos Aires: vida cotidiana y alienación.* 15th ed. Buenos Aires: Ediciones Siglo Veinte, 1979.

———. 1981. *Fútbol y masas.* Buenos Aires: Editorial Galerna.

———. 1984. *Los deseos imaginarios del peronismo.* 4th ed. Buenos Aires: Editorial Legasa.

———. 1986. *La saga de los Anchorena.* Buenos Aires: Sudamericana.

Sedgwick, Eve Kosofsky. 1990. *Epistemology of the Closet.* Berkeley: University of California Press.

Seidler, Victor J. 1994. *Unreasonable Men: Masculinity and Social Theory.* New York: Routledge.

Shaw, Donald A. 1982. "Notes on the Presentation of Sexuality in the Modern Spanish-American Novel." *Bulletin of Hispanic Studies* 59: 275–282.

Silverman, Kaja. 1992. *Male Subjectivity at the Margins.* New York: Routledge.

Soble, Alan. 1986. *Pornography: Marxism, Feminism, and the Future of Sexuality.* New Haven: Yale University Press.

Sola, Graciela de. 1961. *Proyecciones del surrealismo en la literatura argentina.* Buenos Aires: Culturales Argentinas.

Sommers, Joseph. 1979. "Critical Approaches to Chicano Literature." In *Modern Chicano Writers: A Collection of Critical Essays,* edited by Joseph Sommers and Tomás Ybarra-Frausto, 31–40. Englewood Cliffs, N.J.: Prentice-Hall.

Sontag, Susan. 1982. "The Pornographic Imagination." In *A Susan Sontag Reader,* 205–233. New York: Farrar/Strauss/Giroux.

Soto, Francisco. 1991. "Reinaldo Arenas's Literary Legacy." *Christopher Street* 156: 12–16.

Stabb, Martin. 1967. *In Quest of Identity: Patterns in the Spanish American Essay of Ideas, 1890–1960.* Chapel Hill: University of North Carolina Press.

Steimberg, Alicia. 1989. *Amatista*. Barcelona: Tusquets.

Streinberg, Warren. 1993. *Masculinity: Identity, Conflict and Transformation*. Boston: Shambhala.

Summers, Claude J., ed. 1995. *The Gay and Lesbian Literary Heritage: A Reader's Companion to the Writers and Their Works, from Antiquity to the Present*. New York: Henry Holt.

Tatum, Charles M. 1979. "The Sexual Underworld of John Rechy." *Minority Voices* 3 (1): 47–52.

Taylor, Clark L. 1986. "Mexican Male Homosexual Interaction in Public Contexts." In *Anthropology and Homosexual Behavior*, edited by Evelyn Blackwood, 117–136. New York: Harworth Press.

Taylor, J. M. 1979. *Eva Perón: The Myths of a Woman*. Chicago: University of Chicago Press.

Thénon, Susana. 1987. *Ova completa*. Buenos Aires: Sudamericana.

Trevisan, João S. 1986. *Perverts in Paradise*. Translated by Martin Foreman. London: GMP Publications, 1986.

Trujillo, Carla, ed. 1991. *Chicana Lesbians: The Girls Our Mothers Warned Us About*. San Francisco: Aunt Lute Books.

Turner, Bryan S. 1984. *The Body and Society: Explorations in Social Theory*. Oxford: B. Blackwell.

Vidal, Gore. 1968. *Myra Breckinridge*. Boston: Little, Brown.

Villanueva, Alfredo. 1976. "Machismo versus Gayness: Latin American Fiction." *Gay Sunshine* 29–30: 22.

Villanueva-Collado, Alfredo. 1991. "(Homo)sexualidad y periferia en la novelística de Marta Brunet y Silvina Bullrich." In *El descubrimiento y los desplazamientos: la literatura hispanoamericana como diálogo entre centros y periferias* edited by Juan Alcira Arancibia, 79–94. Buenos Aires: Instituto Literario y Cultural Hispánico.

Villordo, Oscar Hermes. 1986. *La otra mejilla*. Buenos Aires: Sudamericana.

Viñas, David. 1958. *Los dueños de la tierra*. Buenos Aires: Losada.

———. 1967a. *Cayó sobre su rostro*. Buenos Aires: Centro Editor de América Latina.

———. 1967b. *Los hombres de a caballo*. Havana: Casa de las Américas.

———. 1979. *Cuerpo a cuerpo*. Mexico City: Siglo Veintiuno.

Webber, Andrew Lloyd, lyricist, and Tom Rice, composer. 1979. *Evita: The Legend of Eva Peron (1919–1952)*. New York: Avon Books.

Wetsel, David. 1994. "Copi." In *Latin American Writers on Gay and Lesbian Themes: A Bio-Critical Sourcebook*, edited by David William Foster, 116–121. Westport, Conn.: Greenwood Press.

Williams, Tennessee. 1958. *Suddenly Last Summer*. New York: New Directions.

Wittig, Monique. 1975. *The Lesbian Body*. Translated by David Le Vay. New York: William Morrow.

Young, Allen. 1981. *Gays under the Cuban Revolution*. San Francisco: Grey Fox Press.

Zamora, Carlos. 1979. "Odysseus in John Rechy's *City of Night*: The Epistemological Journey." *Minority Voices* 3 (1): 53–62.

Zapata, Luis. 1979. *Las aventuras, desventuras y sueños de Adonis García, el vampiro de la colonia Roma.* Mexico City: Grijalbo. Translated by E. A. Lacey under the title *Adonis García: A Picaresque Novel* (San Francisco: Gay Sunshine Press, 1981).

———. 1985. *En jirones.* Mexico City: Posada.

———. 1989a. *Ese amor que hasta ayer nos quemaba.* Mexico City:

———. 1989b. *La hermana secreta de Angélica María.* Mexico City: Cal y Arena.

———. 1992. *¿Por qué mejor no nos vamos?* Mexico City: Cal y Arena.

ndex